SUCCESSFUL GARDENING

THE INDOOR GARDEN

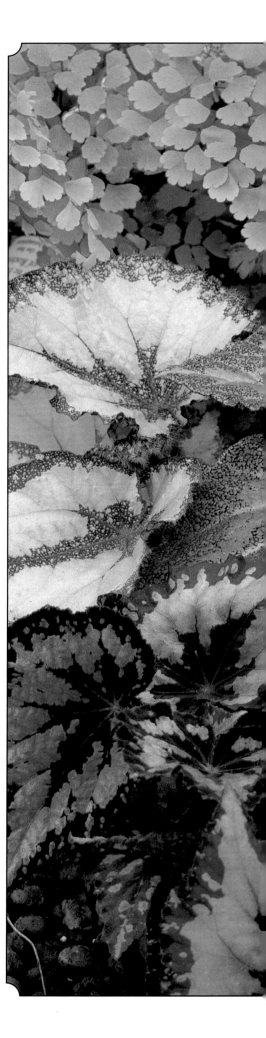

Published by The Reader's Digest Association Limited.

Consultant editor: Lizzie Boyd

Typeset by SX Composing Limited in Century Schoolbook

PRINTED IN SPAIN

ISBN 0 276 42093 4

Opposite: Rex begonias are among the most spectacular foliage plants. Their large,
heart-shaped leaves display stunning colour combinations and markings.

Overleaf: A window display of foliage plants is brightened by the addition of a red-
fruited annual winter cherry.

PUBLISHED BY THE READER'S DIGEST ASSOCIATION LIMITED
LONDON NEW YORK MONTREAL SYDNEY CAPE TOWN

Originally published in partwork form
by Eaglemoss Publications Limited

SUCCESSFUL GARDENING
THE INDOOR GARDEN

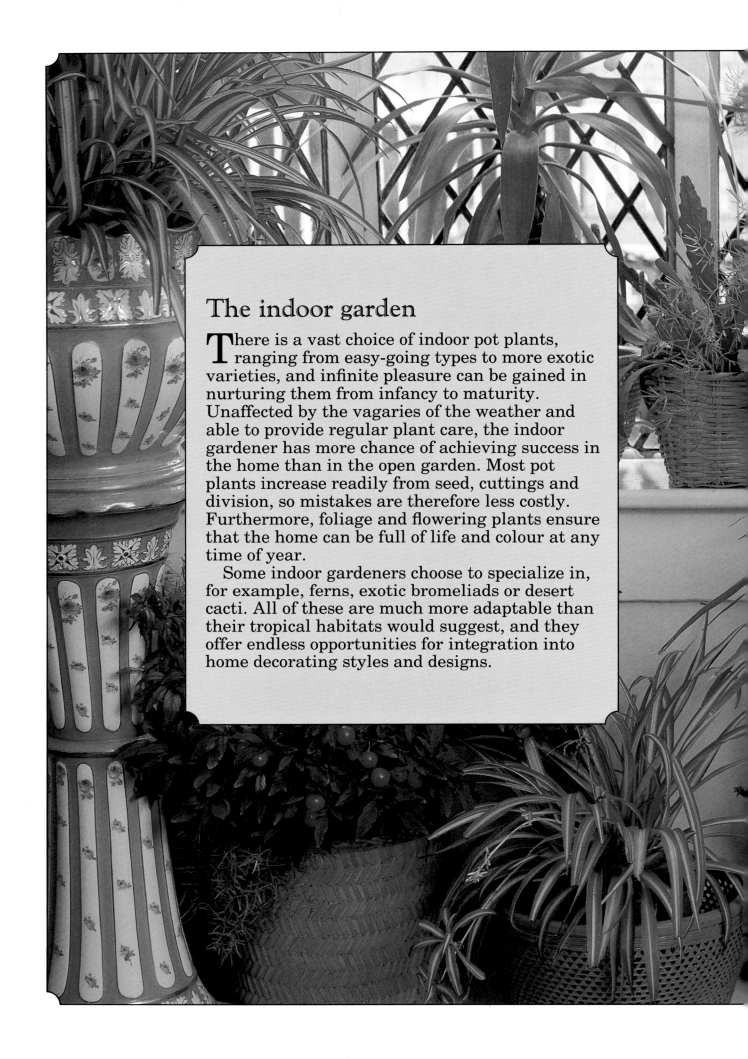

The indoor garden

There is a vast choice of indoor pot plants, ranging from easy-going types to more exotic varieties, and infinite pleasure can be gained in nurturing them from infancy to maturity. Unaffected by the vagaries of the weather and able to provide regular plant care, the indoor gardener has more chance of achieving success in the home than in the open garden. Most pot plants increase readily from seed, cuttings and division, so mistakes are therefore less costly. Furthermore, foliage and flowering plants ensure that the home can be full of life and colour at any time of year.

Some indoor gardeners choose to specialize in, for example, ferns, exotic bromeliads or desert cacti. All of these are much more adaptable than their tropical habitats would suggest, and they offer endless opportunities for integration into home decorating styles and designs.

CONTENTS

Colourful plants Crotons, caladiums and bright red poinsettias need good light and constant temperatures.

Caring for house plants

Indoor plants depend entirely on their owners for their compost, water, light, air and heat requirements. Although the majority of indoor plants cannot tolerate outdoor winter conditions, they do not need hot-house treatment either – more house plants are killed by over-kindness than by neglect. Their basic needs vary enormously according to their origins. For example, foliage plants from steamy tropical rainforests differ greatly from cacti which grow naturally in arid deserts, where hot days alternate with cold nights. Such differences must be taken into consideration when caring for house plants.

No plant will survive in complete shade, but bright sun reflected through glass can be just as harmful. Good air circulation is essential, but draughts can be lethal. A compromise between such extremes suits most indoor plants, and as pot plants can easily be moved from one spot to another, it should be easy to determine the most suitable site. The majority adapt surprisingly well to the artificial conditions found in the home, and as long as pot plants are provided with adequate light, water and food they will develop steadily. Their well-being can be further improved if their individual needs regarding humidity, minimum temperatures and a dormant winter rest are met.

Poor health may be attributed to a few pests and diseases, but it is more often caused by poor growing conditions, which can usually be improved. With regular care, the indoor garden can be as striking as any outdoor garden.

Plant window Trailing, climbing and upright foliage plants display a diversity of shapes and colours.

HOUSE PLANT CARE

Indoor plants vary in their needs, but certain conditions are essential if they are to thrive and remain healthy.

All plants have the same basic requirements – air, light, water, nutrients, humidity and a suitable range of temperatures – though individual species vary enormously in the quantity and quality of these needs. The balance must be just right if they are to thrive and flourish under the artificial conditions of the home. A knowledge of how and where the plant grows in the wild can help in deciding how it ought to be grown indoors. It's always best to choose plants which favour a particular home environment, rather than trying to alter conditions to suit a particular plant.

Air and air flow
Plants breathe, just like animals, but through pores in their leaf surfaces. They do not compete for air with animals during the day, since they breathe in carbon dioxide – rather than oxygen – to use in their food-making process. At the same time, they breathe out

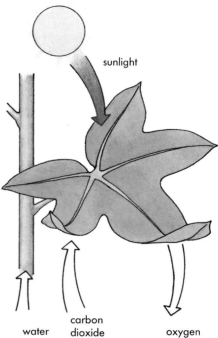

1 During the day carbon dioxide is absorbed through pores on the underside of the leaf, and oxygen is released.

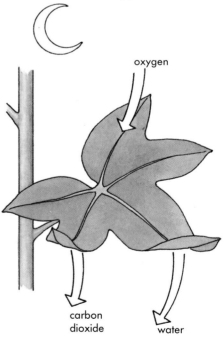

2 At night the process is reversed – oxygen is absorbed, and carbon dioxide and water vapour are given off. The daytime process of food manufacture – photosynthesis – requires energy from sunlight plus water from the soil, while the conversion of food into plant energy – respiration – can be carried out in total darkness.

◄ **Indoor plants** In spite of their varying cultural needs, many house plants, grown for foliage or flowers, will adapt to indoor conditions. Light is the most important factor for their continual well-being.

oxygen. At night, this process is reversed and small amounts of oxygen are used up and carbon dioxide is breathed out – hence the custom of taking plants away from a sick-bed at night. So, fresh – oxygen-rich – air is not necessarily essential and, indeed, many plants will thrive in the almost closed environment of a bottle garden or terrarium. However, there must be a balance with other essential conditions.

Far more important is the flow of air. Stagnant air can create an increase in temperature and humidity. Although such conditions can be good for a plant in moderation, they can encourage fungal diseases such as botrytis when plants are grown very close together. Draughts, too, always damage plants – causing leaf curl, yellowing, brown tips or margins and sudden leaf fall. A room shouldn't be ventilated when out-side temperatures are dramatically less than those indoors. Also, an accumulation of toxic gases, such as those from an open coal fire or paraffin heater, can be equally damaging.

Light

No plant will grow properly without sufficient light. Energy from sunlight is absorbed by the green pigment chlorophyll in the leaves and used as the fuel for converting carbon dioxide (from the air) and water into essential food substances. Most plants do not 'feed' like animals, but manufacture their own food.

Flowering plants, as a general rule, need more light than foliage plants since the formation of flowers (the reproductive organs of the plant) uses up a lot of additional energy.

Foliage plants from deep jungles, such as philodendrons, monsteras

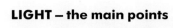

LIGHT – the main points

- ☐ Flowering plants need the most light.
- ☐ Pale-leaved plants need more light than darker ones.
- ☐ Certain foliage plants tolerate shade, but none survive prolonged heavy shade.
- ☐ Most plants grow towards light, so turn them regularly.
- ☐ Don't suddenly move plants, especially those in bud, into much stronger light – do so gradually over a few days.
- ☐ Avoid positions where direct sunlight strikes through glass.
- ☐ Diffused but bright light is usually best.
- ☐ The human eye is a poor judge of light intensity since it self-adjusts – use a light meter if you are unsure.
- ☐ Dirty windows transmit up to 10% less light, so keep them clean.
- ☐ A dull room can be brightened by painting it white.
- ☐ Artificial lighting can be installed to supplement natural light – fluorescent tubes are ideal, but avoid ordinary domestic spot lamps as they give out too much heat and scorch the plants.

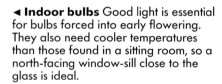

◄ **Indoor bulbs** Good light is essential for bulbs forced into early flowering. They also need cooler temperatures than those found in a sitting room, so a north-facing window-sill close to the glass is ideal.

▼ **Mobile plant stand** Indoor flowering plants generally need the best possible light though on summer days they are liable to sun scorch. A plant stand on castors makes it easy to move plants in and out of diffused light.

Day length
This is as important to certain plants as light intensity. Poinsettias are short-day plants – red bracts only form if they are given a maximum of 10 hours of light (a short day) with no less than 14 hours of uninterrupted darkness (a long night) every day for 8 weeks.

and ficus, can survive in fairly low levels of light. They often have very dark green leaves saturated with chlorophyll, so they can make maximum use of what little light there is. They are usually slow-growing and rarely flower in the home, but are excellent for darkish corners. With a slow 'metabolism' in low light, they also use up less water and need less frequent watering than flowering plants.

Plants with variegated leaves, such as spider plant (*Chlorophytum*) and wandering Jew (*Tradescantia* and *Zebrina*), with little or no chlorophyll in the pale leaf regions and, therefore, less ability to absorb light, need brighter positions than all-green plants. So, too, do plants with entirely pale leaves, but there is another important consideration here – such leaves are often soft and easily scorched by direct sun shining through glass.

In the Northern Hemisphere, south-facing windows are often too bright for all but cacti and flowering plants, unless summer sun is diffused by net curtains, blinds or outdoor foliage. (In the Southern Hemisphere, the sun's orientation is reversed.) Plants in an east- or west-facing window, however, will only receive sunlight when the sun is at its coolest in the morning or late afternoon – so these are usually ideal positions for sun-loving plants. Bright but filtered light is the most suitable for the majority of sun-loving plants.

Partial shade is found near a north-facing window or in any area several paces from a sunny window. Areas well away from any window will have continuous shade – conditions only suited to certain foliage plants. As a rule of thumb, if there isn't enough natural light during the daytime to read a newspaper comfortably without turning on the electric lights, there isn't enough light to grow plants.

When light comes from just one source – from a single window for instance – leaves turn to face it and in so doing turn or lean away from the room interior. To overcome this effect, turn the pots regularly. Young flower buds may, however, object to being suddenly brought into stronger light, and fall off.

Rooms with white or pale-coloured walls are obviously much brighter than those decorated in darker shades. White walls in particular are effective as they reflect some of the available light back on to the plants.

Temperature
As many house plants come from tropical climates, some people assume that they need equally high temperatures when grown in the home. This is certainly not the case. Temperatures much above 24°C (75°F) are only acceptable when daylight hours are very long, light is very strong and humidity is near saturation point. Most of us do not live in such environments.

At the other end of the scale, few house plants tolerate temperatures much below 13°C (55°F). The best temperature, and the acceptable temperature range, vary according to the particular plant species, together with the associated conditions of light, air, water and humidity (see chart below).

Above all, avoid any sudden and dramatic fluctuations in temperature. Centrally heated homes maintain an even daytime temperature, but when heating is turned off at night, a drop of several degrees – in fact, up to 11°C (20°F) – is common, which can be quite damaging to plants. Also, temperature in a hallway may

TEMPERATURE REQUIREMENTS

Plant type	Growth	Temperature range
Ferns	Active	18-24°C/65-75°F
	Dormant	13-18°C/55-65°F
Hardy palms	Active	15-24°C/59-75°F
	Dormant	7-24°C/45-75°F
Tender palms	Active	15-24°C/59-75°F
	Dormant	13-24°C/55-75°F
Orchids/ Succulents	All year	18-24°C/65-75°F
Desert cacti	Active	18-24°C/65-75°F
	Dormant	4-7°C/40-45°F
Jungle cacti	All year	15-24°C/59-75°F
Other plants	Active	15-24°C/59-75°F
	Dormant	13-18°C/55-65°F

Note: Normal comfortable living-room temperature is 18-24°C/65-75°F.

fluctuate widely when exterior doors are opened.

To minimize these effects, take sensitive plants off window-sills at night, especially during frosty spells in winter, and seal draughts as far as possible. Heavy curtains do much to reduce night-time heat loss through glass.

Humidity
Water is essential to all plants, whether they come from the driest desert or the wettest rain forest. Air humidity is a general environ-

INCREASING AIR HUMIDITY

1 Mist plants daily with a hand sprayer, using tepid water. Allow time for moisture to evaporate before nightfall.

2 Put pebbles or coarse grit in the saucer, and keep this layer wet — but never let the pot stand in water.

3 Sink the whole pot within a second larger one and infill the cavity with a water-retaining peat substitute or coir.

4 Stand the pot on a block within its saucer so that a small pool of water can be maintained below pot level.

5 Special humidifiers can be hung on radiators, improving the room humidity — especially just above the radiator.

6 Small plants which thrive on very high humidity are grown most successfully in a bottle garden.

mental factor related to temperature and is essential to plant health. In technical terms it is the relative humidity – measured on a range 0-100%, completely dry to fully saturated with water vapour – which needs checking. Cold winter air quickly becomes saturated with moisture, but as the temperature rises its capacity to hold on to water vapour increases. Under central heating conditions, the amount of available water in the air is no longer sufficient to keep it 'moist'. For a pleasant indoor atmosphere, for people and plants alike, 40-60% air humidity is ideal.

The only way to find out the exact humidity level of any room is to use a hygrometer. In a centrally heated room with double-glazed windows and draught excluders, a reading will frequently be as low as 15% humidity, which is as dry as in a desert.

The problem of dry air can be

WHAT'S GONE WRONG?

Light
- □ Spindly growth or no new growth at all — too little light.
- □ Leaves paler or smaller than normal (eventually turn yellow and fall) — too little light.
- □ Flowering plants fail to bloom — too little light.
- □ Variegated foliage turns all green — too little light.
- □ Foliage wilts in peak light conditions (may shrivel and die) — sensitive plants should be moved away from direct sun, especially around midday when the sun is hottest.
- □ Scorched brownish patches on leaves, especially thick and succulent foliage — too much direct sunlight through glass.

Temperature
- □ Leaves rapidly turn yellow and/or fall off — sudden and considerable temperature fluctuation.
- □ Leaves curl up, then turn brown and fall off — temperature too low.

- □ Weak spindly shoot growth despite suitable light conditions — temperature too high.
- □ Leaves at the base of plant turn brown and crinkly at their edges after first wilting, then fall off — temperature too high and light too poor.
- □ Flowers wither or fall off prematurely — temperature too high.
- □ Flower buds fail to develop — temperature too high, humidity too low.

Humidity
- □ Leaves turn yellow along their margins, sometimes wilting — air too dry.
- □ Leaf tips turn brown and crinkly, and/or leaves fall — air too dry.
- □ Flowers and buds die prematurely — air too dry.
- □ Grey mould appears on leaves, stems, flowers or buds, often stunting growth — air too moist, together with poor ventilation and too high temperature.

overcome by installing automatically controlled electric humidifiers to increase the overall indoor level of air moisture. Cheaper methods include water-filled humidifiers suspended near radiators or bowls of water stood on suitable surfaces. The most effective remedies for plants are cultural ones. Growing plants together in small groups creates a micro-climate in which moisture evaporating from the compost accumulates within the mass of foliage. Air flow is decreased and therefore relative humidity is increased. Do not overcrowd plants, however, where the temperature is high and ventilation is poor, since fungal diseases may be encouraged.

Individual plants can be planted in pots or stood on trays of pebbles kept constantly moist: mist-spraying also helps to increase air moisture. Additionally, bottle gardens are ideal for plants that require a higher humidity than can be comfortably provided in a room.

Routine chores
More house plants are killed by over-watering than by any other factor. The amount of water to be given depends on the type of plant, the room temperature and the time of year. Every plant also needs various nutrients in order to grow satisfactorily. A newly bought plant should have a supply of the necessary nutrients already in the potting mixture, but eventually these must be replaced.

Watering
You need to be aware of how much and how often each plant needs water. The amount that a plant requires depends to some extent on the natural environment of its country of origin – plants come from all over the world, from dry deserts to wet rainforests.

A cactus which would get almost no water at all for much of the year in its desert home will use much less water in the living room than, say, a potted rush which is used to marshlands. An angel's wings (*Caladium × hortulanum*) resting in winter needs only enough water to prevent the tuber from shrivelling, while a winter-flowering begonia has to be watered moderately throughout the winter months.

The conditions under which a house plant is grown also affect its requirements. In hot, dry weather or in a well-heated room, a large amount of water is lost through the leaf pores and by evaporation from the potting compost. If hot sun shines directly on to a pot, the evaporation and drying out of the mixture is rapid. In situations where temperatures are naturally cool, pot plants lose much less moisture.

During the active growth period, developing leaves and flowers need their full ration of water. Yet, when resting, the same plant can often survive with very little. Whether active or resting, the more roots a plant has, the more quickly it will use up water.

The type of container used also influences the rate of water loss – unglazed clay pots lose more water by evaporation than glazed ceramic or plastic types. The size of a plant relative to its container makes a difference too – the larger the plant, the quicker the compost will dry out.

Finally, the type of potting compost used affects water requirements. Peat-based composts hold less water than loam-based ones, and those which contain sand or perlite lose water faster than standard mixtures.

Because of these different but interacting factors, never water routinely by the calendar. The best way to determine when to water is to examine all plants every day or two to assess individual needs.

Water quality Tap water is normally quite satisfactory for most house plants. However,

◄ **Slow-release fertilizers** Granular plant foods are specially formulated to release the vital nutrients — nitrogen, phosphorus and potassium — over several months. They are pushed into the potting mixture, preferably well away from the roots.

WATERING METHODS

1 For indoor use, choose a lightweight watering can with a long spout which can direct a gentle stream of water with reasonable accuracy. Apply water to the compost surface without wetting the foliage.

2 If the coverage of leaves permits little or no free entry of water to the compost surface, or if the leaves are hairy or borne in a low rosette, water from below, but don't let pots stand permanently in water.

3 Bromeliads do not take up water through their roots – these are for anchorage only. Instead they absorb water through their leaves, so keep the leaf rosette – which forms a reservoir – constantly topped up.

azaleas and other lime-hating plants such as camellias may develop yellow leaves if they are permanently watered with hard water, so use collected rainwater whenever possible. (Hard tap water is lime-rich – it can be distinguished from soft water by its habit of 'furring' a kettle and by lathering soap less well.) Alternatively, use distilled or boiled water. Never use water-softening liquids or powders.

Use lukewarm water, or at least at room temperature, since cold water can impede growth and stray drops can spot the leaves. **Amount of water** Plants vary in their need for water. Some should be watered plentifully, some moderately and others sparingly.

Generally, plants in full growth, and especially those with delicate leaves, need continuously moist compost. Thick-leaved and succulent foliage plants and cacti store water in their tissues and tolerate periods of dryness; they need moderate amounts of water. During the winter rest when growth slows down, water should be given sparingly; this also applies to plants kept in a cool room, where transpiration (emission of water vapour) is much less than in a warm atmosphere.

With plants requiring plentiful watering, keep the potting compost moist throughout at all times – do not permit even the surface to dry out. Give enough at each watering to let some water flow through the drainage holes in the bottom of the pot. Except in rare cases – bog and water plants, for instance – do not let the pot stand in excess water. Remember that even plants that require a lot of water will suffer if given too much.

When to water The most obvious sign that a plant requires water is drooping or wilting leaves, but this is not the most useful indication, since it may come too late. Although thin leaves that have wilted can usually be revived quickly, thicker ones often cannot. In any case, repeated periods of

◄ **Mist spraying** Regular tepid sprays with fine mist keep plant foliage free of dust. Mist spraying also helps to increase the immediate air humidity, but cannot replace day-to-day watering. Never spray plants which have hairy or felted leaves or opening flower buds.

wilting and resuscitation inhibit plant growth and flower formation, and cause leaves to turn brown and fall off. Wilting can also result from too much water – roots can be damaged or destroyed by waterlogging.

Testing the potting compost is the only really sure guide to a plant's water requirements, but don't take too much notice of superficial evidence – a dry surface can hide a lot of underlying moisture. Probe for moisture below the compost surface with your finger, a pencil or thin wooden stake. Moist compost will stick to the probe.

If still in doubt, lift the pot up and test its weight in your hands. Dry compost weighs much less than moist, and with a little practice you should be able to assess the water content with some accuracy. Another clue, when growing plants in clay pots, is the difference in sound when the pot is tapped with a hard object between one filled with moist compost and a dry one – the moist one makes a much duller sound.

You can buy small moisture-indicator sticks. These are simply pushed into the compost as a permanent feature and display the moisture level by changing colour. For the real enthusiast, there are also moisture meters for measuring the moisture content of the compost on a very precise scale. These are rather elaborate for ordinary home use, but are useful for checking large tubs and containers – they incorporate a long probe which can be pushed deep into the root system.

Watering methods Long-stemmed and woody plants may be watered from the top of the pot, but tap water will eventually leave a lime deposit on the compost. Rosette-type plants whose leaves grow straight from a low rootstock or corm – African violets (*Saintpaulia*) and cyclamen, for instance – should not be watered from the top as this may cause the roots to rot. Pour the water into the plant tray or saucer on which the pot stands and allow the compost to draw it up.

Avoid getting drops of water on hairy-leaved plants, such as gloxinias (*Sinningia*) and African violets, since they cause discoloration and rotting of the leaves.

How to water To water plants from the bottom, continue filling the saucer until the compost can absorb no more and the surface feels moist to the touch. Pour out any water that remains in the saucer for longer than half an hour.

To water moderately moisten the compost right through, but allow the top 1.5cm (½in) to dry out before watering again. When watering, stop in time to prevent more than a few drops from seeping through the drainage holes. If watering from the bottom, put only a little at a time into the saucer – to a depth of about 6mm (¼in) – and wait until all this has been absorbed before adding any more. As soon as the surface of the compost feels moist, pour away any water that remains in the saucer.

To water sparingly make the compost barely moist throughout and allow as much as two-thirds of the mixture to dry out before watering again. Give enough to dampen the entire surface area, and then stop. Allow this to seep down through the compost, then use a thin wooden stake to test the depth to which the water has penetrated. If the compost still has dry areas, repeat the procedure. (With experience, you will be able to short-cut these tests.) Never give so much water that it seeps through the drainage holes.

When watering sparingly from the bottom, put no more than 6mm (¼in) in the saucer at a time. Test the compost for dry areas and add a little more water if necessary – remember, that too little water is probably better than too much.

Containers without holes in the bottom must be watered with caution. Let only a little at a time flow in. Even when watering plentifully, don't continue once the compost has absorbed nearly all it can. If a surplus is left on the surface, turn the container on its side to drain away the excess.

▶ **Maidenhair fern** A dainty maidenhair fern (*Adiantum capillus-veneris*) needs filtered light and good humidity. Set the pot in a tray of moist pebbles.

KEEPING LEAVES CLEAN

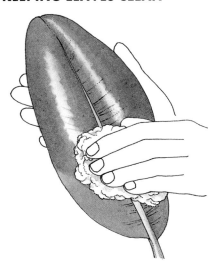

1 From time to time, gently wipe both sides of large-leaved plants with a damp pad of cottonwool or soft kitchen tissue to clean dust thoroughly from their pores. Use soft rainwater or distilled or boiled water if tap water is hard. You can mix a little milk with the water to give a glossy sheen.

2 'Leaf shine' aerosol sprays containing natural oils can be used on glossy-leaved plants to restore their sheen. Such sprays may include a dust-repellent and a mild insecticide. Never use these sprays on hairy or felted foliage – these should be cleaned with a soft paintbrush.

Feeding

Three chemical elements are essential for the balanced growth of all plants: nitrogen, phosphorus and potassium. Nitrogen – in the form of nitrates – is vital for stem and leaf growth. Phosphorus – as phosphoric acid or phosphate – promotes healthy root formation. Potassium – as potash – is required for the production of flowers and fruit as well as general sturdiness. In addition, every plant needs minute quantities of a number of other minerals, known as trace elements.

Plant foods sold specifically for house plants have a balanced content and may be formulated for flowering plants, foliage plants or both types. Those for foliage plants have a relatively high nitrogen content. They may be used for flowering plants in their early stages of growth when leaf and stem growth is required in preference to flowers.

There are also soluble foliar feeds for spraying over foliage. These have an immediate tonic effect on almost any plant that looks starved. Foliar feeding is useful for plants that absorb little food through their roots – brome-liads, for instance. Take plants outside to spray, or put them in the bath, since the chemicals stain fabrics.

Standard house plant feeds come in several forms – liquids, solid 'spikes', pills, granules and soluble powders or crystals. Liquids must be diluted in water, then applied when plants have just been watered. Follow the manufacturer's recommendations carefully for dilution rates.

Pills and spikes are easy to use – push them into the compost according to the manufacturer's instructions. Most modern solid fertilizers release food chemicals gradually without scorching nearby roots.

Applying fertilizers Newly bought or repotted plants should not require immediate feeding. A plant in a soil-based compost may not need to be fed for three months, since the soil contains its own minerals apart from those in any added fertilizer. The fertilizer in peat-based composts, however, is used up in six to eight weeks, and so feeding should begin within two months for newly bought plants or those repotted in such mixtures.

Feed plants only when they are in active growth. If fertilizer is given to a plant during its rest period, it may cause spindly growth with abnormally small, pale, fragile leaves. Don't give fertilizer to a plant just because it seems sickly – fertilizer provides food; it is not a medicine. Consider whether the trouble may be due to over-watering, draughts or the wrong temperature.

FEEDING HOUSE PLANTS

1 Solid plant food spikes are an easy means of feeding house plants. Push one spike into each pot. Nutrients will be released continuously over a period of several weeks. Slow-release granules are also available, which should be pushed deeper into the compost.

2 Liquid feed should be applied directly to the compost surface during the active growing season after the plants have been watered – never to dry plants, as it will scorch their roots. Follow the manufacturer's instructions precisely for rate of application and dilution.

3 Special 'feed-and-grow' mats consist of a fibre cushion which is filled with slow-release fertilizer granules. Simply place one mat under each individual pot; always water from the bottom to release nutrients which can last for up to one year.

REVIVING HOUSE PLANTS

**Sometimes house plants suffer a period of
neglect, but in most cases proper care and treatment
can restore their health and vigour.**

Some house plants are more easy going than others, but all types will become limp, discoloured, straggly, and eventually die if they are not treated properly.

The most common form of neglect is as a result of a long holiday or an unplanned absence from the home. Though measures can be taken to give house plants a slow-release supply of water and nutrients while you are away, the reservoir may dry up in time.

Sick and neglected plants can usually be brought back to health provided they are not completely dead. However, the procedure may have to be drastic, so be prepared for some failures.

Among the most frequent causes of plant ill-health are lack of water and humidity, lack of soil nutrients, lack of space and air, insufficient sunlight, inappropriate room temperatures and cold draughts. Many of these problems can be put right immediately, but damaged plants may take weeks or months to recover fully, though watering a wilted plant may give an almost instant response.

Emergency watering

If a plant's leaves or stems are limp and withered and the compost is bone dry, water must be given straight away.

However, if the compost has shrunk away from the sides of the container, watering from the top is useless – the water simply flows down the sides of the root ball and out through the container's drainage holes without wetting the roots. This sort of problem is common with peat-based composts, which dry out and shrink quickly. Once it is dry, peat is quite difficult to re-moisten.

The best way to saturate dry compost is to submerge the entire pot and root ball in a bucket or bowl of fresh water, so that the water comes right over the top of the pot. With a light-weight peat-based compost combined with a light-weight plastic pot, you may have to hold the pot down to stop it floating. If the surface of the compost is hard and compacted, first scrape it loose with an old kitchen fork, taking care not to damage the plant's roots.

Keep the pot submerged until air bubbles cease to rise from the compost. This may take fifteen minutes or more if the compost is really dry and compacted. Then lift the pot out of the water – it will be much heavier now – and let it drain thoroughly on the kitchen draining board, or in the garden if the weather is calm and mild. Finally, return the plant to its place in the home, standing it in a drip saucer as necessary.

Do not feed a limp plant until it has fully recovered from lack of water, as dry roots are easily scorched by fertilizers.

If lack of water is the only problem, the plant should recover within a few hours, and certainly within a day or two. Any small leaves which don't stand up again should be cut off, otherwise they may rot.

Over-watered plants

It is just as easy to harm a plant by over-watering as by under-watering. More house plants are killed by over-watering than by any other cause. If the foliage is wilting but the compost is wet rather than bone dry, over-watering is probably to blame. Other symptoms include yellowing of the leaves, bud drop and premature flower drop, and rotting of stems and leaves. If green slimy algae appears on a clay pot, it is a sure sign of over-watering.

Over-watering is a common problem in winter. Many plants go into a period of partial dormancy and require little water, but, in trying to be too kind to the plants, many people often water as frequently and as generously as in the summer.

Unlike under-watering, the effects of over-watering can be quite difficult to put right – in bad cases, the roots will have partially or completely rotted.

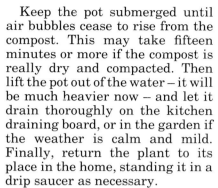

◄ **Speedy revival** Dried out compost, high temperatures and hot sun reflected through glass, can quickly lead to collapse. Immersion in a tepid bath usually revives a plant.

WATERING DRIED-OUT POT PLANTS

1 Before watering, break up the surface of the compost if it has become encrusted with lime from hard tap water. Loosen the top 12mm (½in) so that it will soak up water more readily.

2 Submerge the entire pot in a bowl of tepid water so that the water comes right over the rim. Don't remove the plant until air bubbles stop rising from the surface of the compost.

3 Move the saturated plant on to a kitchen draining board or stand it outdoors so that excess water can drain from the compost before returning the plant to its original site.

Move an affected plant to a warmer spot and don't water it again until the compost has dried out. Even then, let the plant stand dry for another week. Drying out may take several weeks in winter because a combination of damaged roots and partial dormancy means that little water is being taken up by the plant.

In summer, drying out may be much quicker. To prevent additional damage due to dry air while the plant is recovering, mist-spray the foliage frequently with tepid water – this won't affect soil moisture.

Before resuming normal watering, knock the plant out of its pot and check the roots. If new whitish, fleshy roots are discernible, the plant should recover without further treatment. However, if there are only black or brown shrivelled roots visible, tease away most of the soil, cut off the worst affected roots and repot the plant in fresh compost.

Cleaning dirty leaves
When leaves are dusty their pores become clogged, preventing air from reaching the respiratory tissues within. Dust also blocks out light – another vital component for plant growth and health – from the leaf as well as ruining the appearance of the plant.
Washing with water To clean dust and dirt from a relatively small, smooth-leaved house plant which can be picked up and moved easily, put the plant in the bath or kitchen sink and spray it with water at room temperature. Don't

use cold water as this can damage delicate foliage.

An even easier way is to cup the top of the pot with the palm of your hand to contain the compost and invert the whole plant, dipping the leaves and stems in a large bowl of water. Use slightly soapy water if the leaves are very dirty, but be sure to rinse the leaves in clear water afterwards. Never use detergents.

Smooth-leaved plants which are too big to move, as well as those with large leaves, can have each leaf washed individually. Use a sponge or soft cloth moistened with water. Again, if the dust is thick and won't wash off readily, use soapy water followed by a clear-water rinse.

When washing a single leaf, support the leaf blade with one hand and gently sponge or wipe the upper surface with the other hand. Don't try to clean new leaves in this way, since they are too soft and bruise easily. In general, the undersides of leaves need much less attention.

After washing a plant, do not let water remain on the leaves or in the angles between stems and leaf stalks – lingering moisture can scorch the leaves of plants which are standing in full sun, and rot those in shade.
Brushing Hairy leaves, scaly leaves and those which have a waxy or powdery bloom present special cleaning problems which are not always easy to solve. Hairy leaves cannot be washed individually, for instance. Some can be sprayed lightly, as long as persis-

tent drops of water are shaken off afterwards, but others – such as African violets – hate having their leaves moistened.

Clean hairy leaves with a small soft brush. The type of brush used for cleaning camera lenses is ideal for this purpose, or a small soft-bristled artist's paintbrush may also be used.

However, never use even the softest of brushes or cloths for scaly, waxy or powdery coated leaves. A gentle spraying with some cautious shaking to dry off the moisture is as much as these easily damaged surfaces can bear.
Leaf sprays The use of special leaf-shine aerosol sprays or milk to add lustre to smooth leaves is recommended only for waxy surfaced, quite leathery leaves, such as those of rubber plants and other members of the genus *Ficus*, mother-in-law's tongue and many philodendrons. Even then the treatment should be infrequent.

Never use leaf-shine sprays on felted, hairy or soft-textured leaves and always keep it off the undersides of the leaves.

Damaged leaves
In addition to yellowing and general discoloration due to food starvation or incorrect watering, the leaves of neglected plants are often physically damaged by passers-by or scorched by too much sunlight. This produces unsightly brown tips or patches, or bending or breaking of the leaves.

Brown patches or tips indicate dead tissues which will never recover. The only solution is to cut

SIX WAYS TO REJUVENATE HOUSE PLANTS

1 Trim off all dead stems, branches and individual leaves. If they are not removed, further die-back may result and the dead leaves will eventually become infected with mould. Also remove any dead leaves and other debris which has fallen on to the compost at the base of the plant.

2 Dead patches at the tips and edges of leaves look unsightly, but the complete removal of each affected leaf could seriously reduce the plant's vigour. Instead, trim off just the brown areas. If leaves die back further, cut off whole leaves one at a time over several weeks to spread the leaf loss.

3 Support floppy stems with thin house plant stakes. Don't insert thick bamboo canes into the compost — they look obtrusive and may damage the roots. Use soft twine or raffia to tie in the stems, knot it to the stake, then loop it round the stem and finally knot it behind the stake.

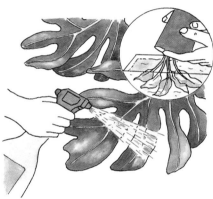

4 Clean dust-laden leaves to allow the pores to breathe freely and to allow essential light energy to reach the food-producing tissues. Dust delicate hairy or felted leaves with a soft brush and use a small sponge or soft cloth moistened with tepid water to wipe the upper surfaces of large shiny leaves.

5 Spray pest- or disease-infected plants with a proprietary liquid, granular or aerosol house plant insecticide or fungicide. If spraying is impracticable in the home, invert the container and immerse the top-growth for a few seconds in a bowl of spray-strength liquid pesticide.

6 Flagging African violets and some semi-succulent, tropical house plants can be given a boost by exposure to steam from a bath of boiling water for a few minutes. Ensure that the base of the pot is raised above the boiling water so that the roots are not scalded; don't let moisture collect on the leaves.

---

off the damaged parts. Cut off the whole leaf if the damage is in the middle. But if only the edge or tip is brown, trim these sections off with a sharp pair of scissors, leaving as much healthy green tissue as possible.

In the long term, trimmed leaves may die back further and need repeated treatment, but substantial defoliation caused by cutting off several whole leaves, just for the sake of eliminating a few brown patches, could seriously weaken the plant. However, if a cut leaf 'bleeds' a lot of sap or white latex, it may be better to cut it off at the stalk where only a small cut surface will remain.

Sometimes it is possible to splint a bent leaf and in time the tissues will harden across the damaged area. Spider plants (*Chlorophytum*), for example, look unsightly if any of their gently arching leaves are creased.

Make a tiny collar-like splint out of a length of sticky tape rolled into a cylinder with the sticky side outwards. Feed the collar over the tip of the bent leaf and position it so that the leaf is bent back to its normal contour — experiment to get the right sized collar, since if it is too tight the leaf will be bruised.

Carefully slip off the splint after a week or so during active growth, or after about a month if the plant is in its resting phase.

Dead stems and branches
Many unsightly house plants can be transformed by simply pruning away dead or dying stems and branches. Though the remaining stems may be rather wide-spaced, the plant should soon flourish provided that it is watered, fed and given adequate light.

Using sharp secateurs, scissors or a pruning knife, cut back dead stems and branches to a point at least 12mm (½in) below the base of the dead material, leaving a clean cut through completely healthy tissue. Cut just above a leaf or bud, or just above a collar-like node if no buds are visible. Cut to an outward-facing bud so the plant can develop a uniform shape.

Lanky growth

Plants which have never been pruned, or which have been grown in insufficient light, are often tall and straggly with long sections of thin stem between each leaf. In severe cases, the base of the plant may have no leaves at all.

Ruthless cutting back of the plant is invariably the only solution, since bare stems never regrow leaves. Using secateurs or scissors, cut hard back close to the base. This should encourage new shoots to form and if the plant is now grown in more suitable conditions, and given adequate food

◄ **Leggy begonia** A new lease of life can be given to an overgrown begonia which has lost most of its lower leaves. Cut the stems down to near the base — use the leaves as propagation material — knock the root ball out of its pot and repot in fresh compost. New shoots should soon sprout from the base.

and water, the new shoots should be compact and healthy.

If the trimmed-off top growth is not too weak it can be salvaged for cuttings. In this way, if the remaining stumps don't produce a satisfactory new plant, the cuttings can provide new stock.

Floppy stems

Climbing and scrambling house plants, such as rhoicissus, may be self-supporting when they are young, but as the stems lengthen they fall over unless a means of support is supplied. Though floppy growth may be perfectly healthy, the effect is unattractive.

Even bushy plants, such as busy Lizzies, can flop over with age, especially if they are grown in poor light where the growth becomes elongated. Straightening them up gives an immediate improvement in appearance.

Thin canes or stakes sold specially for house plants are ideal for supporting single stems. Use small metal ring ties, twine or raffia to tie them in place. For multi-stemmed plants, use indoor plastic trellis. Don't worry if the undersides of some of the leaves face downwards or upwards after the stems have been tied in – they will soon twist around to face the light.

Pests and diseases

Many different pests and diseases can attack house plants, and the symptoms of damage are wide ranging. Once weakened, leaves, stems and flowers often succumb to secondary disorders.

Eradicate pests and diseases as soon as they are spotted. Better still, carry out routine protection measures. Chemical treatment is the usual method, but if a plant has been neglected and the pest or disease has overwhelmed the leaves and stems, a more radical approach may be necessary. This is often the case with red spider mites and whiteflies. These small pests hide on the undersides of the leaves and can remain undetected until they reach plague proportions. Put affected plants in quarantine before they can infect other plants.

Where possible, cut off and destroy just the affected material; otherwise, cut down and destroy almost the entire top growth. If the roots are not affected, the remaining stumps should regrow healthy shoots.

A STRAGGLY PELARGONIUM

Due to insufficient light and nutrient starvation, this zonal pelargonium shows signs of deterioration — yellowing and brown leaves, long thin stems and poor flowers. New growth can be encouraged by cutting the stems down to about 2.5cm (1in) above the compost and repotting. This half-wilted top-growth is unsuitable for cuttings.

PROPAGATING POT PLANTS

**It is easy, inexpensive and immensely
satisfying to multiply house plants by a range of
propagation methods, ranging from seeds to cuttings.**

There are a number of reasons for propagating pot plants – you may want to grow something new that has caught your eye in someone else's home, in a book or catalogue, or in a garden centre; you may want to grow extra plants of your own stock, perhaps as gifts for friends; or you may need to revitalize old, untidy plants. Whatever the reason, the propagation process itself can be so fascinating that many indoor gardeners spend time increasing certain house plants for their own pleasure.

Two main types of propagation are possible. The first – commonly known as vegetative propagation – involves using part of an existing plant, such as an offset, stem or leaf, or it may simply involve the division of a clump. Although this method is in some cases a natural way by which plants increase themselves, most vegetative propagation methods have been devised by man.

Nature's main method of increasing plants is by means of seeds that result from the sexual process of flower pollination. Most house plants can be propagated very successfully by this second method. Indeed, there is no other way to increase annual plants grown for their one short season of flowers. Even raising perennial house plants from seed can be an engrossing and inexpensive source of pleasure and pride.

However, because it is often difficult to obtain viable seed – especially from species which rarely or never flower indoors – and because it is sometimes difficult to make seeds germinate, the vegetative methods are much more common among amateur growers of house plants. Also, bringing a seedling to maturity is invariably a much slower process than any of the vegetative methods.

The use of special indoor propagating frames, or mist benches in a greenhouse, can improve the success rate with certain species, but little equipment is needed for most house plants. All that is required is sterilized seedling/cutting compost – never use garden soil as it probably contains pests, diseases and weed seeds, and won't provide suitable drainage conditions in a pot. Old yoghurt pots and food containers are ideal for raising cuttings or seedlings cheaply, but they must have drainage holes punched through the bottom.

The vegetative method of propagating plants may be further divided into two broad categories – those which use only a small, expendable part of the parent plant, such as a leaf, shoot tip or plantlet, and those which largely destroy the parent. The first of these methods is most appropriate when you are taking material from a plant which is in particularly good health.

Destructive methods – such as division, air layering and stem cuttings from single-stem plants – are only recommended where the parent plant has completely outgrown its allotted space or reached the end of its life.

▶ **Pelargonium cuttings**
Pelargoniums make fine house plants but tend to grow leggy with age. Tip cuttings of young shoots taken at the end of summer root after two or three weeks, although they are notorious for developing black leg disease. This is often due to incorrect treatment.

TAKING SOFT TIP CUTTINGS

1 Several cuttings can be taken from the stems of a zebrina throughout summer. Cut 7.5cm (3in) long cuttings from the tips of side-shoots and remove the lower leaves.

2 Trim each cutting cleanly just below a leaf node. Make planting holes round the edge of a 9cm (3½in) pot. Insert each cutting so that the stem rests against the rim.

3 Cover the pot with a polythene bag held in place with a rubber band. Keep it in a shaded place indoors until the cuttings have rooted — indicated by the appearance of fresh growth.

4 Carefully separate the rooted cuttings. Pot the new plants singly into a proprietary potting compost. Water the potted cuttings and keep them in a shaded place for a few more weeks.

TAKING LEAF-STALK CUTTINGS

1 Cut young, healthy leaves from hairy or fleshy leaved species, such as African violets, in summer or early autumn. Trim the stalks cleanly.

2 With a small stick, make a few planting holes in a pot of compost. Insert each cutting so that the leaf blade is just clear of the compost.

3 Firm the compost with your fingers, but avoid damaging the stalks. Fill the pot to the top with water and let it drain. Cover with a polythene bag.

4 When a tuft of new leaves has grown from the base of each old leaf stalk, pot the cuttings individually in a proprietary potting compost.

CUTTINGS

The increase of plants by cuttings is the type of vegetative propagation most widely practised by indoor gardeners. A small section of a plant is removed and treated so that it becomes a new individual.

Shoot tip cuttings

Cuttings from hollow-stemmed or fleshy stemmed house plants such as busy Lizzie (*Impatiens wallerana*) and wandering Jew (*Tradescantia* and *Zebrina* species and varieties), and from ivies (*Hedera* species and varieties), root easily in a number of ways.

Take cuttings from the tips of young, non-flowering stems or side-shoots between early and late summer. If only flowering shoots are available, trim off all the flowers and flower buds. Strip the lower leaves from a 7.5-10cm (3-4in) cutting and trim it cleanly just below a leaf node. The node is frequently marked by a slightly raised ring of tissue, often with a noticeable sheath that forms at the base of the leaf stalk. On woody plants, where the ring and sheath may not be visible, the node can usually be identified by a thickening of the stem and the presence of a leaf scar and a bud if the leaf has fallen off.

Place the cutting in a glass of water in a well-lit position, but shaded from direct sunlight. Roots will appear within 10-14 days and the cutting can then be potted.

With other house plants, insert the cuttings at once in a rooting medium — any proprietary seedling or potting compost is suitable or use a mixture of equal parts by volume of peat substitute and coarse sand. Fill a 9cm (3½in) pot to just below the rim.

Using a sharp knife, cut off the top 7.5-10cm (3-4in) of a non-flowering stem or side-shoot. Pull off the lower leaves and make a clean cut across the stem, just below a leaf node. The best tip cuttings come from sturdy plants with stems whose nodes are relatively close together.

For certain woody stemmed plants, such as African hemp (*Sparmannia*), a heel cutting is recommended. This consists of a side-shoot pulled off the main stem with a downward tug in such a way as to take with it a heel or small piece of the stem's bark.

Before inserting cuttings into

containers of rooting mixture, it is sometimes advisable to dip the cut ends into a proprietary hormone rooting powder to stimulate root production. With or without the powder, it is best not to push the prepared cuttings directly into the rooting mixture unless this is extremely soft.

Use a small dibber or stick to make a number of 2.5-3.5cm (1-1½in) deep planting holes in the compost – a 9cm (3½in) pot will accommodate four to six cuttings. Make the holes round the edge of the pot so that the stems can be supported on the rim. Firm the compost gently round each cutting, then fill the pot to the rim with water and leave it to drain.

Cover the pot loosely with a polythene bag and secure it with a rubber band or piece of string. Set the pot in a lightly shaded position where a temperature of about 18°C (64°F) can be maintained. Alternatively, place the pot in a heated propagator case. Remove the cover occasionally to check the moisture content of the compost – keep it damp at all times, but not wet. Discard any cutting which shows signs of rotting.

After three or four weeks the cuttings should have rooted and the tips will be showing fresh growth. Remove the polythene bag and invert the pot. Separate

ROOTING CUTTINGS WITHOUT COMPOST

1 African violets and other soft-stemmed plants can be rooted in water alone. Tie polythene across the top of a water-filled jar. Insert a leaf stalk or stem through a hole punched in the plastic. Roots and plantlets form under water, and cuttings can then be potted up.

2 Tubs of rooting gel make a convenient and reliable means of rooting cuttings. Simply punch holes in the top and insert the stalk of each cutting into the transparent gel. When strong roots are visible, the cuttings should be removed and potted up individually.

the rooted cuttings carefully and pot them singly into 7.5-9cm (3-3½in) pots of a proprietary potting compost.

Water the young plants carefully and keep them in a lightly shaded, draught-free place until they are growing well. Once established, move them to their permanent positions.

TAKING LEAF-SECTION CUTTINGS

1 Mother-in-law's tongue is propagated by leaf sections. Cut a leaf away from the crown of the parent plant.

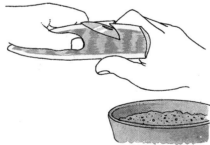

2 Using a sharp knife, cut the leaf cleanly into several 5cm (2in) deep horizontal segments.

3 Insert the segments, lower edge down, in a pan or shallow pot of moist potting compost. Cover with polythene.

4 After about six weeks the leaf segments will develop into young plants, which can be potted up singly.

Leaf cuttings

House plants with thick, hairy or fleshy leaves – African violets (*Saintpaulia*), begonias, gloxinias (*Sinningia*) and peperomias, for instance – are best increased by leaf cuttings. The best time for this method of propagation is between early summer and early autumn.

Cut healthy leaves, each with a 2.5-3.5cm (1-1½in) stalk, from the parent plant. Take only a few leaves, otherwise the parent will be seriously depleted of strength.

Almost fill a 9cm (3½in) pot with a proprietary potting compost. Make a few planting holes, slightly less deep than the leaf stalks. Trim the end of each leaf stem cleanly across with a sharp knife. Insert the leaf stalks into the holes. The base of each stalk should just touch the bottom of the hole, but the leaf blade itself must be clear of the compost, otherwise rotting may occur.

Firm the cuttings gently with your fingertips, taking extra care not to bruise the slender, fragile stalks, and water them in. Ideally, the cuttings should be left to root in a propagating unit with additional heat, but a suitably warm, humid atmosphere can be produced by enclosing the pot in a polythene bag. If a lot of condensation forms on the inside it can rot the cuttings – remove the bag and turn it inside out.

LARGE-LEAF CUTTINGS

1 Increase *Begonia rex* and other large-leaved begonias from leaf cuttings. Cut off a healthy leaf and trim the stalk to about 12mm (½in) from the leaf base.

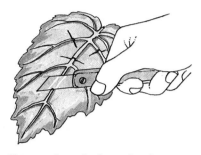

2 Using a sharp knife, make short cuts on the underside of the leaf where the main veins meet. Lay the leaf, cut side down, on moist potting compost in a pot or tray.

3 Weight down the leaf by placing a few crocks or pebbles around the edge. Alternatively, insert pieces of bent wire or hair-pins through the leaf blade into the compost.

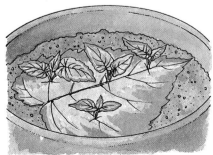

4 Cover the container with polythene and maintain a temperature of about 21°C (70°F). After a few weeks, small rooted plantlets will appear from the cut vein intersections.

After three to five weeks roots should have formed and new leaves will appear from the base of the leaf stalk. Invert the pot and separate the rooted cuttings carefully, without breaking the fine roots. Pot up the cuttings singly in 6cm (2½in) pots and keep the young plants in a warm, lightly shaded position for two to three weeks until they are established.

Leaf sections

Mother-in-law's tongue (*Sansevieria*) is propagated by a special type of leaf cutting – the strap-like, fleshy leaves are cut into horizontal sections, each of which will produce a new plant.

During spring or summer, select a young leaf (preferably one year old) and cut it away close to the plant's crown. Fill a 12cm (5in) pot with moist potting compost. Using a sharp knife, cut the leaf crossways into 5cm (2in) segments, remembering which is the top and which is the bottom of the cuttings, because they must be inserted the right way up. When preparing many leaf segments at once it is advisable to mark the top edge of each with a small V-shaped nick – those which are inserted upside-down won't root.

Insert three or four segments, lower side down in the compost to about a third of their depth. Spray the cuttings with tepid water, then place a polythene bag over the pot. Keep the cuttings in a shaded position at 21°C (70°F).

When each segment begins to produce a new leaf – often after a considerable time – remove the polythene and pot the young plants singly in 7.5cm (3in) pots of potting compost. Yellow-margined varieties of sanseverias do not produce variegated offspring and must be increased by division.

Large-leaf cuttings

Several new plants can sometimes be grown from just one leaf – if it is large enough – as in the case of *Begonia rex* and its many varieties with coloured leaves.

At any time between early summer and early autumn, detach a mature leaf and trim the stalk to within 1.2-2.5cm (½-1in) of the base. Using a sharp knife, make a number of cuts on the underside where the intersections join the main vein. Place the leaf, cut side down, on a seed pan or broad pot of moist potting compost. Secure the leaf to the compost by weighting it down with small pebbles or crocks, or with hair-pins or wire loops pushed through the leaf.

Cover the container with polythene and leave it in a lightly shaded position with a constant temperature of about 21°C (70°F).

After about four weeks, small plantlets will appear from the cuts. Remove the polythene and leave the container in a warm shady place for two to three weeks. Then plant up the rooted plantlets individually in 6cm (2½in) pots of potting compost. Keep them lightly shaded and at a steady, warm temperature.

PROPAGATING PEPEROMIAS

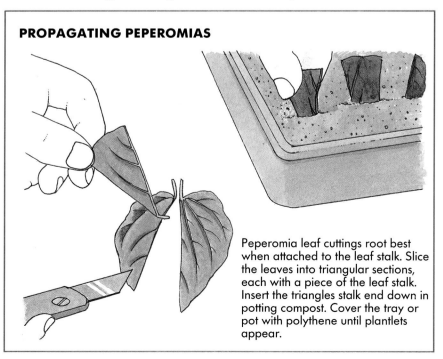

Peperomia leaf cuttings root best when attached to the leaf stalk. Slice the leaves into triangular sections, each with a piece of the leaf stalk. Insert the triangles stalk end down in potting compost. Cover the tray or pot with polythene until plantlets appear.

OTHER WAYS

Besides the various types of cuttings, several other methods of vegetative propagation are suitable for house plants. Some of these leave the parent plant more or less intact, but others involve splitting up the parent plant or mutilating it entirely.

Using plantlets

A few house plant species have a natural ability to increase their numbers by producing miniature replicas of themselves on leaves or stems. These little plants can be detached and grown on.

In some species, plantlets are produced complete with roots, and these develop readily when potted up. More often, however, plantlets are rootless. In such cases they need more careful treatment in order to develop properly after separation from the parent.

On mother-of-thousands detach the thread-like runners, each of which bears a plantlet at its tip, from the parent plant. Nip off the runner from the plantlet.

Almost fill a 6cm (2½in) pot with moist potting compost. Make a shallow depression in the surface and set the plantlet in it. Firm the compost round the base of the plantlet. Do not water further, but place a polythene bag over the pot. Keep out of direct sun and at a temperature of 18-21°C (64-70°F). Ensure that the compost remains just moist at all times.

After about ten days, the plantlet should have rooted. Remove the bag and place the pot in a brighter and cooler place.

Spider plants often bear a number of plantlets on tough flowering stems. Larger plantlets often develop roots and can be severed from the parent plant and potted up individually. Lacking roots, the plantlets can be layered into individual 5cm (2in) pots of potting compost and secured with staples. After about three weeks, the plantlets should have rooted and the stalks can be cut.

Division

Splitting a plant – known as division – is the easiest method of propagation and new offspring develop quickly. However, only certain types of house plants can be increased in this way. Each plant must have at least two, and preferably several, stems arising

PLANTLETS AND RUNNERS

1 Mother-of-thousands (*Saxifraga stolonifera*) produces thread-like stolons or runners that bear plantlets. These can be pinched off and grown on.

2 Firm each plantlet into a pot of potting compost. Cover with polythene and keep the pot in a warm, shaded place until roots have formed.

THE RANGE OF NATURAL PLANTLETS

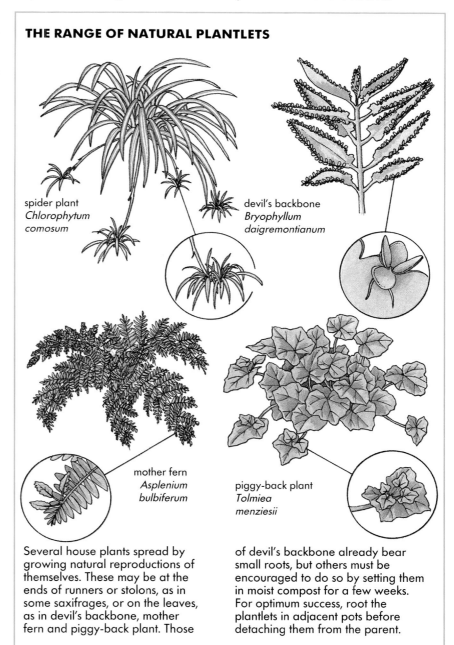

spider plant
Chlorophytum comosum

devil's backbone
Bryophyllum daigremontianum

mother fern
Asplenium bulbiferum

piggy-back plant
Tolmiea menziesii

Several house plants spread by growing natural reproductions of themselves. These may be at the ends of runners or stolons, as in some saxifrages, or on the leaves, as in devil's backbone, mother fern and piggy-back plant. Those of devil's backbone already bear small roots, but others must be encouraged to do so by setting them in moist compost for a few weeks. For optimum success, root the plantlets in adjacent pots before detaching them from the parent.

DIVIDING MULTI-STEMMED PLANTS

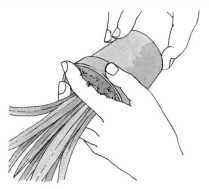

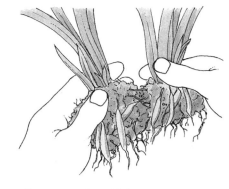

1 Invert the pot and place your fingers around the stems. Knock the rim of the pot against the edge of a table or work-bench to dislodge the compost and the roots.

2 Ease away the old, loose compost and carefully pull the crowns and roots of the plant apart. Cut away any damaged or dead roots with a sharp knife or a razor blade.

3 Set each divided piece in a pot part-filled with potting compost. Spread out the roots and trickle in compost so that the crown will sit just below the rim of the pot.

4 Fill the pot with more compost and level it about 12mm (½in) below the top of the rim. Water sparingly at first and grow the division on in a warm, lightly shaded position.

from or below the crown, each with an independent, well-developed root system.

Suitable plants for division include aspidistra, maidenhair fern (*Adiantum*), fittonia, umbrella grass (*Cyperus*), nephrolepis fern, peperomia, spider plant (*Chlorophytum*) and mother-in-law's tongue (*Sansevieria*).

House plants can be divided at any time during the growing period – late spring to early autumn. Knock the plant out of its pot and tease away the compost around the crown and root ball. This will expose the points at which the plant can be divided.

Grasp the base of the plant in both hands and pull it gently but firmly apart. If the crown or root-stock is thick and tough, sever the largest roots or the underground stems with a sharp knife. Pot the separated pieces at once in potting compost. Water sparingly at first and keep the pots in a shaded, warm position for a few weeks.

Certain plants – especially the shrimp plant (*Beloperone*), wandering Jew (*Tradescantia* and *Zebrina*) and pilea – are often grown commercially from three or more cuttings in the same small pot. As these grow, they form one single plant which can later be divided by pulling it apart. Pot up the pieces individually.

Separating offsets

Most of the bromeliads – such as vase plants (*Aechmea*), queen's tears (*Billbergia*) and flaming sword (*Vriesea*) – as well as other house plants, including false castor oil plant (*Fatsia*), amaryllis (*Hippeastrum*), agalonemas and several cacti, readily produce offsets or suckers. These small plants, which appear at the base of the parent, either close to it or a short distance away, may eventually overcrowd the pot.

Offsets which have reached about a third of the height of the parent plant can be removed easily and potted up separately. The best time for this type of propagation is between early and late summer.

Remove the plant from the pot and crumble away the excess soil. Hold the root ball, stems upwards, in one hand and tear or cut away the offset complete with roots, but take care not to break them.

Put a layer of moist potting compost in a 7.5-10cm (3-4in) pot, and set the offset on top so that the top of the crown is just below the rim of the pot. Trickle in more compost and firm with your fingers. Fill the pot with water and let drain.

Tall offsets will need staking for a couple of months until the root systems are well established and able to support the top-growth. Insert a thin cane close to the plant and secure it with wire ring ties, raffia or string.

Set the plant in a well-lit position, but out of direct sun for a few weeks – a north-west-facing window-sill is the ideal place. Keep the compost moist.

Stem sections

Sections from the lower part of the main stem of certain woody plants can be chopped into pieces and encouraged to produce roots and shoots. Each piece is trimmed just above a node and the top section is

BROMELIAD OFFSETS

Separation of the leaves of a blushing bromeliad (*Neoregelia*) reveals an offset suitable for separation. After removing the plant from its pot, sever the offset as close as possible to the main stem, using a sharp knife. Insert the detached offset in a rooting mixture at the same depth as it was growing before.

prepared and treated as a tip cutting. Suitable plants include good-luck plant (*Cordyline*), dracaena and dumb cane (*Dieffenbachia*). Gifts of the Polynesian ti plant – a variety of *Cordyline terminalis* – are often in the form of short pieces of cane ready to plant.

Stem section propagation can be adopted when cutting back the stem from which a tip cutting has already been taken – in fact, it is often necessary to remove such stems if the plant has grown leggy in an attempt to regain a more attractive shape. If the stem is a thick one, short pieces may be used. Each piece need be no more than 5cm (2in) long, provided it has one or two nodes. The position of the cuts in relation to the nodes is unimportant. Nick the base of each section to indicate which way it should be potted up.

Insert the short, thick cuttings into the rooting mixture vertically and half-buried, with a node or leaf bud facing upwards and the nicked edge in the compost. Or lay the sections vertically on the compost and cover them lightly until roots develop at one end.

Air layering

Eventually rubber plants (*Ficus elastica*), false aralias (*Dizygotheca elegantissima*) and certain other upright plants grow too tall and lose their lower leaves. Rather than throw the plant away, propagate it by air layering in spring to produce a shorter stemmed plant.

Using a sharp knife, remove the leaves 15-23cm (6-9in) below the growing tip. Cut flush with the stem, but without damaging the stem tissues. Then make a shallow upward-slanting cut about 3.5cm (1½in) long, starting below a node. Tie the stem to a stake, above and below the cut. Prop the cut open with a small wedge or matchstick. Brush both sides of the wound with hormone rooting powder.

Fold polythene around the cut. It should be about 15-18cm (6-7in) wide and long enough to come 7.5-10cm (3-4in) below and above the cut. Seal with adhesive tape below the cut to create a tube or sleeve. The use of clear polythene makes it easier to see when rooting has taken place, but black polythene excludes sunlight and may encourage better rooting.

Fill the polythene tube with moist sphagnum moss, moss peat or coir fibre, pressing it into and

STEM SECTION CUTTINGS

1 An overgrown *Dracaena fragrans* that has lost its lower leaves may no longer be attractive. It is an obvious candidate for propagation from thick stem cuttings.

2 Using a sharp knife or secateurs, cut the main stem into several short pieces, each of which should take root and produce shoots as long as it contains at least one healthy leaf node.

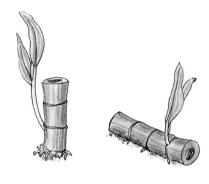

3 Stem sections may be placed in the compost either horizontally or vertically, the same way up as the original plant — stems inserted upside down will not root successfully.

4 Leaf shoots develop from nodes exposed to the air, while roots sprout from buried nodes. When a couple of leaves have unfurled, pot each cutting individually in potting compost.

AIR LAYERING A RUBBER PLANT

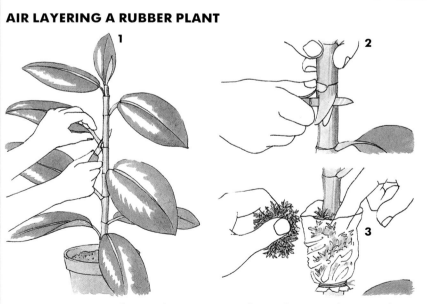

In spring, remove any leaves about 15-23cm (6-9in) below the top cluster on an overgrown plant (**1**). Cut the leaves flush with the stem. Make a slanting, upward cut, 3.5-5cm (1½-2in) long, from below

a node (**2**). Open out the cut and brush with rooting powder. Secure a polythene tube over the cut and pack with moist sphagnum moss or coir (**3**). When roots are visible, sever the shoot and pot it up.

PROPAGATION BY SEED

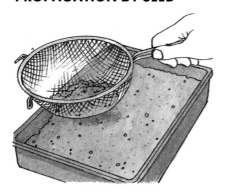

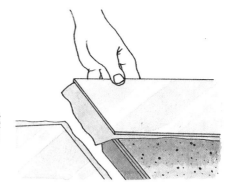

1 Before sowing dust-like seed in seedling compost, sift some of the mixture through a fine strainer. This finely ground top layer will stop the seeds from sinking too deeply.

2 Scatter the seeds thinly. With experience, you can shake them directly from the seed packet; or, mix them with some sand and sprinkle small pinches between finger and thumb.

3 To avoid the need for frequent watering, cover the tray or pot with glass or polythene, which maintains humidity. Some surface-sown seeds must be shaded from light.

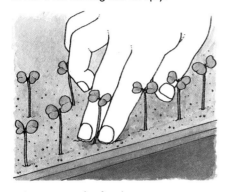

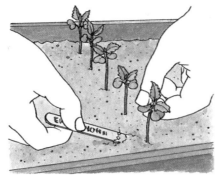

4 As soon as the first leaves appear, thin out the seedlings drastically – they need space for their developing root system. After thinning, gently firm the compost around the seedlings.

5 When each seedling is growing strongly, and before its roots become entangled, ease it out of the compost – a small plastic plant label makes a useful tool for this purpose.

6 Transplant each seedling singly into a small pot of proprietary compost. Hold the seedling by a leaf, which is expendable – not by its delicate and irreplaceable stem.

around the cut with a small stick or dibber. Seal the top of the tube with tape, so that the rooting medium will remain moist.

After eight to ten weeks the open wound should have produced roots. When this has occurred, sever the shoot below the tube and carefully free the roots from the polythene and moss. Discard the old plant or let it grow on to produce side-shoots.

Pot the new plant in a 10cm (4in) pot of compost. For the first few weeks – until the new root system has established – grow the plant at 18-21°C (64-70°F) and syringe the leaves daily with tepid water.

Seed propagation
House plant seed is becoming more readily available – in addition to the common busy Lizzie, cyclamen, celosia, coleus, cineraria, primula and streptocarpus, exotics such as bird of paradise flower (*Strelitzia*) banana plants (*Musa*) and angel's trumpet (*Datura*) are offered. Though mature

plants are slower to develop from seed than from other forms of propagation, this is the only way of growing hybrid strains, and is a rewarding way of growing many house plants.

Seeds come in all sizes, from dust-like specks to stones the size of an avocado pear. The tiniest ones are best mixed with a little sand in a saucer to make them more visible and hence easier to sow thinly and uniformly.

Sowing time and the required temperature for germination vary – follow the recommendations given on the packet. Most house plant seeds need a minimum temperature of 18°C (64°F), but some need as much as 27°C (80°F).

Sow seeds thinly on a proprietary seedling compost – it's better to waste some seeds than to sow too many, since well-spaced seedlings develop a better shape and are less prone to damping-off disease. Large seeds often benefit from being soaked overnight in water before sowing. Others have

tough coats, which must be nicked with a sharp knife to weaken them – barely perforate the coating using a slicing action without injuring the embryo inside.

Cover small but visible seeds with a thin sprinkling of finely sieved compost. Cover larger seeds with a layer equivalent to twice their diameter. Dust-like seed, on the other hand, should not be covered at all – merely mist spray with water to settle the seeds into the surface of the compost.

Keep the compost moist, but not wet, at all times – tiny seeds in particular shrivel and die even after a few hours of dryness. But constant watering disturbs seeds, so it is best to maintain a humid atmosphere which will reduce the need to water. Place the container in a propagating unit or cover it with a sheet of glass or clear polythene until seedlings emerge.

When they are large enough to handle, transplant seedlings into small pots of potting compost and grow them on.

HOUSE PLANTS FOR FREE

**Exotic and unusual house plants can be grown
from the stones and pips which are usually discarded
from tropical edible fruits.**

Don't throw away the stones and pips of edible fresh fruits which you buy from the greengrocer or supermarket, especially if they are exotic types from abroad – many are fertile and can be germinated to produce handsome pot plants for the home, greenhouse or conservatory.

Even if unsuccessful as house plants in the long term, the experiment will be educational and fascinating for children and adults alike – sometimes the most enthusiastic gardeners do not know what the parent plants of many imported fruits look like. Remember, though, that the stones and pips found in canned fruits and roasted and salted nuts will never germinate.

Easy-grown exotics

If you are not experienced in growing unfamiliar plants from seeds, the following types are quite easy and will give reliable results. Children in particular will enjoy the exercise and the final plants will look attractive indoors.

Avocado pear (*Persea americana*, syn. *P. gratissima*) has one huge stone in the centre. When the fruit is ripe and ready to eat the stone is potentially capable of germination – in fact, when a very ripe avocado is cut open the stone's mahogany-brown skin is often already split.

Gently wipe away any green flesh from the surface of the stone, then soak it for about two days in a bowl of tepid water. Keep the water warm by placing the bowl over a radiator or by putting it in an airing cupboard – cold water can inhibit the germination of this tropical plant.

Don't peel the stone unless the brown skin is flaky. To encourage germination, suspend the pre-soaked stone in the neck of a jar filled almost to the top with water. The simplest way of providing support for the stone is to push the tips of three matchsticks into the sides. This causes no real harm and the bruising may actually stimulate germination.

The egg-shaped stone must stand fattest end downward. Also ensure that the base of the stone remains submerged to a depth of 1-2cm (⅜-¾in) until a root sprouts from it – this generally takes five to eight weeks, perhaps more in winter. If the water turns cloudy, throw the stone away and start afresh – it has rotted inside.

The first sign of successful germination is a worm-like white taproot emerging from the base of the stone, though the stone may start to split open before this happens. A few weeks later a shoot will

◄ **Sweet potato** Related to the morning glory rather than the ordinary potato, sweet potato (*Ipomoea batatas*) is an edible tuber from the tropics. In the wild, it grows naturally as a scrambling climber with lush foliage and scarlet trumpet flowers.

The tubers can be grown indoors for ornamental purposes. Simply wedge them, root end downwards, in the neck of a bottle or jar of water; long fibrous roots and clambering shoots will soon develop, though the plant will not bear flowers.

GROWING AN AVOCADO PEAR

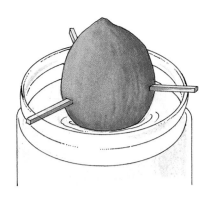

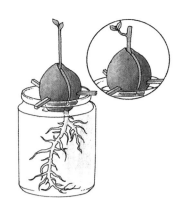

1 Soak a stone for two days in tepid water. There is no need to remove the skin unless it peels away easily. Then push the tips of three matchsticks into the sides of the stone and balance it in the neck of a jar filled almost to the top with water.

2 Keep the water topped up at all times – the base of the stone should be submerged to a depth of 1-2cm (3/8-3/4in). Roots should appear after five to eight weeks followed by a slender shoot. When the shoot reaches 15cm (6in) in height, nip off the top (inset).

3 A new shoot will soon develop from just below the cut top and this will be less vigorous than the original shoot, making a better-shaped final plant. Carefully pot up the seedling so that the top of the stone stands just above the surface of the compost.

4 Avocado plants grow rapidly and will need annual repotting. They tend to produce a tall, bare stem with several large, slender leaves at the top. Pinch out the tip of the main stem when the required height is reached. Support the stem with a cane if necessary.

appear from the top of the stone. At this time the avocado needs plenty of light, so put it on a sunny window-sill.

The shoot elongates quickly. When it is about 15cm (6in) tall cut off the tip, leaving just a bare stalk – left untrimmed it grows lanky and fails to develop side-shoots.

Surprisingly, a new shoot soon grows from the top of the cut stalk and this is much slower growing and more compact in habit.

At this stage – or earlier if you prefer – pot up the young plant, setting the stone with its neck just above the surface of moist potting compost. Large evergreen leaves develop and within 1½-2 years you will have a stately house plant.

Citrus fruits, such as lemons (*Citrus limon*), oranges (*C. sinensis* and *C. aurantium*), tangerines

(*C. reticulata*), grapefruits (*C. paradisi*) and limes (*C. aurantiifolia*), contain pips (seeds), though some are seedless.

If the seeds are plump they can be germinated in pots of seedling compost to produce attractive foliage plants which have a tangy aromatic scent. Though they are unlikely to yield edible fruits indoors, their white flowers are pretty and powerfully scented.

If you have a conservatory or heated greenhouse, citrus plants can be grown on into large shrubs or small trees which will bear edible fruits.

The best time of year to sow citrus pips is early spring, but gentle warmth should promote germination at any time of the year. Use a coir-based seedling compost for best results.

There is no need to store the pips or treat them in any way – simply sow them fresh, on their sides and at a depth equal to twice their diameter. Citrus pips sprout within a few weeks.

If you sow a single seed from an orange or lime, you may find that two or three shoots emerge. Only one is a true seedling – the others are a special form of vegetative off-spring which develop asexually within the seed shell.

The true seedling has features which are slightly dissimilar to the parent and are least likely to bear edible fruits. The vegetative offspring are identical to the parent and are potential bearers of edible fruit.

Within a few years seedlings develop into bushy plants about 90cm-1.2m (3-4ft) tall.

Coffee beans (*Coffea arabica*) can be obtained from some delicatessens and specialist coffee shops in a fresh, unroasted state. Sow them in spring in pots of seedling compost. Roasted coffee beans will not germinate. Maintain a temperature of 21-25°C (70-77°F) until the seedlings emerge.

Coffee plants are bushy with evergreen, dark green, glossy leaves. They may eventually produce clusters of attractive white, strongly fragrant flowers followed by green berries which turn red and then nearly black as the coffee beans ripen within.

However, coffee plants are chiefly grown indoors for their foliage value – the beans will be of poor quality.

Date palms (*Phoenix dactylifera*) can be grown from fresh date stones, making elegant plants with a tropical air for the home or conservatory. The stones are fairly difficult to germinate, but the effort can be worthwhile.

Being a tropical plant, the date needs plenty of warmth to start growing. Begin by lightly sand-papering or filing the surface of the stones to roughen their surfaces and allow moisture to penetrate more easily.

Next, soak the stones in tepid water for two days. Prepare several stones even if you want just one plant, because many are infertile.

Mix the soaked stones with a few handfuls of moist compost in a watertight plastic bag. Seal the bag and put it in a warm airing cupboard. Check the contents

▶ **Peanut plants** These little annuals are fascinating plants for a warm, sunny spot in the home. Their clover-like growth is not spectacular, but yellow pea flowers produce seed pods which the plants self-sow by bending their stems downwards into the ground or compost. Peanuts develop and ripen underground within the pod.

weekly and re-moisten the compost as necessary.

When small shoots or roots appear, pot up the seedlings individually with the stone about 2.5cm (1in) below the surface. Place the pots in a sunny spot and keep them moist.

Growth is slow and for several months each seedling will resemble a blade of grass. After two or three years young plants will have developed a small spray of fan-like leaves, but don't expect flowers or fruits on pot-grown palms.

Keep plants moist during active growth, but let them dry out between waterings in winter. Don't over-pot date palms – they like to be slightly pot-bound.

Peanuts (*Arachis hypogaea*), sometimes called groundnuts or monkey nuts, will germinate, provided they have not been treated, to produce unusual, low-growing or scrambling house plants.

The peanut plant is an annual, closely related to peas, beans and clover. In temperate climates, it is grown mainly for its curiosity value. The edible part is a kernel, not a true nut.

Choose nuts sold in their husks, shell them carefully and discard (or eat) any nuts which have split in half. Alternatively, leave the peanuts in their husks, but gently split one side to let in moisture. Pre-shelled, unroasted peanuts are also suitable, but again use only whole ones. However, the germination of pre-shelled peanuts tends to be less reliable.

Sow peanuts about 2.5cm (1in) deep, three to four in a 13cm (5in) pot filled with moist coir-based seedling compost. The best time of year is spring, but they can be sown at any time of year.

Keep the pot at a minimum temperature of 21°C (70°F), preferably in a heated propagator until seedlings emerge. This usually takes a couple of weeks.

Once the seeds have germinated, move the pot to a warm, sunny window-sill and keep it well watered. Growth resembles that of clover, though peanut plants are more robust.

Yellow pea flowers appear in summer and these are followed by seed pods – the plant's curiosity feature. As they age, the pods bend downwards and bury themselves in the soil, hence the need for a soft, porous compost.

Pineapples (*Ananas comosus*) are bromeliads and can often be grown from the leafy tuft at the top of each fruit. When buying a pineapple, select one which has an unbruised healthy looking top. Greyish leaves are normal and not a sign of disease.

GROWING LEMONS FROM PIPS

1 Fill a 10cm (4in) pot with seedling compost, water thoroughly and leave it to drain. Bury four to six fresh lemon pips about 12mm (½in) deep, positioning them on their sides.

2 Cover the pot loosely with a piece of clear polythene and secure it with an elastic band. Keep the pot in a warm place with a minimum temperature of 18°C (64°F) until seedlings emerge.

3 Pot up the seedlings individually as soon as they are large enough to handle. Repot whenever the lemon plants become pot-bound, using a proprietary potting compost.

GROWING-ON A PINEAPPLE TOP

1 Select a pineapple with a healthy tuft of unbruised leaves. It has the best flavour and it may be possible to root the top. Cut off the crown below the upper row of 'pips' on the skin.

2 Store the top on its side for one or two days until the cut surface of the flesh has dried out. Then plant the pineapple top in a pot filled with a lime-free potting compost.

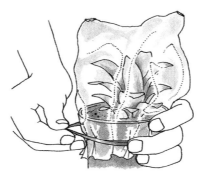

3 Sprinkle fresh compost around the crown of the pineapple so that the fleshy base is just buried – beware of the spiny leaves. Firm in with your fingers and water well.

4 Cover the pot with a clear polythene bag and secure it with an elastic band. Cut off the corners of the bag to allow a little air to circulate inside. Keep the plant warm (minimum 18°C/64°F.)

5 Rooting is indicated by new growth from the centre of the leaf rosette and by freshening of the existing leaves. At this time remove the bag. Repot the plant into a larger pot as necessary.

Cut off the top with a 12mm (½in) thick slice of the juicy flesh attached. Put this aside for one or two days until the cut surface of the flesh has dried out. Peel away any brown leaves around the base of the tuft.

Plant the pineapple top in a pot filled with a coir-based, lime-free potting compost. Water the compost and cover the pot with a clear polythene bag until new leaves appear at the centre of the tuft and the existing leaves start to grow larger – a sign that the pineapple top has rooted.

After several years, the plant may flower and produce a small, inedible fruit, but it is for the stiff, spiny leaves that pineapples are valued indoors.

Other fun plants

Try germinating the seeds, pips or stones of kumquats (*Fortunella japonica* and *F. margarita*), loquats (*Eriobotrya japonica*), lychees (*Litchi chinensis*) and pomegranates (*Punica granatum*).

Also experiment with any of the curious fruits, such as uglis, jujubes and feijoas, which are becoming more and more familiar on supermarket shelves – they will all prove fascinating in their individual ways.

For small quantities of seed, 7.5-10cm (3-4in) pots are ideal, but for larger numbers sow in a seed tray. As a general rule, sow seeds at a depth equal to twice their diameter in a proprietary seedling compost.

A warm, humid atmosphere is likely to encourage germination of tropical species, so cover the pot or tray with a plastic bag, or place it inside a propagating unit. A temperature of about 18°C (64°F) is suitable for most types.

When seedlings are large enough to handle, transplant them into individual small pots filled with a proprietary potting compost – John Innes No. 1 is ideal. Pot on into larger pots with a stronger compost, such as John Innes No. 2, when the root balls become congested and fill the pots – usually after one year.

Large stone seeds may require special treatment before they will germinate. Peach stones, for example, need to be subjected to low temperatures (maximum 4°C/39°F), perhaps in a refrigerator, for several weeks before sowing – in nature, the fallen fruit would have to overwinter in the cold before the stone seeds are ready to germinate.

Climbing plants, such as grapes (*Vitis vinifera*), kiwi fruits (*Actinidia chinensis*), melons (*Cucumis melo*) and passion fruits (*Passiflora edulis*), don't make good long-term house plants, but can be grown in a conservatory or greenhouse, either in large pots or in open borders. They must be provided with suitable support.

GROWING INDOOR BULBS

Pots and bowls of brightly coloured and sweetly scented flowers add a touch of spring to the indoor garden in mid-winter.

Every year in late summer and early autumn, thousands of spring bulbs are on sale in garden centres and nurseries. Many have been specially bred under controlled conditions so that they can be induced or forced to flower indoors months before they would open in the garden. Hyacinths, narcissi, early tulips and large-flowered crocus are the most popular bulbs for forcing and can be brought into bloom by Christmas if given special care.

All bulbs and corms contain immature leaf and flower buds which begin to develop when they are set in a suitable growing medium – compost, bulb fibre or plain water. However, in order to produce a fine flowering display, it is essential to first establish a strong and healthy root system; this is achieved by exposing the potted bulbs to cool, moist and dark conditions for a couple of months.

Forcing bulbs
All kinds of containers can be used for growing indoor bulbs – ordinary flower pots, or ceramic, glass and terracotta bowls (many bulbs for forcing are offered in kit form complete with container, bulb fibre and precise growing instructions). Special bulb fibre or proprietary loam-based compost are equally suitable, though bulb fibre is preferable for containers without drainage holes as compost can become water-logged.

Moisten the fibre or compost thoroughly before placing it in the chosen container and set the bulbs on top, packing them close together. Small bulbs should ideally finish with their tops about 2.5cm (1in) below the rim of the container, while the top halves of large bulbs (such as hyacinths and narcissi) can be left exposed above the compost. Fill in the spaces with more fibre to hold the bulbs firm; leave a space of 12mm (½in) below the rim and top up with water.

Wrap the containers in newspaper and place them in the coolest and darkest room available.

Ideally, they should be placed outdoors, against a north-facing wall or in a plunge bed beneath 15cm (6in) of soil covered with black polythene. Every two or three weeks, check that the containers have not dried out; moisten the compost if necessary. When the shoot tips are 2.5-5cm (1-2in) tall, move the containers into better light with temperatures of no

▼ **Spring-flowering bulbs** Dainty narcissi and cheerful crocuses are familiar sights in spring. They are ideal for forcing into early bloom indoors and can be planted out in the garden later on. Tender bulbs, such as lachenalia, with strap-shaped leaves and tricoloured flowers, and striking veltheimias with huge, wavy leaves and 60cm (2ft) tall flower stems, need warmer indoor conditions throughout the year and an annual rest period.

POTTING BULBS FOR FORCING

1 In early autumn, pot up bulbs for forcing, using moistened compost or bulb fibre for containers without drainage holes. Bulb fibre encourages roots but contains no nourishment, and bulbs end up shrivelled.

2 Add compost or fibre so that the tops of small bulbs finish 2.5cm (1in) below the container rim. The tops of large bulbs can finish above the rim. Fill in with more compost or fibre and level the top 12mm (½in) below the rim.

3 Fill the container to the rim with water and leave it to soak through the compost for a short time before wrapping the container in newspaper and carefully placing it in a cool, dark place. Check occasionally to see that the compost remains just moist.

more than 10°C (50°F). When the shoots have grown about 10cm (4in) high, the bowls can be moved to their flowering positions. A cool, well-lit window-sill is the ideal position.

Remove the flowers as they fade, but leave the stems and foliage intact to nurture the bulbs; move the containers to a cool room and keep them watered until the foliage dies down. Turn the clumps out of the containers and plant them in the garden.

Water culture

Hyacinths, early narcissi and crocuses can also be grown in water. Special hyacinth glasses are available, but any vase or container with a narrow neck in which the bulbs can sit comfortably is suitable. Fill each glass with plain tap water (a small lump of charcoal keeps the water clean and sweet-smelling) to 12mm (½in) above the neck; place one bulb in each glass so that the bulb base is in contact with the water. Keep the hyacinth glasses in a dark and cool but frost-free place until 10cm (4in) roots and 2.5cm (1in) long shoot tips have developed. Move them into better light and warmer conditions for the flowering period.

Crocuses and Tazetta narcissi can be grown in shallow water-proof containers filled with a good layer of pebbles, which can support the bulbs and keep them upright. Keep the pebbles and bulb bases covered with water and top up as necessary as roots develop and flower stems grow. Narcissi bulbs do not need to be kept in the dark and will often flower on a well-lit window-sill after about six weeks.

Bulbs grown in water culture use up all their stored nourishment and are unlikely to ever recover; they are best discarded after flowering.

Untreated bulbs

Most hardy garden bulbs can be brought indoors to flower, but it is the spring-flowering types that generally give the greatest pleasure. Snowdrops and winter aconites, miniature blue and purple *Iris reticulata* and *I. histrioides*, glory-of-the-snow (*Chionodoxa*), muscaris, scillas and species crocuses and tulips are all compact enough to bring temporary colour to the indoor garden.

At planting time in autumn, reserve some bulbs for putting in pots and well-drained bowls of good potting compost. Leave the pots outdoors or in a cold greenhouse until growth is well advanced; they can be brought indoors from mid or late winter onwards, and will flower about three weeks earlier than in the garden. All do best in a cool and bright site. After flowering, move the pots outdoors again and plant out the bulbs when the ground can be worked.

The lovely, sweetly scented lily-of-the-valley (*Convallaria majalis*) which normally flowers in late spring, can be forced into bloom in winter. In late autumn, before the foliage dies down completely, dig up a clump of the rhizomatous roots, making sure there are plenty of plump buds visible; pot them in compost with added sand for drainage. Keep the pots in a cool greenhouse or cold frame for a couple of months, then bring the pots indoors to good light and a temperature of about 20°C (68°F) for flowering in late winter. Keep the compost moist at all times.

Tender bulbs

Many exotic bulbous plants are not hardy enough for growing in the garden, but make fine indoor flowering pot plants. Flowering at different times of the year, depending on the species, they include hippeastrums, autumn- and winter-flowering florist's cyclamen, summer-blooming glory lilies and the dainty Cape cowslips (*Lachenalia*).

Tender bulbs need slightly different treatment to forced bulbs and should be grown in a proprietary loam-based compost. Large bulbs, such as clivias and hippeastrums, look spectacular as single specimen plants, while freesias, Cape cowslips and star of Bethlehem (*Ornithogalum arabicum*) make a better show when planted six or more to a 12.5cm (5in) pot. Set large bulbs so that their tips are level with the surface of the compost, 2.5cm (1in) below the pot rim; small bulbs should be potted with their tips 2.5cm (1in) below the surface.

Most tender bulbs die down after flowering when the foliage turns yellow; they should then be given a rest period, in cool temperatures and with little or no water, until the growth cycle is restarted with renewed watering.

▲ **Soil-less cultivation** Many bulbs, especially prepared hyacinths and bunch-flowered narcissi, flower easily without compost or bulb fibre. Special hyacinth glasses are readily available in a variety of shapes, but any glass container or vase with a constricted neck is suitable. The bulbs must be forced in the dark until roots have developed and the growing point has expanded by a couple of inches.

▶ **Greigii tulips** Notable for their handsome foliage, striped or marbled with purple-maroon, the Greigii tulips flower in the garden in mid-spring. Growing no more than 23cm (9in) high, the bright scarlet 'Red Riding Hood' can be brought indoors in late winter in order to flower several weeks early. Prepared bulbs of early single and double tulips can be forced to flower by Christmas.

▶ **Bunch-flowered narcissi** The pure white Tazetta narcissi 'Paper White' will flower within six weeks of being planted. When grown in bulb fibre or on permanently moist pebbles, each bulb produces several stems, 30cm (12in) high, topped with sweet-scented flowers. Keep them on a well-lit window-sill where the temperature is not too high. The bulbs are too tender for garden planting.

▼ **Basket wares** Winter is transformed into early spring with a colourful indoor display of polyanthus primroses, blue, pink and red hyacinths and elegant *Cyclamen persicum*. After blooming, primroses and hyacinths can be planted out in the garden for flowering the following spring. After a dry summer rest, the cyclamen is easily induced to flower indoors year after year.

HOUSE PLANT PROBLEMS

**The many difficulties associated with house plants can
be avoided by maintaining a programme of routine care.
A few pests and diseases need special attention.**

Plants growing indoors have the advantage over those in the garden of being partially isolated from pests, especially soil-borne types. So, if you can be sure that all the plants you bring into your home are pest-free, subsequent infestation should be minimal.

However, cut flowers and plants growing in a window-box or on a patio below a window can be intermediate hosts for active pests such as whitefly, caterpillars, aphids and spider mites. Diseases are often airborne and can invade more readily.

In all cases, the best way to keep house plants healthy is to give them precisely the right growing conditions.

When you buy a house plant or transfer one from a greenhouse to the home, give it a few weeks of quarantine in the kitchen, bathroom or a spare room – if pests or diseases are present they could soon spread to healthy plants nearby. During this period, watch out for signs of trouble and take immediate action if pests or diseases are spotted. They can strike at any time of year indoors.

Pot plants which have been growing in a greenhouse or have spent the summer in the garden may harbour some troublesome garden pests – such as slugs, snails and caterpillars. Check the plants thoroughly, examining both sides of the leaves, as well as flowers and buds. Knock each plant out of its pot and check the root ball – earwigs often hide in the compost near the drainage holes.

When chemical control is necessary, choose a proprietary brand which is recommended for use on house or greenhouse plants – most garden chemicals are unsafe to use in a closed environment where you will breathe in the fumes or handle treated plants. Always follow the manufacturer's instructions on the package.

If possible, take infested plants into the garden for spraying – most chemicals, however safe, smell unpleasant and can stain fabrics. Wear rubber gloves and wash your hands afterwards. Never use greenhouse fumigants in the home.

◄ **Mite damage** Mites are serious plant pests and difficult to control as they live within buds and leaf tissues. A badly infested hyacinth shows twisted and badly discoloured flowers.

▼ **Scale insects** These troublesome pests which attack house plants are often first noticed when leaves become sticky. The minute pests form brown, yellow or white scales which disfigure the leaves and sap the plants' energy.

PESTS

Most indoor pests are tiny, so scrutinize all house plants regularly – if you wait until the symptoms of attack are obvious it may be too late. When repotting plants, pay special attention to the roots, which can harbour the larvae (grubs) of many insects, as well as some adult pests – underground pests often go undetected until the plant collapses.

Leaf and stem pests can be grouped according to their method of attack. Mites and aphids suck the sap, causing yellowing or distorted growth, often leaving a sticky or sooty deposit on the leaves. Chewing insects bite stems and leaf edges or eat holes in the leaves. And the larvae of some insects bore tunnels or 'mines' in the leaves just below the surface.

There are a number of safe house plant insecticides based on permethrin, pirimiphos-methyl, pyrethum or gamma-HCH, or systemic insecticides such as dimethoate. These may be in concentrated form for dilution as a spray, in aerosol cans or in tablets for inserting into the compost.

APHIDS

Symptoms Colonies of small, round, green, pinkish, yellow or black sap-sucking insects, mostly wingless but with some winged individuals present. Stems, leaves and flower buds rapidly become distorted, sticky and weak.
Treatment Cut off and destroy badly infested growth. Spray regularly with insecticide.

CATERPILLARS

Symptoms Caterpillars chew leaves, making holes or notched edges. Some spin leaves together with silk threads. They rarely derive from eggs laid indoors, but can be brought into the home on plants moved from a greenhouse, conservatory or garden.
Treatment Pick off and destroy individual caterpillars.

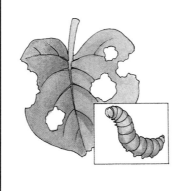

EARWIGS

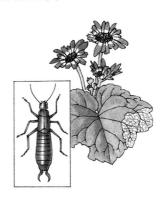

Symptoms Dark reddish brown, narrow-bodied, 2-2.5cm (¾-1in) long insects with a pair of pincers at the tail chew tattered holes in leaves and flowers. They feed at night, remaining hidden under leaves, in flowers or in the compost during the day.
Treatment Shake earwigs out of plants and destroy them by hand.

FUNGUS GNATS

Symptoms Minute gnat-like flies (also called mushroom flies or sciarids) lay eggs in potting compost. Though usually harmless, their white, black-headed maggots sometimes eat roots, weakening growth. They are most troublesome in very moist acid compost.
Treatment Drench the compost with insecticide; avoid over-watering.

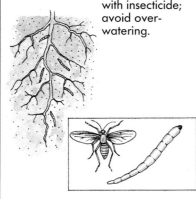

LEAF MINERS

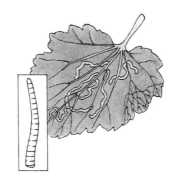

Symptoms Slender sap-sucking maggots burrow or 'mine' through leaf tissues just below the surface, creating a network of pale markings and weakening growth. Chrysanthemums and cinerarias are particularly susceptible to attack.
Treatment Pick off and destroy individual mined leaves; spray with pirimiphos-methyl.

MEALY BUGS

Symptoms Small, oval bugs covered with a whitish cottony secretion form colonies on stems and leaf stalks, especially in sheathed leaf axils. Foliage turns yellow, wilts and may fall.
Treatment Wipe off bugs with a damp cloth or with a cotton bud soaked in methylated spirit; spray with dimethoate.

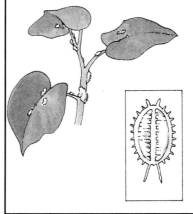

MITES

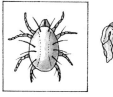

Symptoms Minute sap-sucking insects lay eggs in vast quantities, giving leaves and flower stems the appearance of being coated with dust. Leaves and flower stems become twisted, brittle and scabby; buds wither and open flowers lose their colour. Attacks can often be fatal unless dealt with quickly. The mite most usually found indoors is the cyclamen mite, though this pest attacks many other house plants, including African violets, begonias, busy Lizzies, gloxinias, ivies and pelargoniums.
Treatment Pick off and destroy all infested leaves, buds and flowers. Spray repeatedly with a house plant insecticide, such as permethrin or pirimiphos-methyl until all eggs and mites are destroyed. Maintain adequate humidity.

RED SPIDER MITES

Symptoms Minute reddish sap-sucking insects spin fine, silky webs mainly on the undersides of leaves, which become mottled, turn yellow, curl up and fall. Hot, dry conditions encourage attack.
Treatment Cut off badly infested growth; spray repeatedly with insecticide; mist-spray daily with tepid water.

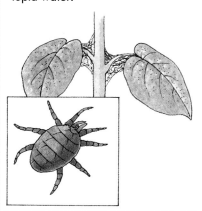

SCALE INSECTS

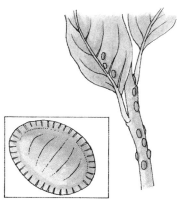

Symptoms Small brown or yellowish motionless scales — each of which covers a sap-sucking insect — infest stems and veins on leaf undersides, causing stickiness and withering.
Treatment Wipe off with a damp cloth or with a cottonwool bud soaked in methylated spirit; or spray with malathion.

SYMPHALIDS

Symptoms Tiny, creamy white, centipede-like creatures eat small roots and burrow inside larger roots, causing loss of vigour, wilting and leaf drop. This pest is found only in unsterilized potting composts.
Treatment Drench compost with insecticide. Use sterilized potting compost.

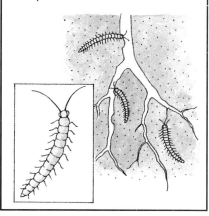

THRIPS

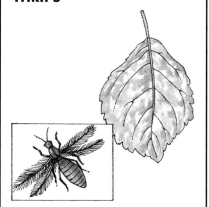

Symptoms Tiny black, feathery-winged jumping insects suck sap from soft tissues. Leaves become mottled or streaked; flowers develop white spots. Blobs of reddish excretion turn black, fouling leaves and flowers.
Treatment Pick off and destroy damaged leaves and flowers; spray with insecticide.

VINE WEEVILS

Symptoms Creamy white, 8mm (⅓in) long, fat grubs eat roots and tubers, causing rapid wilting and plant death. Adult beetle-like weevils chew holes in leaves.
Treatment Pick off and destroy adults. Drench soil with insecticide, but once the symptoms are evident it is usually too late to save the plant.

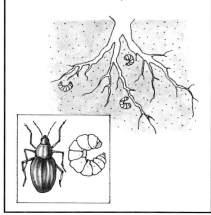

WHITEFLY

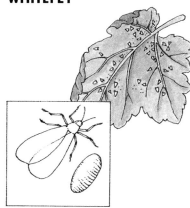

Symptoms Tiny moth-like white flies infest the undersides of leaves, flying away when disturbed. Their whitish scale-like larvae suck sap and excrete sticky honeydew. Whiteflies are unsightly and severe infestations weaken growth and cause yellowing.
Treatment Spray repeatedly with pirimiphos-methyl or permethrin.

DISEASES

Plant diseases result from infection by fungi, bacteria or viruses. Good hygiene is the best preventative measure since diseases are contagious. Space plants well apart so that there is a free passage of air between them – moist, stagnant air encourages the spread of many fungal diseases.

Remove any unhealthy looking or dead material as soon as possible. Also remove bruised or damaged leaves. Always use sterile potting composts, since soil-borne diseases can be very troublesome. Never use garden soil for potting house plants.

As with insecticides, if you decide to use chemicals for the control of house plant diseases do not choose those which are recommended solely for garden plants – they may be noxious indoors. In any case, it is best to take the plants outdoors before treating them. Liquid copper, benomyl, carbendazim and thiophanate-methyl can be used safely and treated plants may be brought back indoors as soon as the leaves are dry and the smell has gone.

CROWN AND STEM ROT

Symptoms Stems become soft and slimy. Crown-forming plants are attacked at their centre by this fungal disease, causing leaves to rot away from the crown.
Treatment Cut away diseased stems, dusting wounds with sulphur; destroy badly affected plants. Avoid over-watering, low temperature and poor ventilation.

GREY MOULD (botrytis)

Symptoms Fleshy leaves, stems and flowers covered with fluffy grey mould, causing stunting.
Treatment Cut away affected growth, dusting wounds with sulphur; destroy badly affected plants. Treat minor outbreaks with fungicide. Avoid high humidity, don't wet leaves when watering and improve ventilation.

LEAF SPOT

Symptoms Brown or yellowish spots on leaves, sometimes with a moist central area. Spots may enlarge and join up, killing the entire leaf.
Treatment Cut off and destroy affected leaves; spray with fungicide and reduce watering until cured. Don't allow water to settle on the leaves.

POWDERY MILDEW

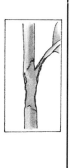

Symptoms White powdery fungus coating or spotting leaves and stems. Flowers are sometimes also affected. Soft-leaved plants are most susceptible. Unlike grey mould, mildew is not fluffy.
Treatment Cut off and destroy affected leaves and stems; spray with fungicide. Improve ventilation.

ROOT ROT

Symptoms Leaves turn yellow, wilt and fall. Roots slimy. Symptoms may not appear until it is too late to save the plant.
Treatment Remove the plant from its pot and shake away all compost, cut away diseased roots, dust the rest with sulphur, then repot. Destroy badly affected plants. Avoid over-watering.

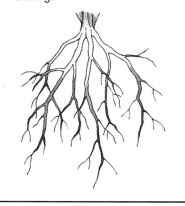

SOOTY MOULD

Symptoms Unsightly black fungus growing on the sticky honeydew secreted by aphids and other sap-sucking pests. Leaf pores become clogged and light is blocked out, reducing growth.
Treatment Wipe leaves with a cloth soaked in warm water; rinse with more water. Control honeydew-secreting pests.

DISORDERS

If house plants show signs of ill-health, but no evidence of pest or disease attack can be detected, the problem is likely to be associated with poor cultural conditions. In fact, most house plant troubles are caused by incorrect watering or temperature control, draughts, dry air, nutrient starvation, cramped roots, poor light or too much direct sunlight.

Remember that those plants which are grown indoors in temperate regions of the world often grow in very different environments in the wild. These conditions must be matched as closely as possible if the plants are to remain healthy. Unfortunately, house plants vary enormously in their origins and you may choose to grow together – perhaps unwittingly – types with widely differing likes and dislikes.

If any of the symptoms featured below occur on your house plants, trim away any growth which has been permanently damaged and take measures to overcome the cause of the problem – for example, by moving the plant.

BROWN BLOTCHES

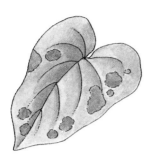

Symptoms Brown or discoloured blotches or spots on leaves.
Causes Areas of dark brown, soft tissue may be caused by over-watering. Pale brown, crisp tissue is a sign of under-watering. Pale blotches often appear when cold water settles on the leaves or if plants are inadvertently sprayed with cosmetic aerosols.

BROWN EDGES/TIPS

Symptoms Leaf edges or tips turn brown.
Causes Brown or yellowish edges are a sign of too much or too little water, scorching by sun through glass, poor light, wrong temperature, over-feeding, too dry air or draughts. If only the leaf tips turn brown (*inset*), the cause is dry air or pot-bound plants.

CURLING LEAVES

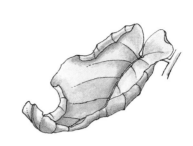

Symptoms Leaves curl up along their edges and eventually fall.
Causes If this disorder occurs in winter the cause is probably cold draughts or generally too low temperatures. Over-watering can cause similar symptoms at any time of year. Unfurl the leaves to check for small leaf-rolling caterpillars.

DRIED-UP LEAVES

Symptoms Leaves dry up, turn brown all over and eventually fall.
Causes If the plant is close to a fire or radiator, the cause is scorching. Elsewhere in the room, the cause may be under-watering, insufficient daylight, or too high temperatures with a combined lack of humidity.

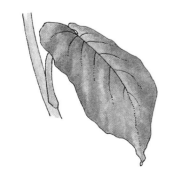

FLOWER BUDS FALL

Symptoms Plump, seemingly healthy flower buds fall off before they open.
Causes Under-watering, erratic watering, dry air or a sudden change in growing conditions are all common causes of bud fall. Insufficient daylight results in poor flower production and bud abortion.

NO FLOWERS

Symptoms Generally healthy plants refuse to produce flowers.
Causes Insufficient daylight is a common cause. Some plants require a precise daylength regime to promote flower initiation. Over-feeding may encourage leaf growth at the expense of flowers. Many cacti need a period of dry rest before they will flower.

SLOW/POOR GROWTH

Symptoms Plants fail to develop at the rate expected during the normal growing season.
Causes Under-feeding or insufficient daylight are common causes. Over-watering can also slow down growth. Knock the plant out of its pot and check that it is not pot-bound — pot-on with fresh compost if necessary. Dust can clog leaf pores, especially those with a felted or hairy surface, preventing them from breathing properly.

Do not expect active growth in winter — many plants go into a period of dormancy during low temperatures and poor light, but this is not a sign of ill-health. Remember that some plants, such as cacti, woody-stemmed shrubs and many tropical palms, are naturally very slow growing.

SPINDLY GROWTH

Symptoms Abnormally tall, soft growth with thin stems and pale leaves.
Causes Under-feeding or insufficient daylight are the causes during the normal active growth period. At other times, when the plant should be dormant, excess warmth stimulates growth but there is too little sunlight.

SUDDEN LEAF FALL

Symptoms Leaves fall off, with no previous signs of ailment.
Causes A shock to the plant's metabolism — for example, a sudden change in temperature, light intensity or water supply. Re-potting into too large a pot can also cause stress. Cold air and shock during transit can defoliate bought plants.

VARIEGATION LOSS

Symptoms Plants which should have variegated or coloured foliage develop all-green leaves on new growth.
Causes Insufficient light is the sole cause. Affected leaves cannot be restored to their correct colour, so remove them. Given more light, subsequent growth should be variegated.

WILTING

Symptoms Leaves become limp; shoots or entire plants may keel over.
Causes Under-watering is a common cause, but over-watering can also be to blame. If the symptoms occur only around midday during summer, too much sun and heat are the causes. Also check that the plant is not pot-bound.

YELLOW LOWER LEAVES

Symptoms Mature leaves at the base of the plant turn yellow and eventually fall.
Causes With many species, it is normal for basal leaves to fall when they reach the end of their active life. If several leaves fall at once, a cold draught or over-watering are probably to blame.

YELLOW NEW LEAVES

Symptoms The leaves on all new growth are abnormally yellow, but otherwise healthy.
Causes The plant is probably an acid-lover, in which case the cause is too much lime in the compost resulting from the continual use of hard water. Use soft rain-water or boiled water and a lime-free compost.

POTS AND CONTAINERS

**Almost any container can be used to display
plants, and decorative items originally designed for quite
different purposes are often the most eye-catching.**

All indoor plants have two basic requirements – a growing medium, usually compost, and a container to hold it. Ordinary garden soil is unsuitable for house plants, partly because it may harbour weed seedlings, pests and disease spores, and partly because it may be short of nutrients and not have a suitable structure, such as adequate drainage or water-holding capacity.

Potting composts

House plants should be grown in sterilized compost, and there are many proprietary brands from which to choose. Some, like the popular John Innes formulations, are loam or soil-based with added fertilizers; they are heavy, retaining water and nutrients well, with

No. 1 being suitable for young plants and seedlings, and No. 2 which has more loam, lime and extra fertilizer, being ideal for most mature pot plants. Lime-free composts for acid-loving plants are also widely available.

Soil-less or peat-based composts are lighter to handle, but are also more difficult to water. They must be kept moist at all times, for once they have dried out, they shrink and leave a space between root ball and pot through which water runs without any benefit to the plants. Soil-less composts, which are now often made with peat substitutes such as coir, should be potted loosely, never tamped down.

In addition, there are special-purpose composts formulated to suit particular plant groups, such

as bromeliads, cacti, ferns and orchids. Perlite, a heat-expanded volcanic mineral, is extremely water-absorbent and can be added to potting mixtures when a particularly open texture is required.

Choosing the correct pot size

Many of our popular house plants grow to enormous sizes in their natural habitats. In the home, however, they remain manageable because their roots are restricted within pots. Eventually, a

▼ **Stylish containers** Choose decorative containers which complement particular types of plants and which suit the style of a room. These elegant planters and pots appear tailor-made for their occupants, each adding to the charm of the other.

▲ **Display case** An elegant bamboo bird cage contains feathery asparagus ferns, trailing tradescantias and philodendrons.

▼ **Teapot cosies** A collection of teapots with a blue colour theme harmonizes with pink and mauve primulas. The plants are grown in plastic pots and can be removed and replaced once flowering has finished.

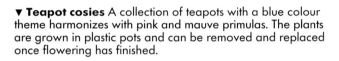

▲ **Plant display** Many ornaments, especially those with a gardening theme, make charming containers. This young asparagus fern (*Asparagus densiflorus* 'Sprengeri'), top-dressed with small pebbles, looks entirely natural in its hand-crafted pottery wheelbarrow.

◄ **Wickerwork baskets** The pleasing soft brown colours of wicker baskets complement flowering and foliage plants alike. Choose shapes to suit plant types — tubs for tulips, oval baskets for a collection of primulas and square baskets for chrysanthemums and trailing ivies.

▲ **Trailing house plant** Tall pedestals are ideal for displaying trailing house plants, such as the wandering Jew (*Tradescantia fluminensis*), especially fast-growing in the green and white-striped variety 'Quicksilver'.

► **Unusual containers** This humorous group includes such unconventional containers as a cat's feeding bowl for mauve campanulas and an old hat box supporting a yucca.

▲ **Victorian jardinière** Popular and almost obligatory in well-appointed Victorian parlours, the highly glazed jardinère consists of a large decorative plant bowl on a tall matching pedestal. Authentic pots have a small inner ledge near the base of the bowl on which a plant pot can rest, allowing surplus water to drain into the cavity below.

Such elaborately decorated containers demand dramatic plant displays — here, a mature spider plant (*Chlorophytum comosum*) drapes slender green- and white-striped leaves amid long flowering stems set with young plantlets.

▲ ▶ **Parlour palm** One of the easiest house plants to grow, the parlour palm (*Chamaedorea elegans*) is an elegant foliage plant that tolerates poor light, air pollution and normal room temperatures. It does object, though, to dry air. It can be mist-sprayed, but it is easier to stand it in a deep container on a layer of constantly moist pebbles.

▶ **Macramé hanger** Available ready-made or in kit form, macramé rope hangers, fringed or trimmed with knotted cord, are ideal for displaying trailing house plants. They should be suspended from sturdy hooks to take the combined weight of plants and moist compost, and positioned where they do not get in the way.

plant will exhaust the compost in which it is growing and fill the pot with a dense ball of roots which cannot absorb water or nutrients. Top growth becomes thin and lanky, and leaves wilt and fall off. Move the plant on by knocking the plant out of its present pot – easiest done when the root ball is moist – and either re-potting it or potting it on.

Re-potting is for plants that have reached their desired size, but are in need of fresh compost. Remove at least a quarter of the existing ball of roots and compost, cutting off all dead roots before setting the plant in a clean pot of the same size and filling in with fresh compost. It can be impractical to re-pot large established plants in heavy and unwieldy containers. It is usually sufficient to scrape off the top of the old compost and replace it with new material.

Potting-on, annually at the start of the growing season, is for plants that have not reached their mature size. It is not necessary to reduce the soil and root ball, except for the removal of dead root tissue, but the plant should be potted on into the next pot size and given new compost.

Clay and plastic pots
Standard clay or plastic pots are measured by the diameter of the rim, from 4cm (1½in) to 38cm (15in) or more. Sizes move up by about 1cm (½in), but popular sizes for house plants are 9cm (3½in), 12cm (5in) and 18cm (7in). Tall-growing shrubs and climbers need correspondingly large tubs.
Clay pots are usually unglazed. They are heavier than plastic pots and are less likely to be knocked over, especially with tall plants grown in a lightweight compost. Clay pots 'breathe' through the pores and water evaporates from the side walls so that the compost dries out quickly with little risk of water-logging. They are good for plants which enjoy dry conditions, such as cacti. All clay pots should be 'crocked', i.e. have a layer of crocks (clay pot shards), clean peb-

bles or stones placed over the single hole in the bottom for added drainage.
Plastic pots are much cheaper than clay pots, less likely to break even though they are quite brittle, and come in various shapes and colours. They are also easier than

clay to keep clean, but because they are lightweight, they topple over easily, and as they are non-porous, they quickly become waterlogged. Plastic pots are equipped with several drainage holes and do not need crocking before being filled.

▶ **Contemporary decor** Modern trends in interior design call for clear, uncluttered shapes and plain, often bold colours. A collection of food cans holds an array of flowering and foliage plants, their bright labels evoking a sense of light-hearted fun.

◄ Spring indoors
Flowering much earlier indoors than in the open garden, a mixed collection of bright flowers brings promise of warmer days to come. A motley collection of containers does not detract from the cheerful display of dainty primulas, forced hyacinths, daffodils, narcissi and tall-growing, wide-petalled *Anemone blanda*.

▼ Decorative cookware
Cake tins of every shape and size can make showy containers for house plants. Aluminium types do not rust, but it is worth lining them with polythene to prevent water dribbling through the seams. For best results, leave the plants in their plastic pots and set them on a base of pebbles to prevent waterlogging.

▲ Terracotta bowls The earthy colour and beauty of unglazed terracotta pots and bowls associate well with greenery. Decorative cereals and grasses are easy to raise from seed and produce lush foliage plants which can be trimmed with scissors like miniature lawns.

Decorative pots and containers
Some clay pots are glazed, which means that they do not lose water through the sides. They look more attractive than either unglazed or plastic pots and can be used for direct planting or as outer pots.

Almost any container can be used to display plants, and decorative items designed for quite different purposes are often the most eye-catching. Copper and other cookware, porcelain, china and glass containers, ceramic bowls and wicker baskets, old teapots and brass coal buckets are all suitable, and they can be swapped from time to time to suit a change in mood or interior style.

Unusual containers can reflect the function of a room. For example, aluminium baking trays, copper cooking pans and decorative serving bowls can double as display containers for house plants in a kitchen. Old-fashioned tea caddies and food tins can also be adapted as plant pots, while glass or plastic sweet jars can be turned into bottle gardens.

Glass containers
Potting compost serves three main purposes – to hold a reserve of water, to supply nutrients and to provide anchorage for the plants. While the compost remains moist, air can still circulate freely between the soil particles to prevent waterlogging.

Because the visual qualities of the rooting medium are generally unimportant, it is usually hidden in non-see-through pots. But transparent glass bowls and troughs make handsome containers, and decorative materials can disguise the compost.

Natural stone chippings or pebbles are ideal means of embellishing the rooting medium. They are available in shades of cream, grey, brown or white. However, these materials will not meet the water- and nutrient-holding requirements of a growing medium. When water is added it fills all the air spaces between the granules and suffocates the roots, so they

must be used in association with a conventional compost.

There are two exceptions to this rule – bulbs and water plants. Bulbs have a built-in supply of nutrients and, provided the bulb itself is kept fairly dry so that it doesn't rot, the roots will tolerate standing in waterlogged conditions (see pages 33-36). True water plants, such as the umbrella sedges (*Cyperus*), grow well in pebbles and water.

The roots of all other house plants need air as well as water and nutrients. Prepare a decorative glass container by building up the walls with pebbles or stone chippings, then filling in the centre with ordinary potting compost. Put the plants in the compost before covering the surface with more pebbles. Another way is to make layers of different coloured chippings, beginning with a generous layer of ordinary compost in the bottom into which the plants

can root. The effect is rather like looking at a geological survey and can be quite a talking point!

Special 'light expanded clay aggregate' granules, known as leca for short, are sometimes available from garden centres. They have the advantage over natural stone pebbles of being able to absorb plenty of water without excluding air. They are attractive and can be used in glass containers instead of potting compost. This system of growing is suitable for most house plants, but regular liquid or slow-release granular feeds must be applied.

Displaying house plants
There's more to displaying house plants than simply putting them in a pot and standing them on a shelf or window-sill – particular styles develop according to how the plants relate to their containers and how the containers in turn relate to the room setting.

▶ **Indoor water garden** Natural water plants – Cyperus, Scirpus and Carex – look particularly effective in glass bowls and tanks. They need a bed of sand, gravel and pebbles to root into, with a few large stones for interest. Bulbs grow readily in special, water-filled bulb vases.

▲ Glass containers Clay granules improve the appearance of the rooting medium and retain a lot of water. They can be used in alternate, undulating layers with ordinary compost. Brightly coloured primulas, hyacinths and narcissi are ideal for this system of growing.

◄ House plant cuttings Many cuttings will root in water, especially those from plants with embryonic root nodules on the stems, such as *Scindapsus* and busy Lizzie (*Impatiens*). When placed in a decorative glass or jar, such cuttings can look just as effective for a short spell as an established plant.

▼ Desert cacti Use decorative materials — stone chippings, small rocks and pieces of driftwood — to create a desert scene for small, slow-growing cacti and succulents of contrasting form.

Try to match the style of the container with that of the plant. Bold designs complement the bizarre structure of many house plants, including yucca, Peruvian apple cactus (*Cereus peruvianus* 'Monstrosus'), flaming sword (*Vriesea splendens*) and Norfolk Island pine (*Araucaria heterophylla*).

Porcelain and china containers are ideal for displaying filigree ferns, and wicker baskets are perfect for temporary flowering plants and for climbers such as Cape leadwort (*Plumbago capensis*), white jasmine (*Jasminum officinale*), wax flower (*Stephanotis floribunda*) and wax plant (*Hoya carnosa*).

Grouping house plants

House plants grow better when grouped together – benefiting from the increased local humidity created by a mass of foliage growing above a relatively large surface area of moist compost. However, if you want to grow several plants in the same container – especially if it is a small one – make sure they all have similar requirements for light, water and nutrition, and that they are slow-growing. Vigorous plants will choke others in the container.

Any type of bowl can be used provided it is reasonably deep. Avoid very shallow ones which will dry out too quickly. Many garden centres offer a range of quite cheap but pretty china planters, or you can opt for a more expensive terracotta or glazed ceramic type.

If the bowl has drainage holes in the bottom it will need a matching saucer or drip tray. Those without holes should be part-filled with a suitable drainage material – pebbles, clay pellets or coarse grit, with some charcoal to keep it sweet – before topping up with potting compost.

Baskets should be lined with a watertight material, such as black polythene sheeting or a small bin liner trimmed to size, before planting up. In this case, don't make drainage holes in the bottom – water will ruin the basket.

There are two ways of planting a mixed bowl or basket. You can either knock each plant out of its original pot and replant them in the compost. Or alternatively, you can keep some or all the plants in their individual pots and sink them in moist peat substitute in the container.

Flowering plants are best kept in their own separate pots so that they can be removed easily from the arrangement once the flowers have faded without disturbing the roots of the others. For a short-term occasion or a table decoration, simply spread a layer of fresh sphagnum moss around the rims of the pots.

The most attractive displays consist of a range of growth habits, leaf shapes and colours. Use upright plants with bold or spiky leaves to produce height and scale. Bushier plants will fill in the bulk of the container, and trailers such as ivy will break up the hard edges. Stagger the plants in a descending tier, preferably with the tallest one positioned off-centre, if the display is to be viewed from one side only. For a table centrepiece, put the tallest plant in the middle of the bowl or basket.

Plants with stunning foliage – such as rex begonias, coleus and marantas – often look better on their own, but several of the same species can be put in one bowl or basket to increase their overall size and impact. A simple planting scheme in a plain container can be as eye-catching as a lavish one in an ornate container – the choice is yours. If you wish, add polished stones, pieces of wood bark or even a pretty ribbon bow for a final decorative touch.

▲ **China bowls** The colour and shape of containers is important in group arrangements. White bowls are perfect for such bright flowers as purple-flowered *Exacum affine*, sapphire flower (*Browallia speciosa*), orange-red kalanchoe and miniature, red-berried bead plant (*Nertera granadensis*). A grassy-leaved sweet flag (*Acorus gramineus*) provides an elegant backdrop.

▼ **Basket plants** A group arrangement of contrasting foliage is always eye-catching. Here, the soft green fronds of maidenhair fern (*Adiantum capillus-veneris*) add airy charm to the more substantial leaves of pink-marbled polka dot plant (*Hypoestes*) and the thick, hairy leaves of African violet.

▲ **African violets** Available in a range of colours, with single or double flowers often with frilly petals, African violets (*Saintpaulia*) are low-growing rosette plants that appreciate close planting for extra humidity. Set them on a layer of moist pebbles in a shallow bowl.

◄ **Spring basket** A lined basket holds a bright spring show of golden cyclamineus narcissi and white polyanthus primulas. Green and variegated ivies tumble over the moss-covered edges.

▼ **Coloured foliage** Rich leaf colours develop best in bright but filtered light. Marbled *Begonia rex*, white-spotted *Dieffenbachia maculata* and trailing, yellow-variegated *Scindapsus aureus* have identical light requirements. A fruit-laden calamondin orange (*Citrus mitis*) does best in full sun.

Identifying house plants

The individual leaf shapes and colours of house plants often provide a good indication of their cultural needs. The large *Ficus* genus, for example, includes the trailing or climbing *F. pumila*, whose thin-textured miniature leaves require a high degree of humidity, and the tree-like rubber plant (*F. elastica*), whose leathery leaves tolerate much drier air conditions. Both grow well in subdued light, but variegated forms of the rubber plant, such as 'Doescheri' and 'Tricolor' only develop ivory and pink markings in bright though filtered light.

All plants with variegated and coloured foliage need well-lit positions as do flowering and scented plants, though they also require some protection from hot midday summer sun. The only indoor plants which revel in full sun are the desert cacti and some leaf succulents. Large-leaved and thick-textured plants are probably the easiest to accommodate – the *Aspidistra*, for example, is virtually indestructible, tolerating less than ideal conditions including shade and dry air.

Specialist plants, like indoor palms and ferns, are easily recognized by their finely divided leaf fans and fronds. They have almost identical needs, though ferns demand particularly good humidity. The distinctive bromeliads or urn plants, with their colourful leaf vases and exotic flower bracts, are in a class of their own, but no more difficult to care for than other vividly-coloured house plants.

Leaf identification House plants range from tiny-leaved miniatures to needle-like leaf sprays and bold jungle exotics.

TINY-LEAVED HOUSE PLANTS

Small-leaved plants fit neatly on window-sills and table tops, and many are perfect for miniature and bottle gardens.

Large bold leaves and bright flowers are a popular choice for indoor plants, but many tiny-leaved plants display even more interesting features – delicate leaf shapes and textures, trailing or creeping stems, intricate colour patterns and unusual flowers and fruits. Their charm can be fully appreciated only by taking a close-up look, though by grouping several plants together even the smallest foliage can have an eye-catching effect. These plants are not suitable for floor-standing containers, but are particularly ideal for shelf displays, table arrangements and hanging baskets.

The size of the container should always be related to plant size for all types of house plant, but it is even more important to choose a container of the right proportions when growing miniature plants, creepers or trailers.

Very low-growing plants are best grown in half pots, bowls or troughs, or they can be used as 'ground-cover' below a larger plant in a full-sized pot. Trailing plants are excellent for hanging baskets or wall-mounted containers, or they may be used to break up the solid edges of a large container filled with larger plants.

With a little artistic flair, you can create a miniature garden. Select a broad bowl or trough with a depth of about 7.5-10cm (3-4in). Fill the bottom with a 2.5cm (1in) layer of gravel or coarse grit for good drainage, then top up with a proprietary potting compost. Draw up a plan of the desired planting scheme – as you would for an outdoor garden – incorporating pieces of wood bark, stones or other decorative items.

Insert the chosen plants one at a time, starting at the centre and working outwards. You may need to trim plants from time to time to keep them within bounds, especially when growing several plants of differing vigour within one container.

Many small-leaved plants need quite humid air conditions in order to thrive – the following pages offer advice on each of the most popular species. Place each pot on a saucer filled with gravel and keep this layer constantly moist – the air around the small plants will then be adequately humid. In centrally heated rooms where the air dries out rapidly, those plants requiring very moist air are best grown in a bottle garden or terrarium. Daily spraying with tepid water also increases humidity, but do not spray hairy or felted leaves.

(The sizes given on the following pages refer to *height × spread* unless otherwise stated.)

◄ **Shelf display** Small-leaved plants show up better when grown in company rather than as isolated specimens. Their diversity in shape, colour and growth habit become truly apparent within an assorted group of plants. Here, trailers, including grey-green string-of-beads (*Senecio rowleyanus*), rosary vine (*Ceropegia woodii*), with its purple-flushed, heart-shaped leaves, and *Sedum sieboldii* 'Medio-variegatum' (bottom shelf), tumble among cacti and ferns.

Adiantum capillus-veneris
Maidenhair fern

Features A delicate-looking fern with light green fronds comprising many fan-shaped leaflets (pinnae) on arching, blackish, hair-like stalks.
Size 25 × 25cm (10 × 10in).
Needs Bright light but no direct sun, moist air, normal room temp., water moderately, liquid feed occasionally during active growth. Mist-spray daily during hot spells.

Bowiea volubilis
Climbing onion

Features Thin, twining stems with sparse, short-lived leaves clamber from a surface bulb. Tiny greenish flowers in spring.
Size 30cm (1ft) or more tall.
Needs Bright light, normal room temp. and humidity, water moderately, liquid feed every month during active growth.

Buxus microphylla
Box (small-leaved)

Features Bushy evergreen shrub similar to the outdoor edging box. Oval, glossy dark green leaves. Variegated forms exist.
Size 23 × 15cm (9 × 6in).
Needs Bright light or semi-shade, normal room temp. and humidity, water moderately, liquid feed monthly in spring and summer. Prune to keep in shape.

Ceropegia woodii
Rosary vine

Features A long-trailer growing from a surface tuber. Purplish thread-like stems bear sparse dark green, heart-shaped leaves marbled silver, and purple beneath. Small pale pink and purple flowers in late summer.
Size Stems trail to 90cm (3ft).
Needs Strong light with some direct sun, normal room temp. and humidity, water sparingly, liquid feed mature plants every month during active growth.

Crassula lycopodioides
Rat-tail plant

Features A small much-branching succulent with slender, upright stems and minute, pointed, fleshy leaves forming four-sided scaly columns. Insignificant green flowers.
Size 23 × 12cm (9 × 5in).
Needs Bright light with some direct sun, normal room temp. and humidity, water moderately during active growth, liquid feed every two weeks. Give a winter rest at 10°C (50°F), water sparingly.

Crassula rupestris
Buttons-on-a-string

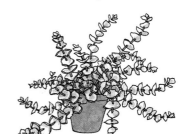

Features A small, spreading succulent, with the stem appearing to pass through the fleshy, almost triangular leaves like a string through beads. Small pink flowers in clusters at the ends of the stems in summer.
Size Stems to 60cm (2ft) long.
Needs Bright light with some direct sun, normal room temp. and humidity, liquid feed every two weeks during active growth.

Ficus pumila
Creeping fig

Features Much-branched species with wiry, trailing or climbing stems; aerial roots cling to moist compost. Small, oval-pointed, glossy dark green and slightly puckered leaves, up to 2.5cm (1in) long. 'Minima' is more compact, with tiny leaves; 'Variegata' is cream-edged.

Size 60 × 30cm (2 × 1ft).
Needs Filtered light, tolerant of shade and light draughts; humid air, mist-spray in hot weather or stand pot on moist pebbles; cool to normal room temp. (winter rest at 10°C/50°F). Pinch out growing tips on trailing plants to induce bushy habit. Water freely during growing season and give fortnightly liquid feeds. In winter, keep the compost just moist.

Fittonia verschaffeltii argyroneura
Mosaic plant

Features A low-creeping plant; slightly pointed oval leaves, olive green with a network of silver-white veins.
Size 5 × 23cm (2 × 9in).
Needs Medium light with no direct sun, brighter in winter; moist air, normal constant room temp. (min. 13°C/55°F), water regularly but sparingly, half-strength liquid fertilizer every two weeks during active growth. Pinch out growing tips to promote side shoots.

Glechoma/Nepeta hederacea
Ground ivy

Features A fast-growing trailer, useful for ground cover or in a hanging basket. The leaves are scalloped and slightly hairy; irregularly edged with white in the variety 'Variegata'.
Size Stems trail to 60cm (2ft).
Needs Light shade, normal room temp. and humidity, water moderately, liquid feed every two weeks during active growth.

Hedera helix varieties
Ivy (small-leaved)

Features Trailing or climbing stems with lobed leaves – vars marked with cream or yellow.
Size Stems to 1.2m (4ft).
Needs Light shade (green foliage) or bright light (variegated forms), normal room temp. and humidity, water moderately, liquid feed every two weeks during active growth.

Hypocyrta glabra
Clog plant

Features Upright or arching stems with glossy, rather fleshy dark green leaves and small, orange, waxy, clog-shaped flowers in summer.
Size 20 × 20cm (8 × 8in).
Needs Light shade, high humidity, min. temp. 15°C (60°F), water freely, liquid feed every two weeks during active growth. Water sparingly in winter. Pinch out tips regularly.

Mimosa pudica
Sensitive plant

Features A branching plant with touch-sensitive feathery leaves which fold in on themselves rapidly when touched. The leaf stalks also bend, returning to their original position after a short time. Tiny pink flowers in summer.
Size 60 × 60cm (2 × 2ft).
Needs Bright light, moist air, normal room temp., water moderately, apply a high-potash liquid fertilizer fortnightly.

Nertera granadensis/depressa
Bead plant

Features Tiny, closely matted, prostrate stems, rooting at the nodes. Mid-green, fleshy leaves. Tiny yellow-green flowers. Shiny, orange-red berries 6mm (¼in) in diameter.
Size 5cm (2in) high, spreading to the width of the container.
Needs Bright light with some direct sun, high humidity, temp. 10-15°C (50-59°F), water moderately all year, liquid feed every month once flowers are over until berries mature.

Pellaea rotundifolia
Button fern

Features Arching and eventually trailing fronds, stalks brownish-black in colour and closely set with pairs of small, almost round, leathery, dark green leaflets. Rootstock is a shallow-growing, creeping rhizome. Moderately vigorous. Unlike any other fern in appearance.
Size Trails to 30cm (1ft), with a similar spread.
Needs Medium light, away from bright sun in summer. Humid air essential at temp. above 16°C (61°F); stand pot on moist pebbles, mist-spray daily with tepid water in hot weather. Normal room temp. (winter min. 10°C/50°F); keep compost permanently moist, give fortnightly dilute feeds during active growth; water sparingly at low temp.

Peperomia prostrata
Creeping peperomia

Features A small trailing plant with tiny rounded leaves marked with bronze-red or silver. The stems have a reddish tinge. No flowers.
Size Stems trail to 20cm (8in).
Needs Light shade, moist air, normal room temp. with a minimum of 13°C (55°F), water sparingly, apply dilute liquid fertilizer every month during active growth. Grow in a peaty or similar compost.

Pilea microphylla
Artillery plant

Features Fine mid-green foliage in flattened sprays — individual leaf fronds are 6mm (¼in) long. Inconspicuous greenish-yellow flowers in summer expel clouds of pollen.
Size 20 × 20cm (8 × 8in).
Needs Semi-shade, moist warm air, min. temp. 13°C (55°F), water sparingly, liquid feed fortnightly during active growth only. Do not pot on to larger than 7.5cm (3in) pots.

Pilea nummulariifolia
Creeping Charlie

Features A fast-growing creeper ideal for a hanging basket. Stems are thin and reddish with pale green quilted leaves. Flowers are insignificant.
Size Stems trail to 30cm (1ft).
Needs Semi-shade, moist warm air, normal room temp. with a minimum of 13°C (55°F), water moderately, liquid feed every two weeks from mid-spring to the end of summer.

Sedum sieboldii
Sedum

Features Succulent trailer with round, slightly toothed grey-green leaves; blotched creamy-white in variety 'Medio-variegatum'. Clusters of pink flowers in autumn.
Size Stems trail to 23cm (9in).
Needs Full sun, normal room temp. and humidity, water moderately, do not feed. Give a winter rest at 10°C (50°F).

Selaginella species
Moss fern

Features Moss-like, low hummocky, creeping or upright bushy plants with tiny leaves in ranks around the stems, giving a fern-like appearance (though they are not true ferns). Species and varieties have green, yellow or silvery-white marked foliage.
Size 7.5-30 ×7.5-30cm (3-12 × 3-12in) according to variety.
Needs Light shade, very moist air, warm room temp, water plentifully, apply one-quarter strength liquid fertilizer fortnightly during active growth. Mist-spray daily. Best in a bottle garden.

Senecio rowleyanus
String-of-beads

Features A prostrate and trailing plant with fleshy stems bearing bead-like grey-green leaves. White, sweetly scented flowers.
Size 5 × 60cm (2 × 24in) or trailing to 60cm (2ft).
Needs Bright light, normal room temp. and humidity, water freely during active growth (sparingly at other times), liquid feed fortnightly during active growth. Winter rest at 10°C (50°F).

Soleirolia/Helxine soleirolii
Mind-your-own-business

Features A low-creeping plant, sometimes also known as 'baby's tears', making good ground cover under larger plants, with fleshy, pink stems that root as they grow. The tiny, densely set, rounded leaves are pale to mid-green.

'Argentea' is silver-variegated, and 'Aurea' is golden-yellow.
Size 7.5-10cm (3-4in).
Needs Bright light but filtered in summer, moist air, mist-spray daily with tepid water; normal room temp., water freely and liquid feed occasionally during active growth. Give a winter rest period at 4-7°C (39-45°F), water sparingly.

BOLD-LEAVED HOUSE PLANTS

Large-leaved house plants of sizeable proportions make stunning focal points in spacious living rooms, large halls and open stairways.

Adequate space is needed to display tall-growing and large-leaved house plants properly. But most homes have at least one corner which is ideal for a container plant of shrubby or even tree-like proportions. Large open-plan living rooms and studios with French windows for good light, spacious stairwells and large well-lit landings are perfect settings for sculptural plants.

A large plant requires a large pot to ensure physical stability, an adequate nutrient and moisture supply to the roots, and well-shaped growth. Ceramic or earthenware pots are much heavier than plastic ones, so they provide better anchorage for top-heavy plants. Similarly, soil-based John Innes potting composts are heavier than soil-less potting mixtures.

Staking may be necessary to keep tall-growing species upright. Use a sturdy bamboo cane and secure the main stem or branches with garden string, raffia or proprietary plant ties.

For plants with aerial roots – such as Swiss cheese plant (*Monstera*) and some philodendrons – insert a moss-covered pole into the compost to provide moist support and a means of anchorage. They can be bought from most garden centres, or you can make your own. Use nylon fishing line to bind sphagnum moss round a length of 2.5-5cm (1-2in) diameter plastic tubing – the type used for simple plumbing is ideal.

Tough-textured aerial roots can be bound to the pole with more fishing line. Alternatively, tie in the main stems with string or raffia to assist support. Spray the moss with water every few days to encourage the aerial roots to grow into the moss, and to increase the immediate humidity.

Most large-leaved house plants either do not flower, or their flowers are small and insignificant. Those with dark, leathery leaves generally tolerate normal room conditions and don't require full sunlight. The species which do flower – such as *Strelitzia* and *Anthurium* – do best in a conservatory or sunroom where fairly high humidity can be maintained.

Keep large leaves clean and healthy by dusting them regularly with a soft dry paint brush. Shiny leaves can be wiped clean on both sides with a damp cloth. Proprietary leaf-shine sprays may be used very occasionally on smooth, leathery leaves to add extra lustre, but never spray the undersides of the leaves or hairy or soft-textured leaves.

(The sizes given on the following pages refer to *height × spread* unless otherwise stated.)

▶ **Bengal fig** In its native habitat of India, the Bengal fig or Banyan tree (*Ficus benghalensis*) grows up to 30m (100ft) tall, but as an indoor container plant it rarely exceeds 2.4m (8ft). Related to the more common rubber plant, the Bengal fig's arching stems bear rich green, leathery leaves covered in soft brown hairs.

Anthurium andreanum
Painter's palette

Features Deep green, glossy, heart-shaped, leathery leaves up to 20cm (8in) long. Vivid red flower spathes from spring to autumn.
Size 45 × 30cm (1½ × 1ft); taller with age.
Needs Filtered light, warm room temp., high humidity, water well, liquid feed monthly.

Calathea makoyana
Cathedral windows

Features Silvery green upright leaves up to 15cm (6in) long, veined, edged and blotched with darker green; undersides similarly patterned with red and purple.
Size 60 × 45cm (2 × 1½ft).
Needs Filtered light, normal room temp., water and feed well.

Codiaeum variegatum pictum
Croton

Features Glossy, leathery leaves up to 30cm (1ft) long, veined and patterned with yellow, orange, red or purple, changing with age.
Size 90 × 60cm (3 × 2ft).
Needs Bright but filtered light, humid air, normal room temp., water well, feed fortnightly.

Dieffenbachia amoena
Dumb cane

Features Elliptic to oblong, cream-marbled, glossy dark green leaves up to 45cm (1½ft) or more long on sturdy upright stalks. Sap poisonous, temporarily paralysing tongue and throat if swallowed.
Size 60cm-1.2m × 60-90cm (2-4 × 2-3ft).
Needs Bright but filtered light, warm room temp. all year, humid air, water moderately, liquid feed fortnightly.

Dracaena fragrans 'Massangeana'
Corn palm

Features Broadly strap-shaped, arching, rich green leaves up to 60cm (2ft) long, patterned with yellow-green central stripes.
Size Eventually up to 1.2m × 75cm (4 × 2½ft).
Needs Bright but filtered light, warm room temp., humid air, mist-spray daily, water plentifully, liquid feed fortnightly.

Fatsia japonica
False castor oil plant

Features Light to mid-green glossy leaves, 23cm (9in) or more across, deeply divided into five to nine coarsely toothed lobes. 'Variegata' has white-edged leaves.
Size Up to 1.5 × 1.2m (5 × 4ft) or more according to pot size.
Needs Shade-tolerant, normal room temp. or less, fresh air, water well, feed fortnightly.

Ficus benghalensis
Bengal fig/banyan

Features Broadly oval, leathery, dark green leaves up to 20cm (8in) or more long with yellowish veins. Young shoots covered with fine russet hair.
Size 1.8-2.4m × 60cm (6-8 × 2ft).
Needs Medium light, normal room temp., water moderately, liquid feed fortnightly.

Ficus elastica 'Decora'
Rubber plant

Features Oval, leathery, glossy dark green leaves up to 30cm (1ft) long with a prominent midrib, usually on an unbranched stem.
Size Up to 3 × 1m (10 × 3ft).
Needs Medium light, normal room temp., water moderately, liquid feed fortnightly.

Ficus lyrata
Fiddle-leaf fig

Features Rich green, violin-shaped leaves often over 30cm (1ft) long, with puckered and wavy margins.
Size 1.2-1.8m × 60-90cm (4-6 × 2-3ft).
Needs Medium light, normal room temp., water moderately, liquid feed fortnightly.

Monstera deliciosa
Swiss cheese plant

Features Heart-shaped, glossy green leaves up to 45cm (1½ft) across on long stalks. Mature plants produce leaves deeply incised and perforated with elongated holes, and trailing aerial roots.
Size Up to 3 × 1.8m (10 × 6ft).
Needs Bright but filtered light, normal room temp., high humidity, water freely, feed fortnightly during active growth.

Musa-acuminata 'Dwarf Cavendish'
Dwarf banana

Features Paddle-shaped leaves with a prominent midrib. Curious flowers and small banana fruits are produced only on mature conservatory plants.
Size 1.2-1.8 × 1.5m (4-6 × 5ft).
Needs Bright but filtered light, warm room temp., humid air, water well, liquid feed fortnightly.

Philodendron elegans
Philodendron

Features Broad, rich green glossy leaves up to 38cm (15in) long, deeply incut into many finger-like segments, borne on long stalks.
Size 1.2-1.8 × 1.2m (4-6 × 4ft).
Needs Medium light, shade-tolerant, normal room temp., humid air, water freely in summer, liquid feed fortnightly.

Philodendron bipinnatifidum
Tree philodendron

Features Broad, dark green, deeply incut leaves up to 60cm (2ft) long, borne on long stalks; stems trunk-like with age.
Size 1.2 × 1.2m (4 × 4ft).
Needs Bright but filtered light, normal room temp., humid air, water freely in summer, liquid feed fortnightly.

Philodendron hastatum/ domesticum
Elephant's ear

Features Narrowly triangular to arrow-shaped, rich green, glossy, fleshy textured leaves up to 60cm (2ft) long.
Size Up to 1.8 × 1.1m (6 × 3½ft).
Needs Bright but filtered light, normal room temp., humid air, water freely in summer, liquid feed fortnightly.

Philodendron selloum
Lacy tree philodendron

Features Similar to *Philodendron bipinnatifidum* but leaves are whole, usually shallowly lobed with wavy margins.
Size Up to 1.8 × 1.2m (6 × 4ft).
Needs Bright but filtered light, normal room temp., humid air, water freely in summer, feed fortnightly.

Schefflera actinophylla
Umbrella tree

Features Glossy, rich green, long-stalked leaves divided umbrella-like into 4-16 separately stalked, arching, oblong, finger-like leaflets.
Size 1-1.8m × 60cm-1.2m (3-6 × 2-4ft).
Needs Bright to medium light, normal to warm room temp., good humidity, water moderately, liquid feed fortnightly.

Spathiphyllum 'Mauna Loa'
White sails

Features Broadly lance-shaped to elliptic, dark green glossy leaves up to 23cm (9in) long, borne on slender stalks in clumps directly from the rhizome. Arum-like flowers backed by a creamy white sail-like spathe appear on tall slender stalks, mainly in spring, but often continuing intermittently until autumn.
Size 60 × 60cm (2 × 2ft).
Needs Filtered light, normal room temp., water freely, humid air, liquid feed fortnightly.

Strelitzia reginae
Bird of paradise flower

Features Paddle-like, grey-green, 38cm (15in) long leaves on long stalks. Exotic orange-and-blue flowers in spring or summer.
Size 90cm-1.2m × 90cm-1.2m (3-4 × 3-4ft).
Needs Bright light with direct sun, normal room temp., water moderately, feed fortnightly.

VARIEGATED FOLIAGE PLANTS

**The decorative effect of foliage in the home
can be heightened and dramatized by the endless patterns
offered by variegated and marbled plants.**

There is green pigment in the inner tissues of every plant leaf, regardless of the surface colour. The function of this green colouring matter, known as chlorophyll, is to carry out the chemical processes (photosynthesis) which enable plants to manufacture food substances using sunlight as the energy source. Sometimes, chlorophyll is absent from part of the leaf, resulting in paler or darker patches. Such variegation can be highly decorative and is in many cases completely natural.

Sometimes the loss of chlorophyll is caused by a virus infection although this is more likely to occur on outdoor plants. The complete yellowing of leaves that are normally green is often due to chlorosis, especially when an acid-loving plant is grown in lime-rich compost or irrigated with hard tap water.

True varigated plants pass on their characteristics to their progeny only through vegetative propagation, and not through seed. Only a few variegated plants flower as house plants.

In most variegated leaves, the basic green is marked with white, grey, silver, cream, yellow or gold. The patterns produced by variegations can be simple or bold. Striped effects may occur from cross-banding as in some dracaenas, or by longitudinal lines as in tradescanias and sansevierias. Patterning can also follow the leaf veins – crotons and calatheas are typical of this type. The leaf edges of some plants may be heavily picked out in gold or silver as in many ivies and peperomias. Yet other plants have marbled leaves where cream or yellow areas appear as irregular blotches over all or part of the leaf surface, as in dumb canes and devil's ivies.

Whether these differences have come about naturally or by skilful plant breeding, variegated foliage looks like the product of artistry and seems perfectly at home among furnishings and fabrics in the living room. There are many different variegated house plants to choose from, ranging from the smallest creepers through bushy types to tall climbers.

The reduced area of green tissue on variegated plants, compared with that of normal all-green types, renders them less able to manufacture food substances, so they may be less vigorous. In order to maintain healthy growth and good leaf colour, variegated plants should be given more light than their all-green relations. How-ever, direct sunlight can be harmful since the paler areas of leaf are often prone to scorching. In summer, indirect but bright light or filtered sunlight is satisfactory.

If an all-green shoot appears on a variegated plant – reversion – prune it away immediately, cutting as close to its point of origin as possible – such growth will be more vigorous than the rest, creating an imbalanced shape.

Don't confuse reversion with loss of variegation due to poor light. Move the plant into a brighter spot – the old leaves may not recover their full colour properly, but new leaves will have the correct variegation.

The following pages review the most common variegated house plants, giving hthe eight and spread of mature specimens.

▶ **Leaf variegations** The patterns on house plant foliage range from intricate markings to simple patches. They may marble almost the whole leaf in gold, white or silver or shade in the leaf veins or edges with narrow bands of colour. Variegated foliage plants look particularly dramatic when set against all-green types.

Abutilon striatum 'Thompsonii'
Flowering maple

Features Vine-like, five-lobed leaves, 12cm (5in) across, richly mottled yellow on dark green. Red-veined, salmon bell-flowers in summer and autumn.
Size Up to 1.2 × 1m (4 × 3ft).
Needs Bright light, some full sun, normal room temp. (min. 10°C/50°F), water moderately (sparingly in winter), liquid feed fortnightly during active growth.

Aglaonema crispum 'Silver Queen'
Chinese evergreen

Features Thick, rather leathery leaves, to 30cm (1ft) long, dark grey-green, heavily marbled with silvery cream, borne on thick, short stems. Flowers rare indoors.
Size Up to 60 × 30cm (2 × 1ft).
Needs Medium light, no direct sun, normal to warm room temp., humid air, water moderately, liquid feed monthly.

Aphelandra squarrosa 'Louisae'
Zebra plant

Features Broad, fleshy, glossy, dark green leaves, 23cm (9in) long, veined ivory-white. Small flowers in a cone-like head with bright yellow bracts (often bought in bloom, but may not repeat).
Size To 45 × 30cm (1½ × 1ft).
Needs Bright but filtered sunlight, warm room temp., humid air, water plentifully, liquid feed weekly during active growth.

Chlorophytum comosum 'Vittatum'
Spider plant

Features Grassy clump of soft, arching leaves, to 30cm (1ft) long, medium green with central creamy white bands. Plantlets form at the ends of long trailing stems. Flowers insignificant.
Size Up to 30 × 45cm (1 × 1½ft).
Needs Bright light, some full sun, normal room temp., water plentifully, liquid feed fortnightly during active growth.

Codiaeum variegatum pictum
Croton

Features Bushy shrub with glossy, leathery, broad or narrow, sometimes incut leaves, up to 30cm (1ft) long, veined or marked with cream, yellow, orange or red.
Size Up to 90 × 60cm (3 × 2ft).
Needs Bright light, some full sun, normal room temp., humid air, water plentifully (sparingly in winter), liquid feed fortnightly.

Dieffenbachia species
Dumb cane

Features Broad, soft leaves up to 30cm (1ft) long, dark or pale green with white, cream or yellowish blotchy markings or marbling, especially around the mid-rib (poisonous).
Size Up to 60 × 45cm (2 × 1½ft).
Needs Bright, indirect light (full sun in winter), humid air, min. temp. 15°C (59°F), water moderately, liquid feed fortnightly.

Dracaena fragrans 'Massangeana'
Corn palm

Features Glossy green, loosely arching leaves, up to 60cm (2ft) long, with a broad central stripe of yellow, usually with one or two narrower yellow stripes alongside. Plants may form a trunk-like stem with age. The variety 'Lindenii' has a similar habit, but with broad, creamy-

gold marginal stripes. Fragrant flowers rarely produced on pot-grown plants.
Size Generally 60 × 60cm (2 × 2ft); up to 120 × 60cm (4 × 2ft) with age.
Needs Bright, filtered light but no direct sun, warm room temp., humid air (stand pot in a saucer of moist pebbles), mist-spray foliage with water frequently, water plentifully (moderately in winter), liquid feed fortnightly during spring and summer.

Dracaena godseffiana
Gold-dust dracaena

Features Dark green, cream-spotted, 7.5cm (3in) long, elliptic leaves in twos or threes up wiry stems. In some varieties the spots merge to form solid patches.
Size Up to 60 × 38cm (24 × 15in).
Needs Bright but filtered light, warm room temp., humid air, water plentifully (moderately in winter), liquid feed fortnightly during active growth.

Dracaena sanderiana
Belgian evergreen

Features Slender and upright, rarely branching; rather stiff, deep green, white-margined leaves up to 23cm (9in) long and 2.5cm (1in) wide.
Size Up to 45 × 38cm (18 × 15in).
Needs Bright but filtered light, warm room temp., humid air, water plentifully (moderately in winter), liquid feed fortnightly.

Euonymus japonicus 'Mediopictus'
Japanese spindle

Features Bushy; leathery, pointed-oval, yellow-centred, rich green leaves up to 5cm (2in) long.
Size To 75 × 45cm (2½ × 1½ft).
Needs Bright but filtered light (some full sun in winter but unaccompanied by any undue warmth), cool temp. (max. 18°C/64°F in summer, 10-13°C/50-55°F in winter), water moderately, feed fortnightly.

Hedera canariensis and *Hedera helix* varieties
Canary island and common ivies

Features *H. canariensis* has large, triangular, slightly lobed leaves; 'Gloire de Marengo' (*illustrated*) has 7.5-10cm (3-4in) long leaves marked with patches of grey-green and silver and white margins. *H. helix* has three to five-lobed, 2.5-5cm (1-2in) long leaves; variegated varieties are popular as house plants, and include 'Glacier' (grey-green blotches and silver-white marginal patches) and 'Little Diamond' (small, thin grey-white edges).
Size Trailing or climbing to 30-90 × 30cm (1-3 × 1ft).
Needs Bright light, some full sun, normal to cool room temp., water sparingly in winter, feed fortnightly.

Heptapleurum arboricola 'Variegata'
Parasol plant

Features Unbranched stem (bushy if pinched out); large rich green leaves, splashed with yellow, divided into seven or more slender leaflets radiating in a circle atop long stalks.
Size Up to 1.8 × 1m (6 × 3ft).
Needs Bright light, some full sun, min temp. 16°C (61°F), humid air, water moderately, liquid feed fortnightly during active growth.

Iresine herbstii 'Aureoreticulata'
Chicken gizzard

Features Bushy; soft, succulent, red stems; rounded leaves up to 7.5cm (3in) long, with a greenish tinge and broadly traced with yellow along the veins.
Size Up to 60 × 30cm (2 × 1ft).
Needs Bright light, some full sun, normal room temp., humid air, water plentifully (sparingly in winter), liquid feed fortnightly during active growth.

Peperomia caperata 'Variegata'
Peperomia

Features Heart-shaped, 2.5-3.5cm (1-1½in) long, corrugated, rich green leaves with broad white borders, borne on fleshy, pinkish stalks. 'Rat-tail' flowers.
Size Up to 20 × 20cm (8 × 8in).
Needs Bright but filtered light, normal room temp., humid air, water carefully (never over-water), apply half-strength liquid fertilizer monthly.

Peperomia magnoliifolia 'Variegata'
Desert privet

Features Robust plant; red stems; fleshy, glossy, oval, dark green leaves mostly 7.5cm (3in) long, marbled and edged with pale green and creamy yellow.
Size Up to 30 × 30cm (1 × 1ft); stems flop over and trail with age.
Needs Bright but filtered light, normal room temp., humid air, water sparingly, apply half-strength liquid fertilizer monthly.

Plectranthus coleoides 'Marginatus'
Swedish ivy

Features Soft stems, squarish in cross-section; hairy, heart-shaped, 5-6cm (2-2½in) long, grey-green leaves, creamy white around the scalloped edges.
Size Trailing to 60cm (2ft).
Needs Bright light, some full sun, normal room temp. (cool in winter), water plentifully (sparingly in winter), liquid feed fortnightly during active growth.

Scindapsus aureus 'Marble Queen'
Devil's ivy

Features Angular whitish stems; heart-shaped, 10-15cm (4-6in) long, glossy, white to cream leaves flecked with grey-green.
Size Climbs to 1.2m (4ft).
Needs Filtered light, tolerates shade. Normal room temp. (cooler in winter), humid air, water moderately (sparingly in winter), liquid feed fortnightly. Best grown on a moss pole.

Senecio macroglossus 'Variegatus'
Variegated wax vine

Features Ivy-like, mid-green, three to five-lobed, 6cm (2½in) long leaves, heavily marked with cream marginal patches.
Size Climbing or trailing to 90cm (3ft).
Needs Bright light, some full sun, normal room temp. (10-13°C/50-55°F in winter), water moderately (sparingly in winter), liquid feed fortnightly during active growth.

Stenotaphrum 'Variegatum'
Buffalo grass

Features Creeping or trailing stems rooting at the nodes; pale cream, 7.5-30cm (3-12in) long, grassy, blunt-tipped leaves marked with fine green lines.
Size Trailing to 60cm (2ft).
Needs Bright light, some full sun, normal room temp., humid air (mist-spray foliage), water plentifully (sparingly in winter), liquid feed monthly.

Syngonium podophyllum 'Imperial White'
Arrowhead vine

Features Arrow-shaped three to five-lobed, 15cm (6in) long, mid-green leaves, centrally marbled with cream; mature plants climb, producing much larger leaves (best prevented by pinching out).
Size Up to 60 × 45cm (2 × 1½ft).
Needs Bright but filtered light, tolerates shade, normal room temp., water moderately, liquid feed fortnightly.

Tradescantia species
Wandering Jew

Features Trailing plants; fleshy stems with prominent nodes, often slightly zigzag; stalkless, pointed-elliptic, 5-10cm (2-4in) leaves. Small white to pinkish flowers at the stem tips. Variegated forms include: *Tradescantia albiflora* 'Albovittata' (green leaves with white stripes); *T. blossfeldiana* 'Variegata' (leaves all-green, all-cream, and half cream and half green all on the same plant, tinged pink when grown in sun); *T. fluminensis* 'Quicksilver' (fast-growing; green-and-white striped leaves).
Size Trailing to 60cm (2ft) or more.
Needs Bright light, some full sun, normal room temp., humid air, water plentifully and liquid feed fortnightly during active growth, water sparingly during dormancy.

COLOURED FOLIAGE PLANTS

Many house plants have brilliantly coloured leaves, often combined with startling shapes and lavish textures, which provide fascinating focal points.

In addition to foliage plants with white and cream, silver, grey and gold variegations there are exotic types with brilliantly coloured leaves. The crotons (*Codiaeum*), for example, are justly known as Joseph's coat: the leaves come in an extensive range of colours and combinations of yellow and green, orange, red and black.

The leaf or rex begonias also come in a wide variety of colours. The large, hairy and corrugated leaves display a kaleidoscope of green, grey, pink, silver and flaming red, usually arranged in distinct patterns. The peacock plants (*Calathea*) are truly outstanding for their intricate leaf patterns and rich colours, which vary from species to species. The similar but easier prayer plants (*Maranta* sp.) are even more exotic, with the leaf ribs picked out in dark crimson.

Unfortunately, several of these multi-coloured foliage plants demand better conditions and more attention than it is possible to provide in a home without a conservatory or a heated greenhouse. They often need much higher temperatures and more air moisture than is comfortable for the human occupants.

Happily, there are many coloured foliage plants that are much less demanding. The flame nettles (*Coleus*) are brilliantly coloured and are some of the easiest plants to grow, thriving outdoors in summer and providing an endless supply of new plants from quickly-rooting cuttings. Purple-coloured setcreaseas, gynuras and wandering Jews, saxifrages and polka dot plants are in the same league and present few problems for the indoor gardener.

Plants with coloured leaves may lose some of their brilliance if grown in poor light, but they rarely tolerate strong direct sun – the paler ones are especially susceptible to scorching. For the best results, grow them in ordinary room conditions away from south- or west-facing windows.

Keep the foliage clean – dust soon clogs the leaf pores and impairs the plant's health and vigour, as well as reducing the lustre of coloured leaves. Glossy leaves can be sprayed occasionally with a proprietary 'leaf-shine' aerosol. Alternatively, wipe tough-textured leaves gently with cottonwool soaked in a mixture of milk and water – don't wipe soft, delicate leaves since they bruise very easily.

Apply a liquid feed regularly to coloured-leaved house plants while they are actively growing – the pigments which produce the unusual colours are built up from trace elements in the soil, so starved plants may develop only weak, poorly coloured foliage.

Some fleshy-leaved plants, such as Christmas cheer (*Sedum rubrotinctum*), turn a richer colour if kept rather dry and warm. In cooler, moist conditions they grow faster, but greener.

◄ **Exotic colours** The glossy-leaved crotons display an astonishing range of colours and leaf shapes that make them the focal point in any group arrangement. Statuesque, yellow-edged mother-in-law's tongue is in fine contrast to the crotons' vibrant colours.

Acalypha wilkesiana
Copperleaf

Features Fast-growing shrub with coppery green leaves mottled copper, red and purple.
Size 1.8 × 1.2m (6 × 4ft); smaller if grown as an annual.
Needs Bright but filtered light, moist air, temp. up to 27°C (80°F) — min. 15°C (59°F) — water moderately, liquid feed every two weeks. Best raised from cuttings every year.

Begonia rex hybrids
Begonia

Features Large offset heart-shaped, rough-textured leaves variably marked with red, pink, purple, silver and green. Insignificant flowers.
Size 45 × 45cm (1½ × 1½ft).
Needs Filtered light, no direct sun, moist air, normal room temp., water moderately, liquid feed every two weeks. Water sparingly during winter.

Caladium × hortulanum
Angel's wings

Features Large arrowhead-shaped, paper-thin leaves on long stalks; suffused, veined or marbled red, pink or white.
Size 38 × 30cm (15 × 12in).
Needs Constant high humidity, bright light but no direct sun, temp. 18-24°C (65-75°F), water moderately and give a weak liquid feed every two weeks. Give five months' rest from autumn.

Calathea makoyana
Cathedral windows

Features Large oblong leaves held upright on slender stalks, patterned with pinkish maroon on the underside, green on top.
Size 60 × 45cm (2 × 1½ft).
Needs Light shade, temp. 15-21°C (59-70°F), mist-spray daily, keep soil constantly moist with lime-free water, liquid feed generously every two weeks. Water moderately when dormant.

Codiaeum variegatum pictum
Croton

Features Bushy shrub with glossy, leathery leaves. Varieties available in a range of leaf shapes and colours — blotched, marbled or veined yellow, orange, red, pink or purple, usually changing with age.
Size 90 × 60cm (3 × 2ft).
Needs Bright filtered light, moist air, normal room temp. (min. 13°C/55°F), water plentifully, liquid feed every two weeks during active growth. Water sparingly while dormant.

Coleus blumei varieties
Flame nettle

Features Bushy, with heart-shaped leaves, sometimes slender or incut; yellow, cream, orange, red, green or purple.
Size 60 × 30cm (2 × 1ft).
Needs Bright light, some full sun, temp. 16-21°C (61-70°F), water well, liquid feed every two weeks, pinch out flowers. Propagate from cuttings annually.

Cordyline terminalis
Cabbage palm

Features Palm-like shrub eventually tree-like as lower leaf fans drop away from erect stems. Clusters of deep green long, pointed and lance-shaped leaves, flushed red when young. Variegated types in shades of green, pink, red, purple and cream.

Size 90 × 60cm (3 × 2ft).
Needs Bright light, filtered in summer; moist air essential, mist-spray daily during active growth. Normal room temp. (min. 10-13°C/50-55°F); water freely to keep compost moist, with fortnightly feeds during active growth; in winter, water only when compost feels dry. Good specimen plant. Brown leaf edges indicate lack of humidity.

Dieffenbachia maculata **varieties**
Dumb Cane

Features Large, arching leaves; pale or dark green with white/cream markings; poisonous.
Size 60 × 45cm (2 × 1½ft).
Needs Bright, indirect light (full sun in winter), high humidity, min. temp. 16°C (61°F), water moderately throughout the year, liquid feed every two weeks during active growth.

Dracaena marginata **'Tricolor'**
Dracaena

Features Narrow, arching leaves, striped pink-red, cream-yellow and green. Old leaves fall off, leaving attractive scars where they were attached to the stem.
Size 1.2m (4ft) or more.
Needs Bright but filtered light, moist air, mist-spray; temp. 18-24°C (65-75°F), water plentifully during growth. Water moderately in winter.

Fittonia verschaffeltii
Painted net leaf

Features Creeping plant with olive-green leaves net-veined with carmine-red/pink.
Size 15 × 23cm (6 × 9in).
Needs Indirect light, brighter in winter, high humidity, temp. 16-18°C (61-65°F), water regularly but sparingly, give weak liquid feed every two weeks during active growth. Pinch out growing tips regularly. Best grown in a bottle garden or terrarium.

Gynura sarmentosa
Velvet plant

Features Twining or trailing plant with rich purple-felted deep green leaves and stems.
Size 90 × 45cm (3 × 1½ft); taller with age.
Needs Bright light, some full sun, moist air, normal room temp., water moderately — don't wet leaves — liquid feed every two weeks during active growth.

Hypoestes phyllostachya
Polka dot plant

Features Compact and bushy, with small, oval and pointed, olive-green leaves spotted soft pink — spots often merge.
Size 38 × 38cm (15 × 15in).
Needs Bright light, normal room temp., water moderately, liquid feed every two weeks during active growth; water sparingly during winter rest. Pinch out flower buds. Propagate from cuttings every few years — bought plants become leggy once a growth-retardant chemical wears off.

Iresine herbstii
Beefsteak plant

Features Fleshy stems and heart-shaped deep red leaves. 'Brilliantissima' has scarlet-veined, plum-red leaves.
Size Up to 60 × 30cm (2 × 1ft).
Needs Bright light, some full sun, moist air, normal room temp., water frequently, liquid feed every two weeks. Water sparingly during winter rest.

Maranta leuconeura erythroneura
Herringbone plant

Features Bushy plant, oval-shaped, deep olive green leaves strongly patterned with pale green midribs and bright red veins; purple undersides. At night, leaves fold up like hands in prayer.
Size 23 × 30cm (9 × 12in).
Needs Filtered light, north- or east-facing position; normal room temp., high humidity, stand pot on moist pebbles and mist-spray with tepid water daily at high temp. During active growth keep compost permanently moist and feed fortnightly; winter rest at 10-13°C (50-55°F), water moderately only when compost feels dry.

Pelargonium 'Mrs Henry Cox'
Zonal pelargonium

Features Bushy plant with round, scalloped-edged leaves, mid-green at the centre with ring 'zones' of red, bronze and yellow; pungent aroma when bruised. Clusters of pale salmon-pink flowers from spring to autumn.

Size 38 × 30cm (15 × 12in); larger if grown for several years.
Needs Bright light with at least some full sun, normal room temp. (min. 10°C/50°F in winter), water moderately, apply a high-potash liquid fertilizer every two weeks when growing actively. Water very sparingly during winter rest period. For compact plants, grow every year from cuttings.

Sansevieria trifasciata
Mother-in-law's tongue

Features Leathery, sword-shaped leaves, marbled grey-green; edged gold in 'Laurentii'.
Size 90 × 45cm (3 × 1½ft)
Needs Bright light but tolerant of shade, temp. 16-27°C (61-80°F), water moderately, give half-strength liquid feed every month during active growth.

Saxifraga stolonifera 'Tricolor'
Mother-of-thousands

Features Stemless with round leaves in a loose rosette, olive-green edged cream and rose-pink; purple below. Sprays of tiny, white flowers. Trailing shoots bear miniature plantlets.
Size 10 × 15cm (4 × 6in).
Needs Bright light, some full sun, moist air, normal room temp., water well, liquid feed every month during active growth. Water sparingly in winter.

Scindapsus aureus 'Golden Queen'
Golden hunter's robe

Features Angular, climbing stems with glossy, golden, heart-shaped leaves.
Size Climbs to 1.2m (4ft).
Needs Bright but indirect light, moist air, normal room temp., water moderately, liquid feed every two weeks during active growth. Grow on a moss pole or allow to trail.

Sedum rubrotinctum
Christmas cheer

Features Fleshy, egg-shaped leaves on thin stems branching from the base; green in colour, turning crimson-red or coppery red under hot, dry conditions.
Size 10-15 × 15cm (4-6 × 6in).
Needs Full sun, normal room temp. (cool in winter), water moderately, do not feed. Water very sparingly in winter. Best grown in shallow pots or trays of sandy compost.

Setcreasea/Callisia elegans
Purple heart

Features Trailer with lance-shaped, rich violet-purple leaves with soft bloom. Small magenta-pink flowers in leaf axils in summer.
Size 30 × 30cm (1 × 1ft).
Needs Bright light, some full sun, normal room temp., water moderately, liquid feed every month during active growth.

Zebrina pendula 'Quadricolor'
Wandering Jew

Features Trailing; sparkling leaves striped cream, silver, pink and green; purple beneath.
Size To 90 × 90cm (3 × 3 ft).
Needs Bright light, normal room temp. (slow-growing if cool), liquid feed every two weeks when growing actively. Keep slightly dry for best leaf colour.

CLIMBERS AND TRAILERS

**A wide range of perennial and shrubby foliage
house plants are ideal as screens and wall plants,
and as foils for flowering plants.**

Rarely exotic but undemanding in their cultural needs, climbing and trailing foliage plants are invaluable for providing green or variegated background colour, as quick-growing screens and room dividers, and for trailing over the edges of tables, hanging baskets and wall planters.

Many climbing plants, notably the ubiquitous ivies and several vines, are as happy trailing as clambering. True trailing species, however, such as the wandering Jews with their brittle stems, cannot be induced to climb upwards.

Very few climbing house plants are self-supporting; most need some support around which they can scramble or twine. Climbing stems grow either clockwise or anti-clockwise and consistently refuse to twine in the opposite direction to their natural growth habit. The course of a young plant may not be obvious, but you can tie the stem loosely to its support until it indicates which way it is going to climb. Various proprietary support systems are available from garden centres and florists' shops, or you can make your own.

☐ Thin bamboo canes and wooden stakes are the simplest and cheapest means of support. Used in conjunction with wire rings or raffia/string ties, these provide good support for individual upright stems. But too many canes in one pot can look rather unsightly.

☐ Spiral supports can be bought or made. Drill a length of bamboo cane or 6-12mm (¼-½in) diameter hardwood dowel at intervals with small holes. Then feed stiff nylon cord through the holes in a spiral configuration up the cane, leaving a series of open loops through which plant stems can be trained.

☐ Wire hoops, generally about 30cm (1ft) in diameter, are suitable for training small twining plants in a circular fashion to limit their upward growth. They are ideal for flowering climbers such as stephanotis and jasmine.

☐ Plastic indoor trellis can be bought in pre-shaped sections in a range of sizes. The bottom of the trellis is simply pushed into the compost in the pot. Usually coloured green, white or brown, plastic trellis provides good support for small multi-stemmed climbers, but does not have a very natural appearance.

☐ Wooden trellis or special timber framework can be built to any size to support tall, heavy climbers. These should be fixed to a wall or other rigid surface – not to the pot.

The wood can be stained with non-toxic wood paint.

☐ Plastic netting can be fixed between two or more canes or stakes in a large pot. As with trellis, this is ideal for multi-stemmed climbers. It can be cut to any desired height and width. Black or dark green netting becomes almost invisible as the climbing plant grows through it.

☐ Moss-covered poles are ideal for supporting plants with aerial roots – ivies, monsteras, scindapsus and some philodendrons. They simulate the plant's natural tree-trunk support, providing anchorage and moisture. They can be bought or made.

▶ **Group display** Climbing foliage plants, including ivies, variegated × *Fatshedera* and ornamental arrowhead vine, give height to a floor arrangement. A trailing tradescantia fills a gap in the foreground.

Callisia elegans
Callisia

Features A sprawling plant resembling *Tradescantia*, with pointed oval, 2.5-4cm (1-1½in) long, white-striped, olive green leaves clasping the fleshy stems; leaf undersides rich purple.
Size Trails to 60cm (2ft); spreads to 30cm (1ft).
Needs Bright light with some full sunlight, normal room temp., liquid feed fortnightly and water plentifully during active growth (sparingly during winter rest).

Ceropegia woodii
Rosary vine

Features Slender purple stems cascade from rounded tubers. The small paired leaves are heart-shaped, marbled silver and green on top, purple beneath. Small lantern-like pink-purple flowers in autumn.
Size Trails up to 90cm (3ft); spreads up to 25cm (10in).
Needs Bright light with some full sun, normal room temp.; water moderately, liquid feed monthly.

Cissus antarctica
Kangaroo vine

Features Vigorous tendril climber with glossy, dark green, pointed oval leaves up to 10cm (4in) long, edged with teeth.
Size Up to 1.8 × 1m (6 × 3ft).
Needs Tolerates shade, draughts, dry air, normal room temp.; water moderately, liquid feed fortnightly. Needs support but can be allowed to trail.

Cissus discolor
Rex-begonia vine

Features Vigorous climber with pointed heart-shaped, rich green leaves up to 15cm (6in) long, strikingly marbled with silvery-white and purple, and crimson beneath. The leaf patterning resembles that of *Begonia rex*.
Size Up to 1.8 × 1m (6 × 3ft).
Needs Bright but filtered light, humid air, normal room temp., (min. winter temp. 10°C/50°F), water moderately, liquid feed fortnightly.

× *Fatshedera lizei* 'Variegata'
Tree ivy

Features Upright climber, but can be kept bushy by pinching out, or can be allowed to trail. Glossy, deep green, white-marked, ivy-like leaves up to 20cm (8in) across.
Size 60cm-1.8m × 30cm-1.2m (2-6 × 1-4ft).
Needs Filtered light, some shade, normal room temp. (cool in winter), water moderately, liquid feed fortnightly, support optional.

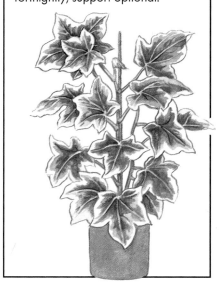

Ficus pumila
Creeping fig

Features Small branching plant with climbing or trailing stems and tightly packed, oval, dark green leaves up to 2.5cm (1in) long.
Size Climbs or trails to 60cm (2ft); spreads to 30cm (1ft).
Needs Bright but filtered light, tolerates shade, cool to normal room temp., humid air, water well, liquid feed fortnightly during active growth; provide support if grown as a climber.

Gynura procumbens
Velvet plant

Features Trailing or climbing stems with toothed, rich green leaves up to 15cm (6in) long, beautifully felted with purple hairs, especially when young.
Size Trails or twines to 1-1.5m (3-5ft); spreads up to 1m (3ft).
Needs Bright light, some sun, normal room temp., humid air, water moderately from below, feed fortnightly, remove flower buds, support optional.

Hedera canariensis
Canary island ivy

Features Vigorous climber or trailer with rich green, leathery, lobed leaves up to 10cm (4in) long; marbled grey-green and edged white in 'Gloire de Marengo'.
Size Climbs to 60cm-3m (2-10ft); spreads 30-60cm (1-2ft).
Needs Bright light (some full sun for variegated types), normal room temp., water moderately, liquid feed every two weeks; support optional.

Hedera helix
Common ivy

Features Vigorous climber or trailer with rich green, lobed leaves generally 2.5-5cm (1-2in) long. Numerous varieties with cream, white or greyish markings.
Size Climbs to 60cm-3m (2-10ft); spreads 30-60cm (1-2ft).
Needs Bright light (all-green types tolerate shade), normal to cool room temp., water moderately, feed monthly; support optional.

Philodendron scandens
Sweetheart plant

Features Climber or trailer with glossy rich green, heart-shaped leaves up to 7.5-10cm (3-4in) long; young leaves may be bronze-tinted.
Size Generally up to 1m (3ft) tall, spreading to 30cm (1ft), but may grow much larger with age.
Needs Bright but filtered light (tolerant of shade), normal room temp., humid air, water well (less in winter), liquid feed fortnightly; good on a moss pole.

Piper crocatum
Ornamental pepper

Features Trailing plant with pointed heart-shaped leaves up to 13cm (5in) long, coloured olive-green with silver and silver-pink markings along the veins; stems and leaf undersides red.
Size Trails up to 2m (7ft); spreads up to 90cm (3ft).
Needs Bright but filtered light, warm room temp., humid air, water moderately, feed fortnightly.

Plectranthus oertendahlii
Swedish ivy

Features Trailing, climbing, somewhat bushy plant packed with almost round, 2.5cm (1in) wide, slightly felted, bronze-tinged green leaves marked with whitish veins and purplish edging.
Size Trails to 90cm (3ft) or can be kept bushy by pinching out; spreads up to 60cm (2ft).
Needs Filtered light, shade-tolerant in summer, normal room temp. (cool in winter), water freely during active growth, liquid feed fortnightly.

Rhoicissus rhomboidea
Grape ivy

Features Tendril climber with slender stems and glossy deep green leaves divided into three 5cm (2in) long toothed leaflets.
Size Up to 1.8-3 × 1.2-1.8m (6-10 × 4-6ft).
Needs Filtered light, tolerates shade, normal room temp., winter rest at 10°C (50°F), water well, feed fortnightly.

Scindapsus aureus
Devil's ivy

Features Climber or trailer with angular stems, aerial roots and glossy, leathery, heart-shaped green leaves up to 10-15cm (4-6in) long, marbled with yellow.
Size Up to 1.8m × 45cm (6 × 1½ft).
Needs Filtered light, tolerates shade, normal room temp., water moderately (sparingly in winter), liquid feed fortnightly; good on a moss pole.

Senecio macroglossus 'Variegatus'
Cape/Natal ivy

Features Ivy-like trailer or climber with purplish stems and triangular, waxy, rich green leaves up to 6cm (2½in) long, irregularly marked and edged with cream.
Size Trails or climbs up to 90cm (3ft); spreads up to 60cm (2ft).
Needs Bright light with some full sun, normal room temp., water moderately (sparingly in winter), liquid feed fortnightly; support optional.

Syngonium podophyllum
Arrowhead vine

Features Bushy at first, but eventually climbing or trailing; glossy green, generally arrowhead-shaped leaves up to 20cm (8in) long on slender stalks; leaves on young plants may be marked silvery-white.
Size Climbs or trails to 1.8m (6ft).
Needs Bright but filtered light, tolerates shade, normal room temp., water moderately, feed fortnightly; good on a moss pole.

Tradescantia fluminensis
Wandering Jew

Features Vigorous trailing plant with fleshy stems, prominent leaf nodes and pointed-oval, stalkless leaves; the variety 'Quicksilver' has green and white striped, 7.5cm (3in) long leaves.
Size Trails and spreads to 60cm (2ft).
Needs Bright light with some full sun, normal room temp., water plentifully, liquid feed monthly.

Zebrina pendula
Wandering Jew

Features Vigorous trailing plant similar to *Tradescantia* (shares same common name — both plants have stems which change direction slightly at each node). The variety 'Quadricolor' has leaves striped with cream, green, silver and pink.
Size Trails up to 90cm (3ft); spreads 30-60cm (1-2ft).
Needs Bright light, normal room temp., water moderately, feed fortnightly.

PARLOUR PALMS

**Although the elegant palms come mainly from the
Tropics, they are surprisingly tolerant of less than perfect
conditions, poor light and low temperatures.**

In their native habitats, most palms develop a tall, unbranched trunk topped by a crown of fan-shaped or feathery fronds, though a few are low-growing, clustering shrubs. As house plants, palms are slow-growing and never achieve the typical gnarled trunk; instead they produce a few new fronds annually from the crown.

Some types have a solitary, unbranched stem that develops into a short trunk or stumpy base even on potted specimens. Others are completely or nearly stemless, forming a cluster of leaf stalks. It is characteristic of every palm that each of the stems has only one growing point from which all the leaves develop. If this is damaged or destroyed, it is not replaced and the whole plant will eventually die. Therefore, although individual leaves may be removed as they yellow, the plants cannot be cut back in any other way.

Palm leaves – fronds – are of two distinct kinds: feathery or fan-shaped. Both kinds of leaf are likely to have stalks with a broad, thickened base. The leaf stalk itself can be smooth and shiny, or hairy, spiny or tooth-edged. The stalk of a fan-shaped frond ends at the base of the broad blade. In the feathery types, however, the extended leaf stalk becomes the midrib of the blade, and the blade is divided into a number of leaflets arranged along the midrib.

In fan-leaf palms, the frond blade spreads out in spray-like fashion from an axis at the tip of the leafstalk. More often than not, the leaf stalks of these fronds are spined or tooth-edged. Indoor palms rarely flower, though the smaller parlour palm (*Chamaedorea elegans*) often produces insignificant sprays of yellow, ball-shaped blooms on plants four or five years old. Even when flowers are produced indoors, they never yield fruit.

Palms are popular plants in large open vestibules, open-plan offices and hotel foyers, where they seem to thrive on neglect. Certainly, most palms tolerate a wide range of light intensity, hot and dry air, and an erratic watering programme. But all will develop into fine plants if given reasonable treatment. They prefer airy conditions with some degree of humidity, but cannot tolerate draughts, extreme heat or sudden changes in light.

Indoor palms normally have a two- or three-month rest period during the poorly lit days of winter. Active, though slow, growth begins in mid-spring and continues until late autumn. Most types benefit from standing in a sheltered but sunny position outdoors during the warmer months, but this is not essential for their well-being.

(Sizes given on the following pages refer to *height* × *spread* of mature pot plants.)

◄ **Elegant palms** Evoking images of Palm Court orchestras and Victorian parlours decorated with pedestals of palms and aspidistras, the graceful palms fit just as easily into modern homes. Their undemanding growth habit and elegant foliage allow them to fit into almost any room.

Caryota mitis
Burmese fishtail palm

Features Greyish stalks carry fronds which are cut herringbone-fashion into sections, and again subdivided into wedge-shaped, folded, ragged leaflets.
Size Up to 2.4 × 1.2m (8 × 4ft).
Needs Filtered light, warm temp. (min. 13°C/55°F), water plentifully, liquid feed monthly from early spring to mid-autumn.

Chamaedorea elegans
Parlour palm

Features Short green trunk with arching fronds; leaflets arranged almost in pairs along a pale leaf stalk. Slow-growing.
Size Eventually 90 × 90cm (3 × 3ft), but generally smaller.
Needs Bright but filtered light, normal room temp., prefers moist air but tolerant of dry air, water plentifully (moderately in winter), give weak liquid feed monthly during active growth.

Chamaerops humilis
European fan palm

Features Erect fan fronds cut into rigid, sword-like segments; stiff, strongly toothed stalks.
Size 90 × 60cm (3 × 2ft).
Needs Good light with some direct sun, normal room temp.; water plentifully, liquid feed fortnightly during active growth.

Chrysalidocarpus lutescens
Yellow butterfly palm

Features Light green, glossy and arching fronds up to 1.2m (4ft) long on tall, deeply furrowed stalks; leaflets arranged in almost opposite pairs.
Size 1.5 × 1.2m (5 × 4ft).
Needs Sun filtered through a blind or curtain, normal room temp. (min. 13°C/55°F), water plentifully,
liquid feed every two weeks during active growth.

Cycas revoluta
Sago palm

Features Feathery-looking, but stiff, arching fronds rising from a pineapple-like, brown-felted, water-storing base; needle-like leaflets. Extremely slow-growing cycad — not a true palm.
Size Eventually 1.2 × 1.5m (4 × 5ft), but generally much smaller.
Needs Bright light essential, normal room temp., not below 13°C (55°F), tolerant of dry air, water moderately, liquid feed monthly except in winter.

Howeia/Kentia belmoreana
Curly palm

Features Slender plant forming a short trunk with age; upright to gracefully arching, rich green, fan-like fronds, incut almost to the midrib.
Size Up to 3 × 1.5m (10 × 5ft) with age.
Needs Bright or medium light, normal room temp., tolerant of quite dry air, water plentifully during active growth (sparingly during the winter), liquid feed fortnightly only during active growth.

Howeia/Kentia forsteriana
Kentia palm

Features Rich green, arching fronds with drooping leaflets.
Size Up to 3 × 2.4m (10 × 8ft).
Needs Tolerant of shade and dry air, but prefers good light, normal room temp., water well (sparingly in winter), liquid feed fortnightly.

Licuala spinosa
Queensland fan palm

Features Clustered stems carrying thorny, slender-stalked fronds composed of radiating, wedge-shaped leaflets which are ribbed and end in a blunt tip.
Size Eventually up to 1.2 × 1.2m (4 × 4ft), but generally smaller.
Needs Bright but filtered light, normal to warm room temp., humid air, water plentifully (moderately in winter), liquid feed fortnightly during active growth.

Livistona chinensis
Chinese fan palm

Features Generally stemless; bright green, glossy, fan-shaped fronds up to 60cm (2ft) across with deeply incut edges, drooping at their tips; toothed stalks.
Size 1.5 × 1.5m (5 × 5ft).
Needs Bright, filtered light out of direct sun, normal room temp., water moderately, liquid feed fortnightly during active growth. Will tolerate temp. down to 7°C (45°F), water sparingly.

Microcoelum/Cocos weddelianum
Coconut palm (dwarf)

Features Shiny, dark green fronds with narrow, herringbone leaflets spread out from a short, thickened base; central rib covered with black scales.
Size Up to 1.2 × 1.2m (4 × 4ft).
Needs Filtered light out of direct sun, temp. 16-27°C (61-80°F), water moderately, liquid feed monthly during active growth. Stand pot on a tray of moist pebbles to maintain humidity.

Phoenix canariensis
Canary date palm

Features Stumpy, almost bulbous stem base; frond bases covered with brown, fibrous hair; dark, stiff, herringbone fronds.
Size 1.8 × 1.5m (6 × 5ft).
Needs Full sun, normal room temp., water plentifully, liquid feed fortnightly during active growth. Give a winter rest at 10-13°C (50-55°F), watering sparingly.

Phoenix roebelenii
Miniature date palm

Features Thick crown of narrow, arching, dark green fronds covered with a thin layer of white scales; plant may develop more than one stem.
Size Up to 90 × 120cm (3 × 4ft).
Needs Bright light filtered through a translucent curtain, normal room temp., water plentifully, liquid feed fortnightly during active growth. Give a winter rest at 10-13°C (50-55°F), watering sparingly.

Rhapis excelsa
Little lady palm

Features Clustered stems covered with a rough, brown fibre; fan-shaped, dark green fronds of blunt-tipped segments.
Size Eventually 1.5 × 1.5m (5 × 5ft), but generally smaller.
Needs Bright but filtered light (with some direct sun in winter), normal to cool room temp. down to 7°C (45°F), water moderately (sparingly in winter), liquid feed monthly during active growth.

Trachycarpus fortunei
Windmill palm

Features Slender stem with fan-shaped fronds on finely toothed, long stalks; young fronds are pleated and covered with fine, light brown hairs. Old main stem covered with coarse brown fibre.
Size Up to 2.4 × 1.8m (8 × 6ft).
Needs Bright light with some direct sun, normal to cool room temp., water moderately, liquid feed fortnightly during active growth.

Washingtonia filifera
Desert fan palm

Features Short, tapered, red-brown trunk; long, spiny leaf stalks; fan-shaped fronds edged with fine, twisted fibres.
Size Up to 1.5 × 1.5m (5 × 5ft).
Needs Bright light with some direct sun, normal to warm room temp., moist air, water plentifully (moderately in winter), liquid feed fortnightly only during active growth.

OTHER INDOOR PALMS

Archontophoenix alexandrae (Alexandra palm) A large palm, suitable for indoors when young. Smooth, short trunk with arching fan-like fronds composed of many narrow leaflets, covered with fine hairs on their undersides, giving a silvery appearance. Plants reach 3 × 2.1m (10 × 7ft). Needs bright but filtered light, normal to warm room temp., plentiful watering and liquid feeding fortnightly during active growth.

Arecastrum/Cocos romanzoffianum (Queen palm) Tall, elegant palm with large fan-like fronds composed of narrow, drooping leaflets. Plants may reach 3 × 2.1m (10 × 7ft). Needs bright to medium light, normal to warm room temp., moderate watering and fortnightly liquid feeds during active growth.

Caryota urens (Sago or wine palm) Similar to the Burmese fishtail palm, with drooping fronds composed of many sets of dark green, somewhat leathery leaflets. The leaflets are more triangular in shape and have less jagged edges than those of the Burmese fishtail palm, and are far less numerous, so that the fronds look looser and lace-like.

Chamaedorea erumpens (Bamboo palm) Clump-forming with smooth, slender, upright stems which are knotted at intervals like bamboo. Fronds are arching, deep green and fan-like. Plants may reach 2.4 × 1.2m (8 × 4ft) with age. Cultural requirements are as for the parlour palm.

Chamaedorea seifrizii (Reed palm) Clump-forming with slender cane-like stems and delicate-looking, lacy, fan-like, bluish green fronds 60-90cm (2-3ft) long. Plants reach 1.2 × 1.2m (4 × 4ft). Cultural requirements are as for the parlour palm.

Corypha elata (Gebang sugar palm) Long-stalked, fan-like fronds deeply incut into up to 80 narrow leaflets. Plants reach 1-2 × 1-2m (3-6½ × 3-6½ft). Needs bright light, normal to warm room temp., moderate watering and liquid feeding fortnightly during active growth.

Jubaea chilensis (Chilean wine palm) Large fan-like fronds with long, narrow, greyish green leaflets; stem base swollen and covered with brown fibres. Plants eventually reach 1.5 × 1.5m (5 × 5ft) with age.

Livistona australis (Australian fan palm) Very similar to the Chinese fan palm, but it has slightly larger, dark green leaves and striking spiny leaf stalks.

Phoenix dactylifera (Date palm) Blue-green, prickly fronds arching from a slender green stem. Similar to the Canary date palm, but somewhat faster growing and less showy as a house plant.

Rhapis humilis (Slender lady palm) Very slender, reed-like stems; fan-like fronds divided into 10-20 pointed-tipped leaflets of rather varying widths. Plants reach up to 2.4 × 1.8m (8 × 6ft) with age. Cultural requirements as for little lady fern (*Rhapis excelsa*).

Thrinax microcarpa (Thatch palm) Rounded heads of fan-like fronds, which are silvery beneath. Plants are slow-growing and very decorative when young, but may grow too large with age.

Washingtonia robusta (Thread palm) Similar to the desert fan palm, but taller, thinner, faster growing and with bright green fronds composed of stiffer, less deeply incut fronds.

INDOOR FERNS

**Ferns, the oldest of all plant groups, neither
flower nor set seed. They are attractive indoor plants
valued for their delicate leaf fronds.**

Ferns belong to several different families of plants, but since they have many features in common they are invariably treated as a single group. Although ferns come from all parts of the world, only those native to the warmest regions are suitable indoors.

Many tropical ferns are epiphytes – in the wild, their roots grow into rotting vegetation and other debris that collects in crevices between tree branches.

Other ferns are terrestrial and thrive in the shady, humid atmosphere at the base of trees or anywhere else at ground level where there is humus-rich soil.

The fronds – equivalent to the leaves of other plants – and the feeding roots grow from rhizomes, which are fleshy stems serving as food stores. Rhizomes usually grow horizontally underground, but those of some ferns, such as *Asplenium* and *Polystichum*, are stem-like, short and branching.

The rhizomatous stems of a few ferns, including *Davallia* and *Polypodium*, can creep or cling above ground. When grown in a pot, these rhizomatous stems – which are often furry – overhang the rim gracefully.

Fronds are a combination of stalk and leaf-like blade, and vary greatly in size and shape. In outline, the blade may be simple and strap-like as in *Asplenium scolopendrium*, divided and feathery as in *Davallia*, triangular as in *Adiantum*, or broad and antler-like as in *Platycerium*.

The segments of a divided blade are called pinnae. When pinnae are divided further, the segments are known as pinnules. Twice-divided blades are described as bipinnate; those divided three times are tripinnate.

Ferns do not flower. Instead, they reproduce by means of dust-like spores which are borne in brownish cases – called sori – on the undersides of the fronds. Ferns don't require direct sun or even very bright light and, in fact, do well where other house plants may fail.

There is one popular genus of flowering plant – *Asparagus* – which has ferny foliage. Though really members of the lily family, asparagus are commonly called ferns and are treated as such.

▼ **Indoor fernery** Tolerant of poor light and low temperatures, this fern collection displays contrasting forms and colours. Graceful maidenhair and arching Boston ferns shelter beneath a canopy of feathery asparagus.

Adiantum capillus-veneris
Maidenhair fern

Features Delicately formed, arching fronds on blackish, hair-like stalks with light green, fan-like pinnae. Rhizomes grow horizontally just below the soil surface.
Size Generally up to 25 × 25cm (10 × 10in), but may reach twice this size in ideal conditions.
Needs Filtered bright light but no direct sun, moist air, normal room temperatures (minimum 13°C/55°F). Water moderately, aiming to keep the compost slightly moist at all times — don't allow fluctuations between excess moisture and dryness. Stand pots on a layer of moist pebbles.

As with most ferns, acid potting composts are ideal, provided that plants are fed every two weeks during active growth with liquid foliage house plant fertilizer.

Adiantum hispidulum
Australian maidenhair

Features Fronds divided into spreading sections, each with rows of small, almost oblong, leathery pinnae, coloured reddish brown at first, maturing to mid-green.
Size Up to 30 × 30cm (1 × 1ft).
Needs As Adiantum capillus-veneris above.

Asparagus densiflorus 'Sprengeri'
Emerald fern

Features Soft, arching plumes of bright green, needle-like branchlets (leaves not produced).
Size 30 × 30cm (1 × 1ft). Species may reach 1.2m (4ft) high.
Needs Filtered light, shade tolerant, normal room temp., water freely (less in winter), feed fortnightly.

Asparagus falcatus
Sicklethorn

Features Climbing stems with clusters of slightly curved 5cm (2in) long, needle-like, fresh green branchlets (no true leaves).
Size To 3.5m × 30cm (12 × 1ft).
Needs Filtered light, normal room tempt., water freely (less in winter), feed fortnightly.

Asparagus myersii (syn. A. 'Myers')
Foxtail fern

Features Soft, upright to arching, foxtail-like plumes of bright green, tightly clustered needle-shaped branchlets.
Size Up to 60 × 60cm (2 × 2ft)
Needs Filtered light, normal room temp., water freely (less in winter), feed fortnightly.

Asparagus plumosus/setaceus
Asparagus fern

Features Wiry, arching stems with flattened sprays of bright green, 6mm (¼in) long branchlets.
Size Climbs to 3m × 60cm (10 × 2ft); 'Nanus' (shown) is dwarf.
Needs Filtered light, normal room temp., water freely (less in winter), feed fortnightly.

Asplenium bulbiferum
Mother spleenwort

Features Lacy, mid-green fronds which look rather like carrot leaves. Small brown bulbils on the fronds produce baby ferns.
Size Up to 60 × 90cm (2 × 3ft).
Needs Light shade, normal room temp. (minimum 10°C/50°F), water plentifully (sparingly in winter), liquid feed monthly during active growth.

Asplenium nidus
Bird's nest fern

Features Shuttlecock-like rosette of apple green, undivided, slightly undulating fronds, each with a blackish midrib and glossy surface.
Size Up to 1.2m × 60cm (4 × 2ft).
Needs Moderate light, normal room temp. (minimum 16°C/61°F), water plentifully (sparingly in winter), liquid feed monthly.

Asplenium/Phyllitis scolopendrium
Hart's tongue fern

Features Glossy green, strap-shaped, undivided fronds, often with undulating edges, forming an upright tuft.
Size Up to 60 × 30cm (2 × 1ft).
Needs Moderate light, normal room temp., water moderately (less in winter), apply half-strength liquid fertilizer fortnightly.

Blechnum gibbum
Blechnum

Features Glossy green, finely divided fronds, in a rosette at the top of a dark rhizomatous stem, which may become trunk-like.
Size Up to 1 × 1.2m (3 × 4ft).
Needs Bright but filtered light, warm room temp., moist air, water plentifully, feed with dilute liquid fertilizer during active growth.

Cyrtomium falcatum
Holly fern

Features Dark green, holly-like pinnae, each 5-10cm (2-4in) long, forming stiff, arching fronds.
Size Up to 45 × 60cm (1½ × 2ft).
Needs Bright but filtered light, normal room temp., water moderately, apply half-strength liquid fertilizer fortnightly.

Davallia canariensis
Deer's foot fern

Features Narrowly triangular, soft-textured, mid-green fronds much divided into tiny pinnae. Creeping scaly rhizomes.
Size Up to 45 × 45cm (1½ × 1½ft).
Needs Bright light, normal to warm room temp., water well (less in winter), liquid feed monthly.

Nephrolepis exaltata 'Bostoniensis'
Boston fern

Features Long, arching to drooping, rich green fronds divided into many narrow pinnae. Variety 'Elegantissima' has more feathery, bright green fronds.
Size Up to 60 × 90cm (2 × 3ft).
Needs Bright but filtered light, normal room temp., water plentifully, feed fortnightly.

Pellaea rotundifolia
Button fern

Features Unusual fern, arching and spreading fronds with dark green, leathery, button-like, 12mm (½in) wide pinnae. Borne alternately or almost in pairs on blackish wiry stalks which are covered with reddish brown scales. Creeping rhizomes produce spreading clumps of fronds when the plant is grown in a wide container.
Size Up to 30 × 45cm (12 × 18in).
Needs Medium light, normal room temp. (minimum 10°C/50°F), mist-spray daily with tepid water in hot temp., water plentifully (sparingly in winter), liquid feed fortnightly during active growth. Button fern is shallow-rooted and is best grown in a half-pot or shallow pan.

Platycerium bifurcatum/alcicorne
Stag's horn fern

Features One small sterile frond, replaced yearly, forms a brown papery shield. From the centre of this grow larger fertile fronds with antler-like segments.
Size Up to 90 × 90cm (3 × 3ft).
Needs Bright but filtered light, normal room temp., moist air, water moderately, feed occasionally. Pack rhizomes in peat substitute and tie to bark slabs.

Polypodium aureum
Hare's foot fern

Features Fronds divided into light green, undulating pinnae. Furry brown rhizomes, like hare's feet, creep over the soil surface.
Size Up to 90 × 60cm (3 × 2ft).
Needs Medium light, normal room temp., water plentifully (less in winter), apply half-strength liquid fertilizer weekly.

Polystichum tsus-simense
Tsusina holly fern

Features Bipinnate, arching fronds divided into slender pinnae, then into tiny, toothed, deep green pinnules like mini holly leaves.
Size Up to 90 × 60cm (3 × 2ft).
Needs Medium to bright light, normal room temp., moist air, water plentifully (less in winter), apply dilute fertilizer fortnightly.

Pteris cretica 'Albolineata'
Cretan brake fern

Features Long-stalked fronds with pinnae in threes. Cream bands mark each side of the ribs.
Size Up to 30 × 45cm (1 × 1½ft).
Needs Bright but filtered light, normal room temp., moist air, water plentifully, apply dilute fertilizer fortnightly.

Pteris ensiformis 'Victoriae'
Sword brake fern

Features Narrowly triangular fronds divided into paired, green pinnae with silvery white midribs.
Size Up to 45 × 45cm (1½ × 1½ft).
Needs Bright but filtered light, normal room temp., moist air, water plentifully (less in winter), apply dilute fertilizer fortnightly.

Pteris tremula
Trembling brake fern

Features Triangular, bipinnate, feathery fronds with lance-shaped pinnae sub-divided into small fresh green pinnules.
Size Up to 60 × 30cm (2 × 1ft).
Needs Bright but filtered light, normal room temp., moist air, water plentifully (less in winter), apply dilute fertilizer fortnightly.

Selaginella **species and varieties**
Moss ferns

Features Not true ferns, but closely related and spore-bearing. Moss-like hummocky plants or highly branched upright plants with creeping stems. Tiny fleshy leaves in orderly ranks around the stems, forming elegant plumes or sprays. Species and varieties are available with pale green, bright green, golden or silvery green foliage.
Size Generally 5-30 × 15-30cm (2-12 × 6-12in).
Needs Full or light shade, warm room temp., moist air, mist-spray with tepid water daily (never use cold water), water plentifully, apply very dilute liquid fertilizer fortnightly during active growth. Ideal plants for a bottle garden or terrarium.

FLOWERING POT PLANTS

A vast number of pot plants with exotic blooms, brilliant colours or delicate scents thrive under indoor conditions.

Every winter, florists' shops and garden centres are stocked with flowering house plants – cyclamen, poinsettias, chrysanthemums, azaleas and primroses, but the range of indoor flowering plants extends far beyond these. You should be careful when purchasing plants sold from windy street corners or in overheated supermarkets – the sudden shock that plants experience when moved to normal home environments can be such that the flowers drop too early, and new buds fail to develop.

These seasonal buys are short-term plants which are intended to be discarded after flowering. However, if treated correctly many can be coaxed into blooming year after year, especially cyclamen and most azaleas. Poinsettias, too, can be encouraged to flower for a second and even a third year, though the flower bracts, while still brilliant in colour, become progressively smaller.

The finest flowering house plants are those which will reward good care with a more or less continuous display, such as the African violets, Cape primroses, busy Lizzies and wax begonias. All are easy to grow indoors.

Some of the exotic types, like *Hoya* and *Stephanotis* species, are more exacting in their requirements, but their flowering seasons are so spectacular and fragrant that they are worth cosseting.

Certain flowering plants are true herbaceous perennials that retire into a period of dormancy when they are best removed to a cool spare room until they start to grow again. Hippeastrums and sinningias belong in this category. The flowers of some house plants, clivias and aphelandras for example, provide an additional attraction to handsome foliage. At the other end of the scale are the carefree annuals that flower for months before coming to a natural end – calceolarias, cinerarias and German violets.

The indoor garden can be bright with flower colour at any time of the year – short-term, long-blooming or temporary plants, and bowls of potted and forced bulbs can form a year-round display. In general, flowering plants are less tolerant of poor light and draughts than foliage plants; temperature fluctuations can result in bud drop and mist-spraying may spoil more delicate petals.

▼ **Unusual containers** Choose pot holders to suit the mood and style of the decor. Ornate containers are out of keeping with functional workplaces, but ordinary cans and tins can add a lighthearted touch, and a little imagination and artistic flair can transform plain clay pots.

Achimenes grandiflora 'Rose Red'
Hot water plant

Features Deciduous perennial of bushy habit; mid-green toothed leaves. Tubular pink-red, purple or violet flowers in summer.
Size 45 × 45cm (1½ × 1½ft).
Needs Bright light out of hot sun; warm temp., min. 13°C (55°F). Keep moist during active growth, mist-spray daily during hot spells.

Anthurium scherzerianum
Flamingo flower

Features Dark green, lance-shaped leaves. Scarlet spathes with twisted spadix, spring to autumn.
Size 30 × 45cm (1 × 1½ft).
Needs Partial shade; constant temp. of 16-21°C (61-70°F); high humidity, mist-spray often. Keep moist during active growth, feed fortnightly.

Aphelandra squarrosa 'Louisae'
Zebra plant

Features Pointed dark green leaves with ivory veins. Yellow bracts in summer and autumn.
Size 60 × 30cm (2 × 1ft).
Needs Bright light, min. temp. 16°C (61°F). Good humidity; water freely and feed weekly during active growth, fortnightly and kept moist for the rest of the year.

Beloperone guttata
Shrimp plant

Features Evergreen and vigorous shrub with small, lightly hairy leaves. Long arching flower spikes of pinkish brown bracts hiding tiny white flowers, appear from spring to autumn.
Size 45-90 × 30-45cm (1½-3 × 1-1½ft).
Needs Bright but filtered light in summer, bright light in winter. Normal room temp., good ventilation and humidity. Water moderately and feed weekly during active growth; water sparingly in winter and keep at a constant temp. of 10°C (50°F).

Pinch out growing tips to encourage bushy plants; prune back by up to half in late winter to maintain shape. Repot or pot on annually in mid-spring. Increase by tip cuttings in spring; pinch out tips and early flower bracts to build up bushy plants.

Calceolaria × *herbeohybrida*
Slipper flower

Features Biennial; large, hairy mid-green leaves. Dense clusters of pouched flowers in red, orange or yellow, often blotched with crimson in summer.
Size To 45 × 45cm (1½ × 1½ft).
Needs Bright but filtered light; cool temp., min. 7-10°C (45-50°F). Keep compost permanently moist. Discard after flowering.

Campanula isophylla
Italian bellflower

Features Trailing perennial; small heart-shaped leaves. Profusion of white or blue star-shaped flowers in summer to autumn.
Size 15 × 30-45cm (6in × 1-1½ft).
Needs Bright light, full sun. Cool site, min. temp. 7°C (45°F). Good humidity, mist-spray often. Water freely and feed fortnightly during growth. Good for hanging baskets.

Clivia miniata
Kaffir lily

Features Fleshy-rooted perennial; arching dark green fans, leathery leaves. Large orange-red flower heads in spring to autumn.
Size 45 × 45cm (1½ × 1½ft).
Needs Bright but filtered light; warm room temp., winter min. 10-13°C (50-55°F). Moist compost and fortnightly feeds during active growth; near-dry winter rest.

Euphorbia pulcherrima
Poinsettia

Features Short-lived deciduous shrub with bright green, lobed and prominently veined leaves. Tiny greenish-yellow flowers surrounded by scarlet flower bracts in winter. Pink, white and lime-green varieties also available.
Size 60 × 45cm (2 × 1½ft).
Needs Brightest possible light; normal room temp., min. 10-13°C (50-55°F); increased humidity at high temps., no draughts. Water thoroughly when compost feels dry at top. Usually discarded after flowering, but can be grown on after cutting hard back when foliage dies and rested dry until late spring. Repot and resume watering; flowers only produced if plants given 8 weeks of bud initiation consisting of 14 hours of darkness and 10 hours of light daily.

Hibiscus rosa-sinensis
Rose of China

Features Evergreen shrub; dark green, toothed leaves. Short-lived but profuse funnel-shaped flowers, crimson, pink, salmon, yellow in summer.
Size To 1.8 × 1.8m (6 × 6ft).
Needs Bright filtered light, warm room temp., good humidity. Constant moist compost, feed fortnightly during growth; near-dry winter rest at 10°C (50°F).

Hippeastrum hybrids
Hippeastrum

Features Bulbous plants; arching strap-shaped leaves. Large, tall-stemmed white, pink, orange or scarlet, often bicoloured flower clusters in spring.
Size To 75 × 45cm (2½ × 1½ft).
Needs Bright light, full sun; max. temp. 19°C (66°F). Water moderately, feed fortnightly during active growth; dry rest period after foliage dies down.

Hoya carnosa
Wax plant

Features Vigorous evergreen climber; oval, fleshy leaves. Scented flower clusters, white to pink from mid-spring to autumn.
Size To 3m × 90cm (10 × 3ft).
Needs Bright light, full sun; temp. 16-24°C (61-75°F). Good humidity; feed fortnightly, water moderately during growth; winter rest at 10°C (50°F). Grow on wire hoops or canes.

Impatiens walleriana
Busy Lizzie

Features Short-lived shrubby perennial; green or bronze leaves. Free-flowering, red, pink, white, often bicoloured, spring to autumn.
Size 60 × 30cm (2 × 1ft).
Needs Bright filtered light; min. temp. 13°C (55°F). Good humidity; water moderately, feed fortnightly. Pinch out tips for bushiness. Discard when plant becomes leggy.

Jasminum polyanthum
Pink jasmine

Features Climbing plant; dark green leaves. Sweetly scented, pink-budded white flowers in winter and spring.
Size 90 × 90cm (3 × 3ft).
Needs Bright light, full sun; cool room temp., 16°C (61°F). Feed fortnightly, water freely during growth. Provide support. Cut back after flowering and rest at 10-13°C (50-55°F).

Pelargonium 'Aztec'
Regal pelargonium

Features Perennial; handsome lobed and toothed leaves. Clusters of red flowers with white frilly edges in summer.
Size To 60 × 38cm (24 × 15in).
Needs Bright light and sun; temp. 16-21°C (61-70°F). Feed fortnightly during active growth, water compost when dry. Winter-rest at min. 10°C (50°F), water sparingly; cut stems back by half.

Plumbago capensis
Cape leadwort

Features Evergreen climber; long elliptic mid-green leaves. Clusters of pale blue, primrose-like flowers, spring to autumn.
Size 120-180 × 90cm (4-6 × 3ft).
Needs Bright light, full sun; room temp. During active growth water freely, feed fortnightly. Winter-rest at 10°C (50°F), water sparingly; prune after flowering.

Saintpaulia ionantha
African violet

Features Evergreen plant; hairy sometimes wrinkled leaf rosettes. Flower clusters in mauve, purple, violet, pink, red, white and bicoloured; any time of the year.
Size 5-20 × 10-40cm (2-4 × 4-16in).
Needs Filtered light; constant min. temp. 18°C (64°F); high humidity. Water from below to keep compost moist; feed fortnightly.

Senecio × hybridus
Cineraria

Features Biennial with heart-shaped, toothed leaves. Daisy-like flowers in a wide colour range in winter and spring.
Size 23-60 × 30-60cm (9-24 × 12-24in).
Needs Bright light incl. sun; cool room temp., 16°C (61°F). Set pots on moist pebbles on a sunny window-sill. Water freely and discard after flowering.

Sinningia regina
Cinderella slippers

Features Tuberous perennial; deep green, purple-backed, veined leaves. Violet-purple bellflowers in late spring and summer.
Size 20 × 30cm (8 × 12in).
Needs Bright filtered light, normal room temp. High humidity; mist-spray. Feed fortnightly, water freely from spring-autumn. Dry winter rest.

Spathiphyllum 'Mauna Loa'
Peace lily

Features Glossy, long-stemmed leaves. Fragrant white flower spathes in late spring and summer.
Size 60 × 30cm (2 × 1ft).
Needs Bright but filtered light, normal room temp. High humidity, mist-spray daily in summer. Feed fortnightly and water freely when in active growth; near-dry winter rest at min. 13°C (55°F).

Stephanotis floribunda
Wax flower

Features Slow evergreen climber; leathery, glossy green leaves. Strongly scented, waxy white flowers from late spring-autumn.
Size 60 × 90cm (2 × 3ft) or more.
Needs Bright but filtered light, normal room temp., min. 13°C (55°F) in winter. Good humidity, mist-spray. Feed fortnightly, water freely during active growth.

Streptocarpus 'Concord'
Cape primrose

Features Evergreen perennial of hybrid origin; large, coarse-textured and wrinkled primrose-like leaves. 'Concord' bears loose clusters of long-stemmed flowers in shades of purple, pink, white or lilac with maroon veins. Other varieties include blue and red-purple types with contrasting throats; many can be in flower for six months or more.
Size To 30 × 38cm (12 × 15in).
Needs Bright light, out of direct summer sun; normal room temp., winter rest at 13°C (55°F). Stand pots on moist pebbles and cover compost with sphagnum moss to keep roots cool during active growth; feed fortnightly and water freely, allowing compost to dry out between applications. Apply water sparingly in winter.

SCENTED HOUSE PLANTS

**Apart from forced spring bulbs, only a few
indoor plants are scented, but these have fragrances
heady enough to fill a room.**

Most indoor plants are foliage plants which never or only rarely bear flowers because conditions in the home cannot match the tropical climates in which the plants grow naturally. Instead we use cut flowers or bowls of pot-pourri to scent our living rooms, particularly during winter.

However, spring-flowering bulbs forced into early bloom are a popular if temporary indoor plant option. For example, bunch-flowered narcissi and Dutch hyacinths are valued for both their flowers and their fragrance. Gently forced freesias have a delicious perfume and some of the tencer primulas, especially *Primula obconica*,

scent the air with promises of spring. Miniature roses, kept at cool temperatures, have a lingering fragrance and lily-of-the-valley, potted up and forced at gentle heat, will release a heady, persistent scent.

Many orchids, with their exotic blooms, are strongly fragrant, notably *Coelogyne*, *Lycaste* and several of the easily-grown odontoglossums with their long-lasting flowers.

A few powerfully scented species make fine pot plants for the home, or can be grown in tubs and open borders in a conservatory, sunroom or heated greenhouse. They include angel's trumpet (*Datura*), gardenia, wax flower

(*Stephanotis*) and wax plants (*Hoya* species).

Some of these are easier to grow than others. Gardenia, for example, is so exacting in its cultural needs that it can be difficult to bring to flower in the average living room. Stephanotis, with its heavily scented, waxy white flowers, drops its buds at fluctuating temperature and humidity levels, while the highly fragrant *Jasminum polyanthum* is less temperamental and becomes smothered with heady-scented white flowers in spring, when grown in a cool room. The Citrus species, too, are accommodating house plants and the little calamondin orange (*Citrus mitis*) is especially sweet-scented, flowering and fruiting when quite young.

In all cases, a living room is more likely to be filled with scent if the plants are positioned where there are moving currents of air, but out of cold draughts.

Plants with aromatic leaves – certain pelargoniums – release their fragrance only when bruised. Stand them where they may be brushed by passers-by.

Scented plants benefit from regular feeding with a proprietary house plant fertilizer which is specially formulated for flowering plants – flower production requires extra potash. One of the best and cheapest sources of potash is the type of liquid fertilizer sold specifically for tomatoes.

Most scented plants thrive in ordinary potting compost – whether soil-based John Innes mixes or peat-based types. However, gardenias dislike even the smallest trace of lime and need an acid (ericaceous) potting compost. Use rain-water or boiled water rather than hard tap-water.

◄ **Sweet-scented hyacinths** Prized for their densely packed flower spikes, Dutch hyacinths have an unmistakable, almost overpoweringly sweet fragrance. They are specially prepared for early indoor flowering and come in a range of colours – pure white, creamy-yellow, pink, red and blue.

Bouvardia × *domestica*
Bouvardia

Features Upright shrub. Tubular red, pink or white, sweet-scented flowers in clusters up to 10cm (4in) across at the tips of the branches in summer and autumn. Mid-green, oval to pointed leaves.
Size Up to 90 × 45cm (3 × 1½ft).
Needs Bright light, normal room temp., water plentifully, liquid feed weekly when flower buds form.

Citrus mitis
Calamondin orange

Features Bushy shrub. Small clusters of white, sweetly scented, 12mm (½in) wide flowers in summer, followed by 3cm (1¼in) wide orange fruits like tiny satsumas. Glossy leaves.
Size 45 × 45cm (1½ × 1½ft) or more.
Needs Bright light with some full sun, normal room temp., water moderately, feed fortnightly.

Convallaria majalis
Lily-of-the-valley

Features Upright rhizome-rooted perennial. Arching sprays of waxy, white, bell-shaped, powerfully sweet-scented flowers in spring (prepared roots can be forced to flower in winter). Paired, mid-green, narrowly oval leaves.
Size Up to 20cm (8in) tall.
Needs Light shade, cool temp., water plentifully, liquid feed fortnightly.

Cyclamen persicum
Florist's cyclamen

Features Tuberous-rooted perennial. Butterfly-like red, pink, mauve or white flowers; small-flowered varieties have more scent than larger ones. Heart-shaped marbled leaves.
Size Up to 23 × 23cm (9 × 9in).
Needs Bright but filtered light, cool temp., water moderately from below, liquid feed fortnightly.

Datura × *candida*
Angel's trumpet

Features Upright shrub. Huge pendent, white trumpet flowers up to 25cm (10in) long in summer; their powerful scent is sweet and heavy, mainly in the evening. Large mid-green, oval leaves.
Size 1-2.4m (3-8ft) tall.
Needs Bright light, warm temp., water moderately, feed fortnightly during active growth. Cool winter rest.

Exacum affine
German/Persian violet

Features Bushy perennial best grown as an annual. Profuse, small, violet-like, lavender-blue or white, mildly fragrant flowers from summer to early autumn. Small, oval, olive green leaves.
Size Up to 30 × 30cm (1 × 1ft).
Needs Bright but filtered light, warm temp., humid air, water plentifully, liquid feed fortnightly, dead-head regularly.

Freesia × *hybrida*
Freesia

Features Corm-rooted perennial. Arching sprays of funnel-shaped, 2.5-4cm (1-1½in) long, very sweetly scented flowers in a wide range of colours, including red, pink, mauve, lilac, orange, yellow, cream and white; flowers often paler in the throat and sometimes double.

Upright to arching grass-like leaves up to 23cm (9in) long.
Size 45-60cm (1½-2ft).
Needs Bright light, cool temp., water moderately (plentifully when in flower), feed fortnightly during active growth. Provide support for the floppy stems. After flowering, dry off the plants, lift the corms and store in a cool, dry place until repotting.

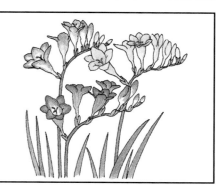

Gardenia jasminoides
Gardenia

Features Bushy shrub. Double or semi-double, creamy white, powerfully sweet-scented flowers in summer and autumn, each up to 7.5cm (3in) across; a brief flush of flowers may also appear in winter. Lance-shaped, dark green, glossy, leathery leaves, generally up to 10cm (4in) long.

Size 60-120 × 60-120cm (2-4 × 2-4ft).
Needs Bright but filtered light, temp. steady 17°C (62°F) when flower buds are forming, normal room temp. at other times and 10°C (50°F) in winter, humid air, water moderately (sparingly in winter) using lime-free collected rainwater or boiled water, feed fortnightly during active growth with special acid-based house plant fertilizer. Dead-head regularly. Use lime-free potting compost.

Heliotropium × hybridum
Heliotrope/cherry pie

Features Bushy annual. Broad heads of fragrant, deep violet or white flowers from summer to mid-autumn. Dark green leaves.
Size 30 × 30cm (1 × 1ft).
Needs Bright light, cool to normal room temp., humid air, water plentifully, feed with weak liquid fertilizer every 10 days.

Hoya bella
Miniature wax plant

Features Arching or trailing shrub. Small, pendent clusters of sweet-scented, starry, purple-centred white flowers in summer. Lance-shaped, mid-green leaves.
Size 30 × 45cm (1 × 1½ft) or more.
Needs Bright light, filtered in summer, normal room temp., water moderately, liquid feed fortnightly with high-potash fertilizer.

Hoya carnosa
Wax plant

Features Vigorous climbing shrub. Pendent clusters of powerfully sweet-scented, red-centred, creamy white, star-like flowers mainly in summer (fragrance strongest in the evening). Glossy dark green, 5-7cm (2-3in) long leaves.
Size Climbs to 3m (10ft) or can be trained to any size.
Needs Bright light with some full sun, normal room temp., water moderately, liquid feed fortnightly.

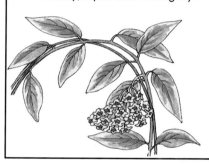

Hyacinthus orientalis **varieties**
Dutch hyacinths

Features Bulb. Cylindrical spike of sweet-scented blue, pink, yellow or white flowers in winter.
Size Up to 30 × 15cm (12 × 6in).
Needs Keep dark until leaves are 2.5cm (1in) tall, then move into bright light. Cool to normal room temp., water moderately.

Jasminum polyanthum
Pink jasmine

Features Climbing shrub. Clusters of sweet-scented, 2.5cm (1in) long, pink-tinged, white trumpet flowers in winter and spring. Mid-green leaves.
Size May climb to 3m (10ft) but can be trained smaller.
Needs Bright light with some full sun, cool temp., water plentifully, liquid feed fortnightly.

Lilium auratum
Golden-rayed lily

Features Bulb. Huge heavily scented, trumpet-shaped, gold-striped white flowers up to 20cm (8in) across in late summer. Lance-shaped, mid-green leaves.
Size Up to 1.2m (4ft) tall.
Needs Bright light, cool temp. during early growth then normal room temp., water moderately.

Narcissus varieties
Narcissi

Features Bulbs. Short-tubed, delicately sweet-scented trumpet flowers, generally in clusters of 3-7, on upright leafless stalks in late winter or spring. Flower colour varies from pure white, through cream and pale yellow to rich golden yellow, and the trumpet may be orange, yellow or white (often contrasting with the outer petals). Upright to arching strap-shaped, mid-green leaves.

Varieties suitable for growing indoors include: 'Cragford' (white with orange central cup); 'Geranium' (white with orange-red cup), 'Grand Soleil d'Or' (*illustrated*); 'Paper White' (all white).
Size Up to 45cm (1½ft) tall.
Needs Grow in shallow bowls or half-pots filled with washed gravel, pebbles, bulb fibre or potting compost. Keep bulbs dark and cool at first then move them into bright light and more warmth when the leaves are 10cm (4in) tall (usually 6-8 weeks after planting). Water moderately.

Pelargonium species and varieties
Scented-leaved pelargoniums

P. capitatum

P. crispum 'Variegatum'

P. graveolens

Features Tough-stemmed, bushy perennials. Flowers generally insignificant. Coarse-textured aromatic leaves in many shades of green, sometimes with darker shading or with paler variegations, and usually with crimped and incut edges. Scent is released when the leaves are touched.

Species and varieties suitable for the home include: *P. capitatum* (rose-scented); 'Chocolate Peppermint' (chocolate-peppermint-scented);

'Cinnamon' (cinnamon-scented); *P. crispum* 'Variegatum' (lemon-scented); *P × fragrans* (nutmeg-scented); *P. graveolens* (rose-scented); 'Mabel Grey' (lemon/grapefruit-scented); 'Prince of Orange' (orange-scented); *P. tomentosum* (peppermint-scented).
Size 45-90 × 45-60cm (1½-3 × 1½-2ft).
Needs Bright light with some full sun, normal room temp., water moderately, liquid feed fortnightly.

Primula malacoides
Fairy primrose

Features Annual. Tiered clusters of softly fragrant, yellow-centred pink, red or white, 12mm (½in) wide flowers in winter and spring. Oval, pale green, slightly hairy, scalloped-edged leaves.
Size To 45 × 25cm (18 × 10in).
Needs Bright light with some full sun, cool temp., water plentifully, liquid feed fortnightly.

Rosa chinensis hybrids
Miniature roses

Features Shrubs. Single, semi-double or double, 1.2-4cm (½-1½in) wide flowers in many colours; some are very fragrant, others are less so.
Size Up to 30 × 30cm (1 × 1ft).
Needs Bright light, some full sun, normal room temp. (cold in winter), water moderately, feed fortnightly.

Stephanotis floribunda
Wax flower

Features Climbing shrub. Waxy, white, powerfully fragrant trumpet flowers in summer and autumn. Oval, dark green leaves.
Size Climbs to 3m (10ft), but can be trained around a small hoop.
Needs Bright but filtered light, normal room temp., humid air, no draughts, water plentifully.

EXOTIC BROMELIADS

Bromeliads are tropical foliage and flowering plants which display strikingly beautiful flower spikes and stunning leaf colours and patterns.

Bromeliads belong to a large family of tropical and sub-tropical plants. The terrestrial species of the group inhabit the rich moist ground deep in jungle forests, while the epiphytes live on tree branches and rocks. They gain only support from their hosts, being in no way parasitic but taking nourishment from surrounding forest debris.

The plants vary greatly in shape, size and colour, but most are characterized by distinctive leathery, strap-shaped leaves arranged in a rosette. This may be a loose, open circle of leaves, or it may be tube-like. In many bromeliads, the leaves overlap one another to form a cup-like, water-tight vessel. In the wild, rainwater and dew collect in the cup, and the plants draw water and food from this reservoir during dry periods.

Bromeliads are unique among plants in that most need to have water around the growing point – situated at the centre of the rosette – and this should be topped up at all times, preferably with rainwater. Nutrients are best supplied by adding dilute liquid fertilizer to the water in the rosette, or by giving a foliar spray.

The majority of bromeliads grown indoors are epiphytic by nature, but both these and the terrestrial types adapt themselves to different conditions provided their basic needs are met.

The flowers, which can appear at any time of year, are striking and often brilliantly coloured. They are often partly encased in showy red- or pink-coloured bracts. In some bromeliads, the blooms barely rise above the water in the rosette. Individual flowers are small, but they appear in succession on a broad, stalkless head. As if in compensation, the leaves or portions of leaves at the centre of the rosette frequently become brightly coloured – usually red or purple – at flowering time.

Other bromeliads have a long, erect and sturdy flower spike that pushes up from the rosette centre. This is topped by a bold, usually brightly coloured flower head bearing flowers that are about 12mm (½in) across, but surrounded by bright and long-lasting bracts. The leaves of this type do not change colour during the flowering period, but they are often attractively overlaid with a white or silvery meal, a scaly covering that acts as protection during prolonged droughts.

Bromeliad flowers are short-lived, but the bracts remain colourful for several weeks, and they may be followed by berries.

In general, each rosette flowers only once, then slowly dies. However, bromeliads usually self-propagate by developing offsets before the main rosette dies. These grow on to replace the old one.

It may take several years for flowers to appear, and nurseries may demand fairly high prices for mature flowering specimens. If you don't mind waiting for results, propagate your own plants from offsets detached when they are about one-quarter the size of the parent plant.

◄ **Tropical jungle effect** Bromeliads, also known as air plants, grow on the floor of tropical rain forests or on tree branches and rock faces. All are rosette-forming, often with brilliant leaf colours, marbled cross bands or variegated stripes and a centre of dramatic leaf colouring as the flowering season approaches.

Aechmea chantinii
Vase plant

Features Tough, greyish leaves with a coating of silvery scales in crossways bands. Flower head of pointed orange-red bracts and yellow-and-red flowers.
Size Up to 90 × 60cm (3 × 2ft).
Needs Bright but filtered light, warm temp. (min. 16°C/61°F), water soil moderately but keep the rosette filled with water.

Aechmea fasciata
Urn plant

Features Grey-green leaves with irregular, powdery white cross-bands and fine marginal spines. Large, long-stemmed flower head consists of bristly pink bracts and short-lived blue flowers, soon turning red. Bracts remain decorative for up to six months.
Size Up to 60 × 30cm (2 × 1ft).
Needs As for vase plant.

Ananas bracteatus 'Striatus'
Red pineapple

Features Tough, variegated leaves with broad lengthways stripes coloured green and cream, suffused with red-pink and edged with spines. Flowers rare.
Size 60-90 × 60-90cm (2-3 × 2-3ft), eventually much larger.
Needs Bright light, some full sun, warm temp., humid air, water compost moderately (don't fill rosette), liquid feed fortnightly.

Ananas comosus 'Variegatus'
Variegated pineapple

Features Similar to the red pineapple, but smaller, with green, spiny leaves broadly edged ivory-cream. Leaf edges acquire a rich pink tint if plants are kept in strong light. Plants which are six years or more old may produce a short, stout flower stem which bears a head of pink/scarlet bracts and bluish flowers. As the flowers fade a tuft of variegated leaves develops above the flower head. Then, a small, inedible pineapple fruit swells below the tuft. (The plant is a variegated and smaller form of the large-fruited, edible pineapple.)
Size Up to 60-90 × 60cm (2-3 × 2ft).
Needs Bright light, some full sun, warm temp., humid air, water compost moderately, liquid feed fortnightly.

Billbergia nutans
Queen's tears

Features Lax, narrow, arching, olive-green leaves, with reddish tints if grown in sun. Pendent flower spikes with pink, blue-edged petals, backed by long pink bracts.
Size To 45 × 30cm (1½ × 1ft).
Needs Bright light, some full sun, normal room temp., water compost moderately, keep leaf rosettes moist, liquid feed monthly.

Cryptanthus bivittatus
Earth star

Features Low star-shaped rosettes of undulating leaves coloured greenish brown with two lengthways red or pink stripes. Never flowers indoors.
Size Each up to 7.5 × 15cm (3 × 6in), forming a larger clump.
Needs Bright light, some full sun, warm temp., humid air, water sparingly (compost only), apply a weak foliar feed occasionally.

Cryptanthus bromelioides 'Tricolor'
Rainbow star

Features Irregularly arranged, undulating leaves coloured mid-green with ivory-white edging and striping. Central leaves acquire a pink hue in full sun. No flowers indoors. May send out runners with offsets at the tips.
Size Up to 23 × 30cm (9 × 12in) with age; clump-forming.
Needs As *C. bivittatus*.

Cryptanthus fosterianus
Pheasant leaf

Features Stiff and fleshy, undulating and crinkly, purplish copper-brown leaves, cross-barred with irregular stripes of greyish scales, forming a broad and flat rosette. Wide-spreading; rarely flowers.
Size Eventually to 7.5 × 45cm (3 × 18in).
Needs As for *Cryptanthus bivittatus*.

Dyckia fosteriana
Dyckia

Features Shiny, stiff, greyish leaves, armed with hooked spines. In bright sun, leaf colour changes to a rich metallic bronze. Slender stalks carry orange-yellow bell flowers in spring.
Size Up to 15 × 45cm (6 × 18in).
Needs Full sun, normal room temp., water compost moderately (don't fill leaf rosettes), give a liquid feed monthly.

Guzmania lingulata
Scarlet star

Features Smooth, rich green leaves. Small yellow flowers at the centre of a cup or funnel-shaped head of crimson bracts.
Size 30 × 45cm (1 × 1½ft).
Needs Bright but filtered light, min. temp. 18°C (64°F), humid air, water compost plentifully, keep rosette filled except when flowering, apply liquid fertilizer fortnightly to soil and foliage.

Neoregelia carolinae 'Tricolor'
Blushing bromeliad

Features Glossy mid-green leaves centrally striped with creamy white, and tinted rose-pink towards the base. As the plant matures, the whole leaf area becomes suffused with pink, and with the approach of flowering the central leaves turn brilliant red. An insignificant flower head forms deep in the centre of the leaf rosette.
Size 23 × 45cm (9 × 18in).

Needs Bright light with at least some full sun each day, normal room temp. (min. 16°C/61°F), humid air (stand the pot in a saucer filled with moist pebbles or spray foliage with water daily), water compost moderately, keep the rosette topped up with fresh soft or rainwater (tip out and replenish the water once a month), apply half-strength liquid fertilizer to the compost and leaves fortnightly, adding some to the water in the reservoir (full-strength liquid fertilizer can burn the foliage).

Neoregelia spectabilis
Painted fingernail

Features Leathery, olive-green leaves with grey stripes on the undersides and tipped at flowering time with 2.5cm (1in) long red 'fingernails'. Flowers are blue and held in a dense circular 'nest' of purple-brown bracts deep within the leaf rosette.
Size 30 × 60cm (12 × 24in).
Needs As for *Neoregelia carolinae* 'Tricolor'.

Nidularium billbergioides flavum
Nidularium

Features Bright green, fine-toothed leaves. Flower stalk topped with yellow bracts which conceal white flowers.
Size 25 × 45cm (10 × 18in).
Needs Bright but filtered light, normal room temp. (min. 18°C/64°F), humid air, water compost moderately, keep the rosette topped up, give half-strength liquid feed monthly.

Nidularium fulgens
Blushing bromeliad

Features Pale green, arching, spiny edged leaves, marbled or flecked with darker green. At flowering time the rosette centre flushes bright cerise. At the same time a flower head consisting of dark violet-blue, white-edged flowers and red, green-tipped bracts appears within it.
Size 30 × 45cm (1 × 1½ft).
Needs As for *Nidularium billbergioides flavum*.

Nidularium innocentii
Bird's nest plant

Features Similar to *Nidularium fulgens* in overall size and shape, but the colour of the shiny leaves is mahogany-red above and wine-red underneath. The rosette centre turns brownish red at flowering time. Flowers are white within rose-red bracts.
Size 45 × 45cm (1½ × 1½ft).
Needs As for *Nidularium billbergioides flavum*.

Tillandsia caput-medusae
Medusa's head

Features Twisted, silver-scaled leaves arising from a swollen base. Tiny blue flowers with showy red bracts on mature plants.
Size Up to 15 × 10cm (6 × 4in).
Needs Bright but filtered light, normal room temp., mist-spray foliage occasionally with water, do not water base or feed. This is one of many air plants suitable for growing on bark slabs.

Tillandsia ionantha
Air plant

Features Arching, silver-scaled, tapering leaves in a compact and congested rosette. The inner leaves develop a red hue as small, stalkless violet flowers appear on mature plants.
Size Up to 5 × 10cm (2 × 4in).
Needs As for *Tillandsia caput-medusae*. All tillandsias can be mounted on any solid surface, without compost.

Tillandsia lindenii
Blue-flowered torch

Features Narrow, pointed-tipped, grey-green leaves in a loose rosette; undersides purplish. A sturdy flower stalk appearing from the centre of a mature plant carries a large fan-shaped head of rose-pink, overlapping bracts. White-throated deep blue flowers appear from between the bracts one or two at a time in succession throughout summer. *Tillandsia cyanea* is very similar, with a shorter stalk, violet-blue flowers and rose-red bracts.
Size Up to 50 × 38cm (20 × 15in).
Needs Bright but filtered sunlight, normal room temp. (min. 13°C/55°F), humid air (stand pot on a saucer of moist pebbles), give half-strength liquid feed monthly. Blue-flowered torch requires little water at ground level, but mist-spray the foliage two or three times a week — epiphytic bromeliads absorb most of the moisture they need through pores in their leaves.

Tillandsia usneoides
Spanish moss

Features Thread-like trailing stems covered with silver-grey scales (minute scaly leaves).
Size Trails to 1m (3ft) or more with age.
Needs Bright but filtered sunlight, normal room temp., mist-spray foliage daily. Requires no rooting medium — attach the base to a twig or bark and suspend the plant in a high position. Detach and submerge in water once a month.

Vriesea fenestralis
Vriesea

Features Arching yellow green leaves decoratively marked with pale green above and purple below. Not noted for its flowers.
Size Up to 60 × 60cm (2 × 2ft).
Needs Bright light, some full sun (filtered in summer), normal room temp. at all times, humid air, keep rosette topped up with water and moisten the compost, give half-strength liquid feed once a month.

Vriesea splendens
Flaming sword

Features Dark green leaves with purple-black cross-banding. Tall flower stalk capped with a blade-like head of vivid red bracts from which emerge yellow flowers.
Size Up to 60 × 45cm (2 × 1½ft).
Needs As for *Vriesea fenestralis*.

DESERT AND FOREST CACTI

Revelling in bright light and tolerant of neglect, cacti come in a vast range of shapes and sizes to suit most tastes.

The immediate appeal of cacti lies in their strange, often bizarre shapes. Apart from a few forest cacti, such as the epiphytic orchid, Christmas and Easter cacti, the plants are native to deserts in the American continent, areas characterized by heat and infrequent though heavy rainfall. The plants have adapted to long periods of drought by evolving into globular or cylindrical plant bodies which are really swollen, water-storing stem tissues.

Most cylindrical and globular cacti have either pleats or ridges on the plant body; these are known as ribs. Others have spirally arranged wart-like swellings called tubercles instead of ribs, but both ribs and tubercles enable the plants to expand or contract with water intake or loss. Prickly pears (*Opuntia* sp.) differ in having segmented, flattened stems known as pads, bearing barbed but fine tips (glochids) which are extremely irritating to the skin. Many forest cacti have flattened, strap-shaped stems that closely resemble leaf segments.

Cactus spines vary greatly in size and shape – some are thick and sharp-pointed and others are merely bristly or hair-like. They may be straight or curved, long or short, hooked or, if hair-like, curly. Wool spines, flowers and new shoots develop from little cushion-like structures called areoles, which are usually arranged in rows.

General needs

Cacti are tolerant of neglect, but several needs must be catered for if they are to remain healthy.

☐ Provide bright light and full sun, except for forest species.

☐ Water well during active growth when the soil is dry, then allow the soil to dry out again.

☐ Feed fortnightly during active growth, using a proprietary tomato fertilizer.

☐ Allow a period of rest in winter with a temperature of 5-10°C (41-50°F); don't water unless the soil becomes bone-dry.

▼ **Diversity of shape** Cylindrical or globular, viciously spined or smooth-leaved, cacti and succulents display a variety of shapes and growth patterns.

Aporocactus flagelliformis
Rat's tail cactus

Features Slender tail-like pendent stems, each with 8 to 14 shallow ribs and areoles of short spines. Crimson-pink flowers in succession all spring, each lasting for about one week.
Size Trails to 1m (3ft) or more.
Special needs Keep constantly moist during active growth.

Astrophytum myriostigma
Bishop's cap

Features Unbranched globular stem — becoming cylindrical with age — with broad indented segments. No spines, but minute silvery scales dotted over the ribs. Bright yellow, many-petalled 5cm (2in) wide flowers in spring and summer.
Size 10 × 15cm (4 × 6in); eventually elongating to 20cm (8in) tall.

Cephalocereus senilis
Old man cactus

Features Upright cylindrical stem almost completely hidden under a shaggy mat of silvery white hairs. Small clusters of 4cm (1½in) long spines lie beneath the hairs, so avoid touching the plant. Flowers are not produced on pot-grown plants indoors.
Size Up to 30 × 15cm (12 × 6in).
Special needs Rinse the hairs with mild detergent to remove dust, but avoid drenching the compost. You can comb the hairs to tidy them, but beware of the spines.

Cereus peruvianus 'Monstrosus'
Peruvian apple cactus

Features A distorted mutant form of *C. peruvianus*, having several growing points and covered entirely with irregular, knobbly bumps, forming a grotesque, but eye-catching plant. Flowers rare.
Size Up to 45 × 30cm (1½ × 1ft).
Special needs Requires winter rest at 5°C (41°F).

Chamaecereus silvestrii
Peanut cactus

Features Young shoots resemble peanut shells. These lengthen rapidly into soft-textured, finger-like stems with areoles of short, whitish spines. Scarlet, 2.5cm (1in) wide flowers, each lasting about one day, appear in succession for several weeks from early summer — a reliable flowerer.
Size 10 × 15cm (4 × 6in) or more.

Cleistocactus strausii
Silver torch cactus

Features Upright, cylindrical stem with about 25 shallow and narrow ribs, completely covered with 2cm (¾in) long whitish spines, giving an overall silvery colouring. Some spines in each areole are longer — up to 4cm (1½in) — and yellowish coloured. The stem may branch at the crown to form a clump. Red flowers are borne only on plants more than 10 years old.
Size Each stem up to 1.2m (4ft) tall; clumps up to 30cm (1ft) wide.

Echinocactus grusonii
Barrel cactus

Features Globular plant with 20 or more ribs separated by deep furrows. Stiff golden spines arise in orderly areoles of 8 to 15, each spine being 12mm (½in) or more in length, but a few spines in each cluster are twice this length. Yellowish or whitish woolly hairs cluster around the base of the spines — they are most noticeable at the top of the plant. Flowers are not produced on small plants indoors, but mature plants may produce 5cm (2in) wide yellow flowers in summer. The plant is sometimes also known as the golden ball cactus.
Size Pot-grown plants rarely exceed 15cm (6in) in girth (but plants grown in open ground *can* reach 45cm/1½ft) or more across.

Echinocereus pectinatus
Hedgehog cactus

Features Squat cylindrical body, becoming elongated and sometimes branching at ground level to form a clump. About 20 broad but low ribs bear close-set aeroles of short whitish spines. Pink flowers, up to 7.5cm (3in) wide, appear in summer, even on quite young plants.
Size Up to 25 × 6cm (10 × 2½in).

Echinopsis eyriesii
Sea urchin cactus

Features Globular stem with 11 to 18 narrow ribs, bearing clusters of short brownish spines from greyish cushion-like areoles. Fragrant white 10cm (4in) wide flowers begin to open at dusk, open fully during the night and wilt by the next afternoon; they appear during summer.
Size Up to 10 × 10cm (4 × 4in).

Epiphyllum 'Ackermanii'
Orchid cactus

Features Flat, notched, clump-forming stems. Tiny bristly spines in the notches only. Large red flowers, up to 10cm (4in) wide, appear in succession all year.
Size Trails to 60cm (2ft).
Special needs Forest cactus. Medium light, mist-spray. Water plentifully during growth; allow a brief rest, with just moist compost, after each flush of blooms.

Ferocactus latispinus
Fish-hook cactus

Features Globular stem with spines in clusters of up to 16, most being up to 2.5cm (1in) long and whitish, but the central ones are up to 4cm (1½in) long and red. One spine in each areole is broad and hooked. Violet flowers are rare indoors.
Size 10 × 10cm (4 × 4in); up to 30 × 20cm (12 × 8in) with age.

Gymnocalycium mihanovichii
Chin cactus

Features Red, creamy or black-stemmed varieties without chlorophyll are popular. Globular stem with prominent, sharply angled ribs. Red cap and Hibotan cactus (*G.m. friedrichii*) have pink-red stems; 'Black Cap' has black flesh, and there is a creamy form.
Size Up to 15 × 7.5cm (6 × 3in).
Special needs Must be top-grafted on to a green rootstock.

Hamatocactus setispinus
Strawberry cactus

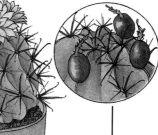

Features Globular stem with notched ribs and 2.5cm (1in) long brownish spines — each areole has up to three stouter, hooked spines in the centre. Short-lived yellow flowers appear in summer and early autumn, followed by red berries.
Size Up to 15 × 10cm (6 × 4in).
Special needs Occasionally rinse sticky gum from areoles with warm water.

Lobivia hertrichiana
Cob cactus

Features Globular stem producing many offsets from the base, eventually forming a clump. Each stem has 11 prominent, deeply notched ribs. Brownish, 12mm (½in) long spines in clusters of six to eight with a single yellowish central spine up to 2.5cm (1in) long. Scarlet, 5cm (2in) wide flowers appear in early summer, several opening at a time but lasting for just one day. However, flowering continues reliably and in succession for a few weeks.

There are a number of similar species, varieties and hybrids with red or yellow flowers, all undemanding and easy to flower in the home.
Size Each stem up to 10 × 10cm (4 × 4in); clumps to 25cm (10in) across.

Mammillaria erythrosperma
Mammillaria

Features Globular stem covered with 12mm (½in) high, spirally arranged, rounded swellings — tubercles — but no ribs. Slender white spines are borne in dense star-like clusters of 15 to 20, each spine being about 12mm (½in) long. One of the central spines in each cluster is hooked. Deep red, satiny, 2cm (¾in) wide flowers appear regularly in spring once a plant is about three years old, forming a ring around the crown of the stem. The flowers sometimes develop into red, fleshy berries which last for months.

The rose pincushion (*Mammillaria zeilmanniana*) is similar in habit with cerise flowers, giving a fine show even on very young specimens.
Size Each stem up to 5 × 5cm (2 × 2in); clumps up to 15cm (6in) wide.

Notocactus leninghausii
Golden ball cactus

Features Globular stem at first, elongating into a many-ribbed column, almost hidden under areoles of spines. Up to 15 of the spines in each areole are 6mm (¼in) long and yellowish, and these surround a few longer golden ones. Yellow, 5cm (2in) wide flowers may appear.
Size Eventually 60 × 7.5cm (24 × 3in).

Opuntia microdasys
Bunny ears

Features Stems divided into oval, flattened pads spotted with minute yellow bristly tufts — glochids — but no true spines. Pale yellow, 4cm (1½in) wide flowers occasionally appear on mature plants.
Size Up to 45 × 30cm (1½ × 1ft).
Special needs Minimum winter temperature 10°C (50°F).

Parodia chrysacanthion
Parodia

Features Gobular stem densely covered with yellow, 12mm (½in) long bristly spines in areoles of 30 to 40. Three to five of the central spines in each areole are about 2.5cm (1in) long and richer in colour. Golden yellow, 2.5cm (1in) wide flowers appear, several at a time, mainly in late spring.
Size Up to 12 × 12cm (5 × 5in).

Rebutia minuscula
Red crown cactus

Features Globular stem with many offsets, covered with rounded swellings — tubercles — each with an areole of 20 to 25 short, whitish spines. Red, 2cm (¾in) wide flowers appear in profusion in late spring.
Size Each stem up to 5 × 5cm (2 × 2in); clumps up to 15cm (6in) wide.

Rhipsalidopsis gaertneri
Easter cactus

Features Flat stems divided into segments with notched edges. Each notch has a minute tuft of soft bristles. Stems upright at first, becoming pendent. Scarlet, 4cm (1½in) long flowers appear in profusion in spring.
Size Trails to 30cm (1ft).
Special needs Water plentifully when in bud and flower.

Schlumbergera truncata **hybrids**
Christmas cacti

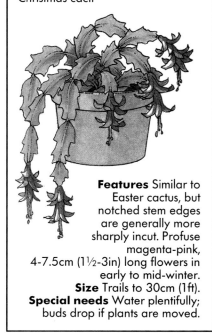

Features Similar to Easter cactus, but notched stem edges are generally more sharply incut. Profuse magenta-pink, 4-7.5cm (1½-3in) long flowers in early to mid-winter.
Size Trails to 30cm (1ft).
Special needs Water plentifully; buds drop if plants are moved.

LEAF SUCCULENTS

Many drought-resistant plants, with their fascinating shapes and colours, are ideal for indoor cultivation.

All succulent plants are alike in having an unparalleled ability to store water in their tissues – the word 'succulent' derives from the Latin *succus*, meaning juice. The water storage tissue is generally concentrated in plump, fleshy leaves (these plants are known as leaf succulents) or in thick, juicy stems (stem succulents).

Stem succulents are often leafless, or nearly so, since the stems of such plants have taken over the food-making process along with water storage. This group encompasses the *Cactaceae* family, whose members are characterized by having areoles – the equivalent of side branches in other plants which are reduced to tiny tissue swellings in cacti. Spines or bristly hairs and flower buds arise from the areoles. Leaf succulents do not bear areoles and usually have thick, smooth leaves though a few, such as the agaves, have spine-tipped edges.

Unlike cacti, leaf succulents belong to several different families which include non-succulent members. The euphorbias, for example, include ordinary annual, perennial and shrubby plants (the poinsettia belongs to the *Euphorbiaceae* family) as well as spiny succulent species that closely resemble true cacti.

All succulents produce flowers in the wild – they generally originate from dry grasslands or semi-deserts – but many are reluctant to flower in the home. Those which do flower reliably include kalanchoës, echeverias and rochea – their colours are often brilliant and the flowers long-lived.

However, those succulents that don't flower in the home are grown for their interesting, often bizarre, shapes or for the attractive colouring of their fleshy leaves. Avoid touching the leaves of succulents with a greyish or bluish bloom on their leaves – it rubs off easily.

Among this wide variety of plants are many that are easy to grow in the home, but others come from such specialized habitats that they are a challenge to even

the most experienced grower. One or two succulents, though attractive, are best avoided – for instance the toad plant (*Stapelia variegata*), with its unusual starry flowers, emits a stench resembling the rotting contents of a dustbin!

Most succulents need as much bright light as they can get and thrive and flourish in the warmth and low humidity of a living room. Water them fairly freely during active growth but allow a near-dry rest period.

▲ **Tree succulent** The near-woody stems of *Aeonium arboreum* bear uniform, fleshy leaf rosettes, almost black in the variety 'Schwarzkopf'.

▼ **Flowering succulents** The winter-flowering *Kalanchoë blossfeldiana* and the jade plant (*Crassula portulacea*) are popular easy-going house plants.

Aeonium arboreum
Aeonium

Features Woody stems branching freely to produce a tree-like plant with age. Spoon-shaped, shiny green, fleshy leaves in tight rosettes 7.5-15cm (3-6in) across (coloured deep purple in the variety 'Atropurpureum' when grown in full sun; almost black in the variety 'Schwarzkopf'). The lowest leaves of each rosette drop off at intervals, extending the length of the branches.
Size Up to 90 × 60cm (3 × 2ft).
Needs Full sun all year, warm room temp. (min. 18°C/65°F) in summer (cool room, min. 10°C/50°F, in winter), water moderately during active growth, less so during the winter, liquid feed fortnightly during active growth.

Agave victoriae-reginae
Century plant

Features Dense rosettes of hard-tipped, dark green leaves, which are triangular in cross-section and strikingly marked with white, mainly along the margins.
Size Up to 25 × 45cm (10 × 18in).
Needs Full sun, normal room temp. (cooler in winter), water moderately (sparingly in winter), liquid feed fortnightly.

Aloe aristata
Lace aloe

Features Dense rosettes of fleshy but hard, grey-green, whitish-edged leaves marked with tubercles. Orange flowers on 30cm (1ft) stalks in early summer.
Size Up to 15 × 20cm (6 × 8in).
Needs Full sun, normal room temp. (cool in winter), water plentifully (sparingly in winter), liquid feed fortnightly.

Aloe variegata
Partridge breast

Features Pointed, triangular leaves in erect rosettes, later spiralling, dark grey-green to purplish with whitish cross-bands. Coral-pink flowers on 30cm (1ft) tall stalks in early spring.
Size 30 × 23cm (12 × 9in), but becoming unstable with age so best propagated from offsets.
Needs As for lace aloe.

Bryophyllum daigremontianum
Devil's backbone

Features Unbranched stem with downward-curving, blue-green leaves; inward-curling, saw-toothed edges carry tiny plantlets.
Size Up to 90 × 15cm (36 × 6in), but unstable once 30cm (1ft) tall.
Needs Bright but indirect light, normal room temp., water moderately, liquid feed monthly.

Crassula portulacea argentea
Jade tree

Features Trunk-like, branching stem with jade green, fleshy leaves. Tiny white, starry flowers on mature plants in winter.
Size Up to 90 × 60cm (3 × 2ft) after many years.
Needs Bright light, some full sun, normal or cool room temp., water moderately (sparingly in winter), liquid feed fortnightly.

Crassula lycopodioides
Rat-tail plant

Features Much-branched with slender, erect stems almost hidden by minute, pointed, fleshy leaves, forming four-sided columns of scaly appearance — plants also known as watch-chain crassulas. Greenish insignificant flowers borne in summer.
Size Up to 30 × 30cm (1 × 1ft).
Needs As for jade tree.

Echeveria derenbergii
Painted lady

Features Cushion-like rosettes of blue-green, fleshy leaves with a waxy bloom and red tips. Orange-red flowers in spring.
Size Each rosette to 7.5 × 7.5cm (3 × 3in), spreading by offsets.
Needs Bright light, normal room temp. (cooler in winter), water sparingly from below, give dilute liquid feed fortnightly.

Echeveria harmsii
Red echeveria

Features Branching stems with loose rosettes of lance-shaped, fleshy, mid-green leaves, thinly edged with brown and covered with short, soft hair. Scarlet, yellow-mouthed flowers on arching stems appear in late spring and early summer.
Size Up to 30 × 30cm (1 × 1ft).
Needs As for painted lady.

Euphorbia milii
Crown of thorns

Features Dense shrub with thick stems heavily armed with sharp spines. Bright green, non-fleshy, short-lived leaves near the growing tips only. Red or yellow-bracted flowers at any time.
Size Up to 60 × 60cm (2 × 2ft).
Needs Full sun, normal room temp., water moderately, liquid feed fortnightly during active growth.

Faucaria tigrina
Tiger jaw

Features Rosettes of fleshy, grey-green jaw-like leaves marked with white dots and edged with softish teeth. Yellow flowers.
Size Up to 10 × 7.5cm (4 × 3in).
Needs Bright light with some full sun, normal room temp. (winter rest at 10°C/50°F), water plentifully (sparingly in winter), apply dilute liquid feed monthly.

Gasteria verrucosa
Wart gasteria

Features Paired, fleshy, tapering, dark green leaves, arranged in two distinct rows, somewhat concave above and rounded on the underside, covered in grey warts.
Size Up to 15 × 15cm (6 × 6in).
Needs Medium light, normal room temp. (winter rest at 10°C/50°F), water moderately (sparingly in winter), do not feed.

Haworthia margaritifera
Pearl plant

Features Cluster-forming rosettes of lance-shaped, tough, dark green, fleshy leaves, thickly spotted with pearly white warts.
Size Up to 7.5 × 15cm (3 × 6in).
Needs Bright light (no direct sun), high room temp., water moderately, never letting the soil dry out completely (sparingly in winter), do not feed.

Kalanchoë blossfeldiana **hybrids**
Flaming katy

Features Loose rosettes of rich green, sometimes red-tinted, rounded leaves on a short stem. Small four-petalled, red, crimson-pink, salmon, orange or yellow flowers appear in large and compact, domed or flattish, long-lasting clusters from mid-winter onwards. Hybrids bought in flower at Christmas or thereafter will flower for two to three months, but then are best discarded, though they can be dead-headed and grown on.
Size Up to 30 × 30cm (12 × 12in).
Needs Full sun, normal room temp., water sparingly, liquid feed fortnightly.

Lithops species
Living stones

Features Buried stem produces a pair of fleshy, semi-globular leaves, joined together for most of their length and resembling stones. The many species vary slightly in leaf colour, most having marbled upper surfaces on a rather greyish or brownish ground. Yellow, white or pink daisy-like flowers appear from slit between the leaf pair generally in early to mid-autumn, opening only on sunny afternoons.
Size Up to 2.5 × 4cm (1 × 1½in); some species form clumps.
Needs Strong light with some direct sun, normal to cool room temp., water sparingly (don't water in winter), do not feed.

Pachyphytum oviferum
Moonstones

Features Sturdy stems carry rosette-like clusters of egg-shaped, grey, pinkish tinged leaves, coated with a whitish bloom which is easily rubbed off.
Size Up to 30 × 30cm (12 × 12in).
Needs Full sun, normal room temp. (cooler in winter), water moderately (sparingly in winter), do not feed.

Rochea coccinea
Rochea

Features Much-branched stems; close-set, rich green, pointed-tipped leaves. Clusters of red or white flowers in spring or summer.
Size Up to 45 × 20cm (18 × 8in).
Needs Full sun, normal room temp., water moderately (sparingly in winter), liquid feed with tomato fertilizer fortnightly when buds first appear.

Sansevieria trifasciata 'Laurentii'
Mother-in-law's tongue

Features Tufts of sword-shaped, dark green, marbled and slightly spiralled leaves, edged golden yellow. Tiny insignificant flowers.
Size Up to 90 × 45cm (3 × 1½ft).
Needs Bright light but tolerant of shade, normal room temp., water moderately (sparingly in winter), give half-strength liquid feed monthly during active growth.

Sedum morganianum
Donkey's tail

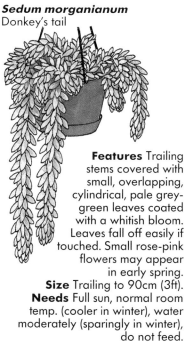

Features Trailing stems covered with small, overlapping, cylindrical, pale grey-green leaves coated with a whitish bloom. Leaves fall off easily if touched. Small rose-pink flowers may appear in early spring.
Size Trailing to 90cm (3ft).
Needs Full sun, normal room temp. (cooler in winter), water moderately (sparingly in winter), do not feed.

Sedum sieboldii
Sedum

Features Nearly circular, slightly toothed, grey-green leaves arranged in threes all along trailing stems; leaves centrally blotched creamy white and tinged pink in variety 'Medio-variegatum'. Small clusters of pink flowers at the stem tips in autumn.
Size Trailing to 23cm (9in).
Needs As for donkey's tail.

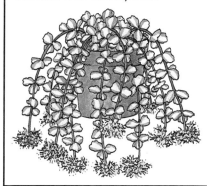

Senecio rowleyanus
String-of-beads

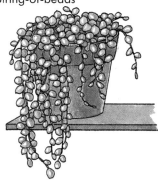

Features Creeping or trailing stems; grape-like leaves with minute pointed tips. Stems root wherever they touch compost.
Size Stems 60-90cm (2-3ft) long.
Needs Bright light with some full sun, normal room temp. (cooler in winter), water plentifully (sparingly in winter), liquid feed fortnightly during active growth.

Decorating with plants

One of the most enjoyable aspects of indoor gardening is arranging pot plants to enhance existing decorating schemes. They can be displayed singly or in group arrangements, or allowed to trail from wall hangers and pedestals and climb round window and door frames.

Window-sills are obvious display areas and are ideal for flowering plants and other light-tolerant species. Decorative containers which harmonize with the colour theme of a room can heighten the whole effect. However, rows of single pot plants can often look disjointed; group arrangements can be much more harmonious. There are numerous ways of arranging plants in groups – all-green foliage plants, for example, chosen for their diverse leaf textures and shapes, can be mixed with perhaps one brightly coloured plant for contrast. Alternatively, you can relieve the formality of a stiff upright plant with an arching fern or a trailing plant. In the final analysis, the only restriction is that all the plants in a group arrangement should require similar growing conditions.

There are plants suited to every room in the house, from kitchens to bathrooms, as well as types which will enhance an empty fireplace or a wall niche. Large, floor-standing plants are perfect for awkward corners, large hallways and open landings, and as room dividers and focal points in workrooms and offices. You can also assemble miniature desert cacti gardens, colourful table decorations and seasonable displays. And there is always the option – not open to the outdoor gardener – of altering a plant arrangement in an instant to suit a change of mood or decorating style.

Window-sill North-facing sites are perfect for flowering pot plants such as African violets and cyclamen.

DISPLAYING HOUSE PLANTS

**House plants add character to a room and
form an integral part of the interior design, making
fine ornaments, focal points and screens.**

The imaginative use of house plants in design schemes is more important in the home than in the garden. Although they are easily moved around, you do have to live with them for many months in a relatively confined space, and thus the arrangement of their individual characteristics – size, foliage shape and colours, growth patterns and flowering habits – can be a creative challenge.

There is more to displaying pot plants than setting them in rows on a window-sill. They should ful-fil a decorative purpose and fit easily into the interior style, yet at the same time command attention as focal points. They must also be in scale with the room; a single African violet would be lost in a large living room and a tall Swiss cheese plant can overpower a room of modest dimensions.

Plant displays should blend with other furnishings, thus making a contribution to the design scheme. Small-leaved and feathery plants disappear next to floral curtains and carpets which are better served by plants with sculptural outlines. Mirrors and lighting can be used to dramatic effect, and paintings and ornaments can also be impressively embellished with plants.

▼ **Window display** French windows screen a selection of foliage plants from outdoor conditions. Tall-growing abutilons and ribbon-leaved dracaenas thrive and flourish in bright light while kangaroo vine (*Cissus*), leaf pelargoniums and avocado plants tolerate filtered light.

▲ **Forced hyacinths** Often flowering by Christmas, deliciously scented hyacinths enjoy a cool but well-lit window-sill once their roots and growing points have developed. Grow bulbs in pots or bowls of bulb fibre or in hyacinth glasses topped up with water to just below the base of the bulbs. Turn the containers often to ensure straight, even growth.

▲ **Cactus garden** All desert cacti and many succulents revel in bright light. A south-facing window is ideal as the summer sun and cooler night temperatures simulate their native habitats. They abhor water around their roots, so in the home they do best on trays of sand that can soak up excess moisture and improve drainage from the pots. When the time for winter rest approaches, the tray, which here holds jade plant, Christmas cheer sedum, noctocactus and grafted gymnocalyciums, can be moved to a cooler place.

The devil's ivy (*Scindapsus aureus*) and variegated *Dracaena sanderana* enjoy bright light but should be kept out of direct sun.

◀ **Plant stands** Useful for displaying small pot plants, decorative stands can be positioned in front of a window to give height to regimented rows of plants placed on narrow window-sills. West or even north-facing windows are perfect for plants that prefer good light but won't tolerate scorching sun.

Here, mauve-flowered sapphire flower (*Browallia speciosa*) and pink African violet (*Saintpaulia*) colourfully frame the trailing stems of *Ficus pumila*.

Window displays

House plants displayed on a window-sill serve several visual purposes. Viewed from indoors, they link the greenery of the garden with the home, or they can create a garden 'view' in themselves – especially valuable in urban settings where attractive outdoor scenery may be lacking.

A window dressed with a variety or a particular type of house plant can provide a living screen which, unlike many fabrics, looks just as good from outdoors as it does from indoors – in fact, leaves and flowers often turn to face the sun and so are even more attractive from outside. And, with the darkness of the room interior as a backdrop, window displays seem almost 'stage-lit' on a sunny day.

Direct sun through glass will scorch most house plants – only a few species, particularly desert cacti and succulents, will survive for long on a south-facing sill in mid-summer. Pot plants can, of course, be moved to a cooler spot when necessary, but west-, east- and even north-facing windows are more suitable for year-round displays of flowers and foliage.

In winter, most window plants dislike being shut behind closed curtains, since the temperature can fall by several degrees. Unless the windows are double-glazed, it is a good idea to arrange plants on large trays or special plant stands which can be moved about easily at night.

Focal points

All too often, the over-enthusiastic indoor gardener fills every spare nook and cranny of a room with house plants, selecting each one according to its individual merits, but paying little regard to how they all look together. Usually, the result of such haphazard design is that none of the plants attracts the attention it rightly deserves.

An impressive mature plant should not be a mere accessory which blends in with the furnishings, but something which captures attention and makes you look at it again and again. There is no need to buy lots of plants – a single, well-placed, 'architectural' specimen or a simple group of plants can be highly effective and provide a striking focal point.

The choice of container also influences a plant's eye-catching potential. A plain plastic pot – however large – rarely draws attention unless it is brightly coloured, but an ornate urn, a sculptured terracotta pot, an elaborate planter or an elegant

▶ **Sculptural foliage** A large-leaved banyan tree (*Ficus benghalensis*) of massive proportions makes a stunning focal point next to a winding staircase. Philodendrons, scindapsus and kangaroo vines (*Cissus*) tumble from the landing, clothing the lofty interior with lush greenery.

▲ **Elegant simplicity** Matching pedestals topped with rich green arching Boston ferns (*Nephrolepis exaltata* 'Bostoniensis') frame a low settee, creating a feeling of understated elegance.

► **Contemporary decor** Capable of reaching 3m (10ft) indoors, *Dracaena marginata*, with its upright stems and tufts of grassy leaves, complements the clean lines of modern designs.

▼ **Matching pairs** Classic style demands finishing touches in keeping with the mood. This large window, framed by pencil-pleated drapes, is dominated by elegant kentia palms.

pedestal chosen to complement the decor of the room will be well worth paying extra for.

Windows, fireplaces, archways and open-plan staircases form natural focal points in any room, and their appeal can be enhanced by a few flamboyant plants. But if a room lacks any kind of focal point, create one with a strategically placed, bold plant. Select a species which has simple but interesting foliage. Much-branched, bushy specimens with a mass of small leaves can look too fussy, whereas open-structured or irregular-shaped, large-leaved types invariably have much greater visual impact.

Room dividers

A large open-plan room is sometimes used for more than one indoor activity, and it's often a good idea to construct some sort of partition between, for example, a dining area and a seating area, or an office and kitchen area. Several types of screens or curtains are available, but for a more informal and flexible – and decorative – barrier an arrangement of climbing, trailing or bushy plants is the ideal solution.

Choose plants with airy foliage to form a visual backdrop without obstructing the flow of air and light – unless you actually do want to hide one particular part of the room. Dense screens can make a room look rather small and cast a lot of shade, which is not good for other plants. If large-leaved plants are preferred, space them a good distance apart.

The most natural group of plants to use as dividers are the climbers and trailers. Plant them in floorstanding troughs, individual pots or tubs, or in raised containers. Some support is essential and will form the foundation of the screen. Since a total coverage of foliage may not be achieved, or be desirable, the supporting structure should look attractive in its own right.

Adopt the same principles as for the outdoor support of plants – use trelliswork, wires, netting or bam-

boo canes – but bear in mind that the materials should be finished to a higher quality. With no alternating weather conditions to worry about, you can choose superior grades of timber.

Room dividers need not be floorstanding; in fact, you may prefer to use rows of hanging baskets or suspended shelving to accommodate trailing or bushy plants. Ideally, they should be of the pulley type so that the plants can be tended and watered without too much difficulty.

The simplest screen is a row of large, bushy potted plants positioned across the floor, perhaps staggered for the best effect. A mixed array of any, or all, of these methods can be used.

▼ **Indoor trailers** Curtains of greenery effectively mask the functional lines and clinical appearance of a high-tech kitchen. Baskets of heart-shaped *Philodendron scandens* and wandering Jew (*Tradescantia albiflora* 'Albovittata') tumble from a shelf suspended from the ceiling.

▲ **Foliage screen** Ornamental figs (*Ficus*) are among the easiest and most popular indoor plants. *F. benjamina* grows up to 1.8m (6ft) tall; its arching branches and glossy green leaves form an airy screen, infilled here with the huge-leaved Swiss cheese plant (*Monstera deliciosa*).

▶ **Indoor climbers** Ubiquitous but immensely useful in decorating schemes, the grape ivy (*Rhoicissus rhomboidea*) can grow 90cm (3ft) in a year. A natural climber equipped with tendrils, it twists its supple stems and green, trifoliate leaves around any support. Its companion here, the asparagus fern (*Asparagus plumosus*), develops a climbing habit when mature; here its bright green fronds lighten the sombre grape ivy foliage.

▼ **Room divider** An array of plants strike a welcoming note and separate the living room from the entrance hall. Weeping figs, ferns, bromeliads and palms thrive in the filtered light admitted by an overhead skylight.

PLANTS FOR DIVIDERS

Climbers and shrubs
Asparagus fern (*Asparagus plumosus*)
Cape leadwort (*Plumbago capensis*)
Grape ivy (*Rhoicissus rhomboidea*)
Heartleaf (*Philodendron scandens*)
Ivy (*Hedera helix* varieties)
Jasmine (*Jasminum officinale* and
    J. polyanthum)
Ornamental fig (*Ficus benjamina*)
Swiss cheese plant (*Monstera
    deliciosa*)

Trailers
Asparagus densiflorus 'Sprengeri'
Candle plant (*Plectranthus
    oertendahlii*)
Columnea microphylla
Rosary vine (*Ceropegia woodii*)
Spider plant (*Chlorophytum
    comosum*)
Wandering Jew (*Tradescantia
    fluminensis, T. albiflora* and
    Zebrina pendula)

It is essential that all containers are waterproof and that surrounding furniture and furnishings will not be harmed by the occasional fine mist sprays that are necessary to keep the plant foliage clean and healthy. With little direct light, the best plants are those that tolerate shade – ivies, × *Fatshedera* and *Cissus* species, scindapsus and several philodendrons. Short-term flowering house plants can be fitted among the greenery for instant colour.

Artificial light

There are several good reasons for growing indoor plants under artificial light. It can be used to supplement natural daylight, or even to replace daylight in poorly lit spots, such as in office reception areas and hallways. It can also improve the growth and health of plants, especially in winter. However, with an appropriate choice of plants, the natural light in most domestic living rooms is adequate enough for growth. Artificial lighting is put to best use, therefore, as a means of enhancing the visual appeal of plants – it can be switched on during the day as well as at night.

Ordinary tungsten filament lamps and spot lamps generate about 70% of their energy in the form of heat rather than light, and are not suitable for supplying the sole source of light to house plants. For this purpose you will need fluorescent tubes or special tungsten filament lamps sold exclusively for plant displays. Ordinary domestic tungsten lamps are suitable, however, for providing strategic lighting effects, but they get very hot and can scorch foliage. Keep them at least 45cm (1½ft) away from the nearest leaf or flower.

The outline and form of many plants are dramatic in their own right, but with directional lighting the effects can be truly stunning. Look at your plants from all angles and decide what their merits are – boldly shaped leaves, delicate filigree foliage, decorative variegations or curious stem structure. Examine the leaves from both sides – some have prominent veins which are seen more clearly from below; others are felted or reddish-purple beneath.

Many of these characteristics can be accentuated by directing light from one particular angle. To enhance vein structures, simply shine light upwards through the plant, or alternatively from behind it. Similarly, use lighting from below the plant to cast startling shadows on walls and ceiling, reflecting the elegant outlines of palm leaves, for instance.

A downward light beam will display low-growing, prostrate plants growing in a shallow trough to better effect. With an appropriately shaped shade and careful adjustment of the lamp height, the light beam can be focused to spotlight the plant.

Lighting solely directed on to the front of a plant produces a dramatic but quite harsh effect, whereas backlighting is considerably softer. The intensity of light can be variably adjusted by selecting suitable bulbs – 25, 40, 60 or 75 watts – or by wiring in a proprietary dimmer switch.

Coloured bulbs can be used to modify or intensify the natural colour of foliage or flowering plants, but you will generally need some additional white lighting nearby to calm the effect. More subtle colouring can be achieved by using a coloured shade over a white bulb.

Spotlights are particularly suitable for large areas, such as spacious open-plan living rooms, staircases and large hallways. They are best fixed to the ceiling so that the light source is far enough away to avoid scorching any plants. If, after a time, the plants become pale and drawn, the spotlight is positioned too far away.

▶ **Lighting effects** The soft light produced by ordinary lamp bulbs can be used to great effect. Diverse foliage shapes are thrown into silhouette against a pale wall, making a focal point of a dark corner.

▲ Tungsten lamps The warm amber tones used throughout this open-plan living area create illusions of balmy evenings on a sandy tropical beach. Floor-standing tungsten lights positioned behind tree-like figs re-create the relaxing effect of the setting sun.

▲ ◀ Mirror images A clever combination of concealed lighting and floor-to-ceiling mirrors provides an endless array of shadows, highlights and reflections. The delicate tracery of fern fronds is emphasized by a spotlight beneath the glass table. Similarly, the fresh green foliage of a kangaroo vine, tumbling from a hanging basket suspended on near-invisible nylon cord, is brought to life by a second spotlight. A single low-slung pendent lamp illuminates the glowing flowers of chrysanthemums.

◀ Fleeting shadows Domestic lamp bulbs emit heat that can scorch foliage. Placed at a safe distance though, the light, while insufficient to maintain healthy growth, creates myriads of delicate shadows on walls and ceilings.

PLANTS FOR SHADY AREAS

**Dull, even draughty and defunct areas can be
turned into decorative features with a surprisingly
large selection of indoor plants.**

Many house plants can be used to great effect in interior design schemes, though they have certain individual requirements which must be met before they can grow successfully. The relationship in scale between room and plant size is very important as are furniture and soft furnishings, but the living conditions the plants will be offered are the most important considerations of all.

Light is probably the most essential factor governing indoor gardening, and while a large range of plants will adapt to less than perfect natural daylight, every home has one or two dull spots where little or no light ever penetrates. Hallways, staircases and landings, inner room corners and fireplaces in particular, are often dark and shady and in need of brightening up.

Luckily, many quite common house plants originate from deep jungle or forest environments where light levels are extremely low. These, together with many plants that prefer light but tolerate shade, are ideal for shady parts of the house.

Few flowering plants will thrive in a dull hallway for long, but there is no reason why certain types should not be moved into the shade for a short time – chrysanthemums, *Primula obconica*, slipper flower (*Calceolaria×herbeohybrida*) and *Cyclamen persicum* for instance. These like quite cool conditions, so actually prefer to be moved out of a sunny window. But never move a flowering plant which is just coming into bud; a change in position often results in bud drop, so wait until several blooms are fully open.

If you do have a bright windowsill in the hallway – perhaps by the front door or on the staircase – you can grow many of the easier flowering house plants. Make sure draughts are kept to a minimum, though, and that the average temperature is suitable. Fit draught excluders to all exterior doors and don't leave the front door open unnecessarily.

Foliage plants which generally prefer shady conditions usually have plain or dark green leaves, but their marvellous variety of shape and texture adequately compensates for their lack of bright colour. There are upright and bushy types as well as others which have either pendent or trailing stems. Those with dark green, sturdy foliage are much more suitable for dark and shady areas than pale-leaved, variegated or soft-leaved plants.

For a large specimen plant choose from the various palms, including Canary date palm (*Phoenix canariensis*), paradise palm (*Howeia forsteriana*) and parlour palm (*Chamaedorea elegans*); also consider the false castor oil plant (*Fatsia japonica*) and Swiss cheese plant (*Monstera deliciosa*). These add considerable impact to a large entrance hall or endow a dull corner with elegance. They are also sturdy and can be planted in containers which are not easily knocked over – an important factor where young children and boisterous pets are concerned.

► **In the shade** Ferns, such as the arching Boston fern, and erect tree ivies (× *Fatshedera*) do well in shady positions or where light is filtered through blinds or net curtains. Ivies (*Hedera* species) will tolerate quite deep shade, but variegated types need some light, as here, to maintain their cream-coloured leaf margins.

◄ Dim interior Boston ferns are displayed most effectively as specimen plants. They do not tolerate bright light and are perfect for relieving the formal style of a dark room, where artificial light throws their arching, rich green fronds into attractive silhouette. Aspidistra would be another good choice for a dark room setting.

▼ Shady hallway The accommodating *Ficus* species tolerate poor natural light, and many have a sculptural beauty that makes them ideal specimen plants. Here, the fast-growing, mature *F. lyrata*, known as fiddle-leaf fig because of the shape of its huge, puckered leaves, has dramatic impact and associates handsomely with the arching rich green foliage of *Spathiphyllum*.

▼ Simple steps A winding staircase makes a suitable platform for foliage plants that prefer subdued light. Pots of *Syngonium podophyllum*, sometimes called goosefoot plant because of the shape of its lobed, arrow-like leaves, occupy the corners of the steps. Above them a sicklethorn asparagus (*Asparagus falcatus*) receives adequate light which is reflected through a window on to the pale-coloured wall.

Asparagus densiflorus 'Sprengeri' trails its dainty, pale green plumes from a window ledge and a rubber plant (*Ficus elastica*) guards the darker recess at the foot of the stairs.

Trailing plants are particularly useful for stairways, where they are free to tumble from hanging containers and window ledges. Ivies (*Hedera helix*) and wandering Jew (*Zebrina pendula*) tolerate dull positions, but avoid yellow-leaved and heavily marbled or variegated ivies, which soon turn all-green in poor light conditions. The fresh green foliage of asparagus ferns (*Asparagus* species) and spider plant (*Chlorophytum comosum*) tolerate poor light conditions and will brighten up the scene.

Smaller, bushy plants are ideal for narrow shelves. Choose from piggy-back plant (*Tolmiea menziesii*), painted net leaf (*Fittonia verschaffeltii*), prayer plant (*Maranta leuconeura*) and the smaller ferns, such as button fern (*Pellaea rotundifolia*) and ribbon fern (*Pteris tremula*).

Empty grates

There is nothing more homely than a roaring open fire in winter, but for the rest of the year an empty grate can look rather drab. And, with the advent of modern central heating, there is often a redundant fireplace all year round – house plants make wonderful fillers for such areas.

The hearth and grate will not suffer from occasional spillages of water, nor sticky nectar drips from flowers. You can even spray moisture-lovers daily – with no wallpaper to worry about.

Beautiful rustic containers are often readily to hand – brass coalscuttles, log boxes and copper cooking pots, for instance. Holders for tongs and pokers can easily double as plant stands. The mantelpiece provides shelving for trailing plants, and taller specimen plants look perfect against the chimney breast. Block up the chimney when not in use, since cold down-draughts are damaging to all plants, however hardy.

▼ **Fireplace fillers** A deep old-fashioned fireplace is a perfect frame for a summer display of pot plants. Containers of flowering begonias and chrysanthemums add a splash of bright colour to the green foliage of spider plant (*Chlorophytum comosum*), maidenhair fern (*Adiantum capillus-veneris*) and grape ivy (*Rhoicissus rhomboidea*).

▲ Shade lovers Many foliage plants, including × *Fatshedera lizei*, castor oil plant (*Fatsia japonica*), wandering Jew and prayer plants (*Maranta*) adapt to less than perfect light conditions.

◄ Temporary display Troughs of tropical foliage plants can be moved to an empty fireplace away from strong sun. In winter, move them to a good source of light.

▼ Indoor fernery Most ferns thrive in light shade and moist air. Their graceful fronds make a focal point of an empty grate.

PLANTS FOR DARK SPOTS

The following shade-tolerant foliage plants are suitable for dull and poorly lit areas. Most of the flowering types are best used as short-stay fillers and can be replaced as they fade.

Foliage plants
Bird's nest fern (*Asplenium nidus*)
Boston fern (*Nephrolepis exaltata* 'Bostoniensis')
Burgundy philodendron (*Philodendron* 'Burgundy')
Cast iron plant (*Aspidistra elatior*)
Dumb cane (*Dieffenbachia maculata*)
Goodluck plant (*Cordyline terminalis*)
Piggy-back plant (*Tolmiea menziesii*)
Rex begonia (*Begonia rex-cultorum*)

Flowering plants
African violet (*Saintpaulia* hybrids)
Azalea (*Rhododendron simsii* hybrids)
Begonia Elatior hybrids
Cape primrose (*Streptocarpus* hybrids)
Flamingo flower (*Anthurium scherzerianum*)
Florists' chrysanthemums (*C. morifolium* hybrids)
Primula obconica

PLANTS FOR HUMID AIR

**Bathrooms and kitchens are often warmer and
more humid than living rooms. They are ideal for a
variety of foliage plants and herbs.**

There is hardly a room in the home that does not benefit from the addition of plant life. Some rooms offer better conditions than others in terms of light and temperature – the two most important factors for plant health – but the great majority of indoor plants will accept and grow in less than ideal sites.

Most house plant purchases are impulse buys or gifts. It is sensible to experiment with the plants and move them around from one place to another in order to discover where they fit in best with the existing decor and where they seem to thrive. Watch the plants carefully, and if they show obvious signs of ill health, move them to a position with higher or lower light levels, or warmer or cooler temperatures or change the watering programme.

The degree of air moisture or humidity can be critical for many tropical foliage plants. Humidity is less of a problem than light and warmth. It can be solved locally by mist-spraying the leaves, standing pots in saucers of pebbles kept permanently wet or by double-potting them in moist peat substitute. Humidity is also automatically increased when plants are arranged in groups rather than displayed as isolated specimens.

In the average house, bathrooms and kitchens often have a higher degree of humidity than living rooms and bedrooms. Such utility areas can provide good homes for many tropical plants.

Bathrooms

In a traditionally designed house the bathroom is sited against an exterior wall – making for easy plumbing. So positioned, it invariably has at least one window and is reasonably light and airy. Frosted glass installed for privacy allows almost as much light as ordinary window glass and without the need for net curtains, the bathroom is often even brighter than elsewhere in the house. Sun-loving plants will, therefore, thrive here, while shade-lovers can be put in darker corners – for instance, on a low-flush cistern, next to a cabinet or airing cupboard or suspended from the ceiling in a hanging basket.

However, a bathroom in a flat, or a second bathroom in a larger house, may have no natural light. This makes permanent house plants an impossibility, but many shade-loving foliage plants can tolerate short periods – a week or so – provided that bright artificial lighting is switched on for a couple of hours a day. Grape ivy (*Rhoicis-sus rhomboidea*), philodendron, creeping fig (*Ficus pumila*) and several ferns are suitable.

Temperature and humidity in a bathroom can vary dramatically during each day. At best, it is warm and often very humid – ideal conditions for most house plants. At worst, it fluctuates wildly from cold and damp and perhaps draughty, to hot and humid. Only the very hardiest of house plants can cope with these variable conditions.

If you want to grow plants successfully, keep some heating on at all times in winter – even if only a heated towel rail – and don't open the window to let bathtime condensation subside when outside temperatures are dramatically lower than indoors. The moisture given off by damp walls, towels and carpets can, in fact, be beneficial to the plants.

► **Steam bath** Most ferns and other plants with thin delicate leaves, such as palms, prefer more air moisture than is found in the average living room. The steamy atmosphere of a frequently used bathroom provides ideal conditions for such plants as umbrella grass (*Cyperus alternifolius*), maidenhair fern (*Adiantum capillus-veneris*), × *Fatshedera lizei* and African violets (*Saintpaulia*).

◄ **Cape primrose** Flowering profusely over many months, the little Cape primrose (*Streptocarpus*) is much easier to grow than its origin would suggest. Available in a range of colours, from pure white to deep purple, Cape primroses revel in good humidity but will also tolerate dry air and the occasional draught. Their leaves resemble those of the common primrose, but are much longer and borne in an irregularly-shaped arching rosette.

▼ **Bathroom greenery** A tropical jungle effect has been created in this bright and warm bathroom. The effect is heightened by natural wood and honey-coloured tiles, a sympathetic backdrop for a collection of ferns whose arching fronds contrast well with the upright leaves of a variegated pineapple (*Ananas comosus* 'Variegatus') and mother-in-law's tongue.

When siting plants, remember that the bathroom is a functional area. Don't clutter shelves and sills with plants – they will become a hazard when you need to grab a towel in a hurry. The atmosphere should be one of comfort and luxury, so choose delicately shaped plants or ones with evocative fragrances such as gardenias, stephanotis and lemon-scented pelargonium.

If space is at a premium, opt for slow-growing species which don't demand huge pots. Hanging baskets provide a useful means of keeping plants off the work surfaces. And if they are suspended over the bath, there's no need to worry about water spillage.

Select plant containers with care. Heavy ceramic pots can do a lot of damage to baths and basins if accidentally knocked over. Lighter-weight plastic containers are preferable and these come in many colours to match your decor. Modern white pots add light to the room; traditional clay-coloured types often clash with pastel-coloured suites.

Spray plants (except those with velvety and hairy leaves) regularly with tepid water to wash off talcum powder, which soon clogs leaf pores. Avoid using aerosol sprays of deodorant or hair lacquer near the plants.

If you intend to set up a display area for plants in a bathroom, never use conventional spot lighting to supplement natural daylight – electric lamps must be isolated from water splashes in all bathrooms for safety.

Kitchen plants

The first consideration in any kitchen, especially where there are children, is safety. Work surfaces should be uncluttered – pots and pans may have to be moved from the cooker quickly and without fear of knocking over other items. Try to keep the functional areas – around the cooker, sink and washing machine – free from plants and ornaments. Instead reserve a few shelves, a cupboard top, the window-sill or even the refrigerator top as decorative focal points for plants.

You may have some attractive pottery or porcelain to display, or interesting cookware and herb and spice bottles. Whatever your taste, house plants brighten up any kitchen and add a feeling of natural freshness.

There are no hard and fast rules as to the choice of suitable kitchen plants – it depends on the aspect, size, light levels and temperature. But, plants which favour humid conditions, such as African violets (*Saintpaulia*), may thrive on a window-sill above a much-used sink and enjoy the extra moist air.

A window-sill is an ideal spot for propagating small quantities of plants and you can keep a regular eye on them. This is also the perfect place for sprouting seeds and for pots of fresh culinary herbs – much nicer to use than dried herbs and instantly to hand in all weathers. Thyme, parsley, bay, lemon balm, rosemary and chives are easy to grow indoors.

▼ **Hanging baskets** *Rhoicissus capensis* and variegated philodendron add a splash of green to a small kitchen without interfering with the work space. Drip saucers attached to the baskets prevent water spillage.

▲ Kitchen decoration With some thoughtful planning, even a busy, humid kitchen can have its share of indoor greenery. Baskets of trailing plants and foliage shrubs in corners do not interfere with kitchen activities, and pots of flowering plants make work surfaces more inviting.

◄ Shelf liners An out-of-the-way shelf in a well-lit kitchen is ideal for plants that need daily cosseting and prefer a humid environment. It is easy to keep an eye on those that may be in failing health or waiting to be propagated.

▼ Propagating units A kitchen window-sill holds a collection of glasses in which avocado stones are being rooted. Cuttings of spider plant (*Chlorophytum*) and *Plectranthus*, as well as busy Lizzies, root easily in jars of water.

Also welcoming a little extra humidity, many indoor ferns are excellent in hanging baskets. This type of container has the advantage of keeping plants above work surfaces. Position them over a sink unit or table-top so they are completely out of the way of passers-by. When watering a hanging container, never let it drip on to food or boiling fat.

Tall plants can be used effectively as living screens or dividers between a cooking and washing area and an eating area in a large kitchen. A sunny breakfast room cries out for lacy foliage, pretty flowers and refreshing country fragrances.

Herbs and vegetables

Many culinary herbs and salad crops, though generally producing few or no flowers, are quite pretty plants in their own right and frequently have an aromatic fragrance when touched. The hardy outdoor types are rarely suitable for all-year cultivation indoors, but are ideal for short stays on the kitchen window-sill, especially when they are nearly ready for harvesting.

The majority of herbs and salad crops are garden plants that mature in summer and will not tolerate long spells in centrally heated atmospheres or poor light. Find the coolest, airiest and sunniest spot possible for them in which to thrive and flourish.

If you want to maintain the most decorative display of herbs possible, choose those from which you pluck just a few leaves, rather than whole shoots, otherwise the plants will soon become bare and unattractive. Marjoram and thyme, for instance, make very good pot plants with their compact and bushy habit and actually grow better when given a regular light trim. They will survive in small pots (7.5-10cm/3-4in) for some considerable time, so you should be able to find room for them in even the most cluttered kitchen. They are both strongly-flavoured, so you need only four to six leaves at

a time for cooking. The small, half-hardy basil is also an excellent pot plant for a sunny window-sill.

More vigorous herbs from which you need to pluck several leaves or shoots at once, such as parsley and mint, can also be grown indoors, but they need larger pots – up to 15cm (6in) in diameter. These hardy herbs are bushy and will not appear sparse when their leaves are plucked.

As soon as any perennial herb shows sign of stress indoors – yellowing leaves, tall spindly shoots or lack of vigour – move it outdoors immediately. Preferably remove it from its pot and plant it in open ground until it is fully revived. In subsequent years, divide the plant or take cuttings from it for potting up indoors, keeping a stock in the garden. If you don't have a suitable place in the garden to grow herbs, replace your kitchen-grown plants from time to

time with new stock bought from a nursery or grown from seed.

All salad crops are annuals and, though generally hardy, benefit from a little extra heat and humidity to encourage quicker, more tender growth – provided they get enough light and water. Such conditions can be adequately provided on a window-sill indoors, but be prepared to water them at least once a day in summer, often more. Most salad crops *can* be grown indoors, but size is usually the limiting factor. Also avoid crops which run quickly to seed, such as lettuces, when high temperatures are combined with full sun through glass.

The best choices are the fruiting vegetables, such as tomatoes, cucumbers, aubergines, peppers and chillis. Don't be deterred by the enormous size usually associated with many of these plants – miniature varieties are available.

► **Kitchen herb garden** Pots of herbs fill a kitchen window with aromatic foliage, ready to be plucked when required. Basil and small bay trees are particularly suitable for growing indoors, and sprouting seeds also do well on a window-sill. Good light and free air circulation are essential.

KITCHEN PLANTS

Culinary herbs
Basil (*Ocimum basilicum* and *O. minimum*)
Bay (*Laurus nobilis*)
Chervil (*Anthriscus cerefolium*)
Chives (*Allium schoenoprasum*)
Lemon balm (*Melissa officinalis*)
Marjoram (*Origanum majorana*)
Mint (*Mentha rotundifolia* and *M. spicata*)
Parsley (*Petroselinum crispum*)
Rosemary (*Rosmarinus officinalis*)
Sage (*Salvia officinalis*)
Savory, winter (*Satureja montana*)
Thyme (*Thymus vulgaris*)

Vegetables and fruits
Aubergine
Chilli pepper
Cucumber (dwarf varieties, such as 'Bush Champion', 'Fembaby' and 'Sweet Success')
Mustard and cress
Sprouting seeds (including alfalfa, buckwheat, fenugreek, lentils, mung beans, adzuki beans, chick peas and triticale)
Strawberry (alpine and compact varieties, such as 'Alexandria' and 'Sweetheart')
Sweet pepper (capsicum)
Tomato (bush and 'cherry' types, such as 'Florida Petit', 'Gardener's Delight', 'Sungold' and 'Sweet 100')

◄ ▲ **Cooking ingredients** Small pots of herbs are handy on a window-sill. Parsley, chives, sage and lemon balm are content in small containers, and salad cress takes up a minimum of space.

◄ **Miniature tomatoes** Cherry tomatoes are popular and several varieties can be grown on a window-sill, and even in hanging baskets. They bear trusses of sweet-flavoured, red or yellow fruit, each about 2.5cm (1in) in size.

▼ **Sprouting seeds** Children love to have their own indoor garden. Salad cress will sprout in less than a fortnight and the tiny seeds can simply be sown on damp cottonwool or a flannel, or in special pottery dishes like this cottage with its own little garden.

TRAILERS AND CLIMBERS

**Baskets of hanging plants and climbers
can decorate windows and walls with greenery,
adding the finishing touch to a room.**

Diminutive leaves are a common feature of trailing plants. For this reason they make the greatest impact when grown in group arrangements, tumbling over ledges or trailing from hanging baskets at or above eye level. They are also useful for hiding the bases of foliage shrubs that have become leggy with age.

Climbers grow in the opposite direction to trailers, extending upwards, although most will only do so when given support. However, many climbers, notably ivies, grape ivies and some philodendrons, are just as happy trailing as climbing.

Trailing plants
Hanging plants make maximum use of space, with a minimum of fuss. In most homes, surface space is usually at a premium, and house plants often have to give way to more functional items. High-level air space, corridors, hallways and odd nooks and crannies provide a perfect setting for displaying trailing plants.

In a window the flowers and foliage of trailing plants filter the light, and provide some privacy at the same time. If the window recess is deep, it can act as a mini-conservatory.

A hanging basket is rather like a living sculpture and should be attractive from all sides in order to merit a prominent position. Left to their own devices, trailing plants will continue to grow downwards with stems that become increasingly thin and leafless. In order to encourage a bushy appearance, the growing tips of young plants should be pinched out from time to time; the side-shoots that result

from this treatment should also be pinched out.

If the stems become straggly, shorten them to just above a leaf. This improves their appearance and encourages the plants to grow bushier. Plants grown in close proximity also benefit from the communal build-up of humidity, but make sure that they all have the same watering, light and temperature needs.

You should be able to reach the plants easily, so don't hang them so high that watering and trimming are difficult. Remember, too, that hot air rises and the air

---

▼ **Conservatory plants** A deep plant window, built as an extension to a living room, is filled with a range of foliage plants. Baskets of trailing plants, suspended by fine nylon wire, receive maximum bright light.

▲ **Living sculpture** The stag's horn fern (*Platycerium bifurcatum*) creates a strong focal point with its dark green fronds, which are divided like the antlers of a stag.

▼ **Space savers** A community of trailing plants take up little space. Filling a window are (top row, left to right) grape ivy, devil's ivy, gynura and columnea; (centre row) ivies; and (bottom row) mother-of-thousands and creeping fig.

▲ **Flowering trailers** The Italian bellflower (*Campanula isophylla*) is an ideal basket plant for a cool, brightly lit room. Its slender stems are covered with mauve or white, star-shaped flowers in summer.

RECOMMENDED TRAILERS

The amount of light reaching house plants can be crucial to their well-being — it's vital to choose the right plants for the right situation.

Direct sunlight
Asparagus fern (*Asparagus densiflorus* 'Sprengeri')
Devil's ivy (*Scindapsus aureus*)
Italian bellflower (*Campanula isophylla*)
Spider plant (*Chlorophytum comosum*)
Wandering Jew (*Tradescantia fluminensis*)

Medium light
Busy Lizzy (*Impatiens walleriana*)
Columnea (*Columnea microphylla*)
Easter cactus (*Rhipsalidopsis gaertneri*)
Grape ivy (*Rhoicissus rhomboidea*)
Gynura (*Gynura aurantiaca*)
Ivy (*Hedera helix* cultivars)
Mother-of-thousands (*Saxifraga stolonifera*)
Stag's horn fern (*Platycerium bifurcatum*)
Sweetheart philodendron (*Philodendron scandens*)

Shade
Boston fern (*Nephrolepis exaltata*)
Creeping fig (*Ficus pumila*)
Maidenhair fern (*Adiantum capillus-veneris*)

near the ceiling is warmer than the rest of the room – for this reason ivies at high level often shrivel and die. Plants suspended from the ceiling should have enough headroom under them for people to move about.

Trailing plants, especially those in loam-based composts, can be very heavy, so fix hooks or brackets firmly to the wall or ceiling. Choose lightweight, waterproof containers for the larger plants – ceramic or brass types could well be too heavy.

Climbing plants

The common feature of all climbing plants is their inability to grow upright without support. However, this is not necessarily a disadvantage – it makes them just right for clothing walls, pillars or partitions. Alternatively, many climbers can be left unsupported to trail downwards from wall pots, niches and shelves.

Many plants can be trained to grow both upwards and downwards around a window or arch. *Philodendron scandens, Rhoicissus rhomboidea* and ivies, for example, grow upwards and sideways with equal success. This can result in some eye-catching arrangements, often giving the impression of a lush garden brought indoors.

The support structure for indoor climbers should be as decorative as possible. Ordinary bamboo canes can be used, but it is better to choose stakes sold specially for the home – they are slimmer than normal bamboo and are generally dipped in dark green preservative to improve their appearance and eliminate harmful moulds. Plastic-coated wire hoops and trellis are also available for training small pot-grown climbers. For larger plants, use plastic netting or well-finished wooden trellis.

Climbers with aerial roots (those appearing from the stems above ground), such as the Swiss cheese plant, philodendrons, ivies and scindapsus, all appreciate humidity and are suitable for growing against moss stakes.

► **Climbing philodendron** Elephant's ear (*Philodendron domesticum*) is named after its 60cm (2ft) long, leathery leaves. In the right cultural conditions, it will slowly climb up to 1.2m (4ft) tall when trained to a stake or moss pole.

These are plastic poles bound with moss and held in place with nylon thread. The moss can be kept moist with mist-spraying so that the aerial roots are encouraged to take a firm hold on the support.

Consider the weight of foliage and stems – the fleshy leaves and stems of wax flower, philodendrons and Swiss cheese plant place a considerable load on ordinary canes, so durable moss stakes are most suitable. Tie in the stems with wire rings or nylon thread.

Flowering climbers, such as black-eyed Susan, passion flower, Cape leadwort and jasmines, provide colour for a few weeks every year, but most indoor climbers are grown for their attractive green or variegated foliage.

▲ **Versatile ivy** The common English ivy (*Hedera helix*) with its different leaf shapes and colour variegations is one of the easiest plants to grow. It will climb or trail and tolerates poor light, dry air and low temperatures.

▲ **Passion flower** Outdoors, passion flower (*Passiflora caerulea*) will climb to 6m (20ft) in favoured sites. As a pot plant, it is usually pruned back annually to 90cm (3ft) and the stems trained round wire hoops. It flowers throughout summer and can sometimes be induced to fruit after hand pollination.

◄ **Points of colour** The huge size of the vigorous climbing Swiss cheese plant (*Monstera deliciosa*) is apparent when compared with a 60cm (2ft) tall clivia. This has elegantly arching leaf fans and fleshy stems topped with brightly coloured flowers.

▼ **Rapid climber** The grape ivy (*Rhoicissus rhomboidea*) can grow 60-90cm (2-3ft) in a year. Its sparse, curly tendrils will attach themselves to many surfaces, but ideally the plant should be trained against wire or netting.

RECOMMENDED CLIMBERS

Arrowhead vine (*Syngonium podophyllum*)
Asparagus fern (*Asparagus densiflorus* 'Sprengeri')
Begonia vine (*Cissus discolor*)
Black-eyed Susan (*Thunbergia alata*)
Black gold philodendron (*Philodendron melanochrysum*)
Blushing philodendron (*Philodendron erubescens*)
Burgundy philodendron (*Philodendron* 'Burgundy')
Canary ivy (*Hedera canariensis* varieties)
Cape leadwort (*Plumbago capensis*)
Elephant's-ear philodendron (*Philodendron domesticum*)
English/common ivy (*Hedera helix* varieties)
× *Fatshedera lizei*

Fiddle-leaf philodendron (*Philodendron bipennifolium*)
Golden hunter's robe (*Scindapsus aureus* 'Golden Queen')
Golden trumpet (*Allamanda cathartica*)
Grape ivy (*Rhoicissus rhomboidea*)
Jasmine (*Jasminum officinale, J. mesnyi* and *J. polyanthum*)
Kangaroo vine (*Cissus antarctica*)
Ornamental pepper (*Piper crocatum*)
Paper flower (*Bougainvillea × buttiana* and *B. glabra* varieties)
Passion flower (*Passiflora caerulea*)
Sicklethorn (*Asparagus falcatus*)
Sweetheart philodendron (*Philodendron scandens*)
Swiss cheese plant (*Monstera deliciosa*)
Wax flower (*Stephanotis floribunda*)
Wax plant (*Hoya carnosa*)

SCULPTURAL PLANTS

**Indoor trees and shrubs make spectacular
focal points in the right setting, bringing colour
and life to large empty spaces.**

Many popular house plants are trees or large shrubs in their native habitats. Scaled-down versions of these make impressive specimen plants for open-plan living rooms, studios and work places. As their roots are confined in large containers, growth is slow, but eventually such plants attain a size and beauty that can have as much visual impact in a room as a piece of fine furniture. Don't crowd a room with large plants – one or two well-positioned specimens are more effective than an overwhelming collection.

Alternatively, some garden centres, florists and house-plant nurseries offer mature specimen plants. But cost is high and transport and acclimatization to a new environment can be difficult.

Almost every home, whatever its size, has the odd corner or empty hallway which is too small for a functional piece of furniture and yet too large to be ignored. A tall plant need occupy only a little floor space, but will fan out above the surrounding furniture, creating a graceful and arresting effect.

Specimen plants

For focal points in spacious areas, choose perfectly formed plants ranging from tree-like types, such as rubber plants (*Ficus elastica*), weeping fig (*F. benjamina*), Swiss cheese plant (*Monstera deliciosa*) or the Norfolk Island pine (*Araucaria heterophylla*), to colourful bromeliads or dracaenas for more modest living rooms.

Leaf shapes are often the deciding factor in the choice of specimen

▼ **Space fillers** The magnificent Swiss cheese plant (*Monstera deliciosa*) needs plenty of space for its climbing stems and huge, deeply lobed leaves, which can grow as much as 90cm (3ft) long. The more delicate foliage of dracaena, araucaria and ferns provides contrasting colours and textures.

◄ **Fiddle-leaf fig** The *Ficus* family includes the edible fig and many ornamental types that vary in height from creeping species to huge rubber trees. The fiddle-leaf fig (*F. lyrata*), with its distinctive violin-shaped, glossy green leaves, easily reaches 1.2m (4ft) as an indoor pot plant placed in good light, and out of direct sun.

▼ **Tropical leaf canopy** The climbing philodendrons, closely related to the Swiss cheese plant, are rapid growers. In their native tropical rainforests they scramble up tall trees, and as house plants they will reach 4.5m (15ft) or more. With adequate support and filtered light, they can be trained up walls and round windows. A weeping fig (*Ficus benjamina*) on the left, grows more slowly to 1.8m (6ft).

plants. Spanish bayonet (*Yucca aloifolia*), for example, has spiky foliage and statuesque form, while the false aralia (*Dizygotheca elegantissima*) has elegant, long-stalked, narrowly divided leaflets, and the umbrella tree (*Schefflera actinophylla*) is distinguished by clusters of glossy green leaves radiating from a central point like the spokes of an umbrella. *Philodendron* and *Ficus* species display huge, smooth or wrinkled leaves, as much as 90cm (3ft) long.

Group arrangements

Floor displays need not be restricted to large plants – an array of small varieties can be just as effective. Choose plants which look good viewed from above, such as bromeliads which have a rosette leaf arrangement. To simplify day-to-day care and to improve humidity, stand the pots on a tray filled with moist pebbles.

The advantage of group arrangements is that they can be moved around to suit a change of decorative style or to give the plants better light, or cooler temperatures during the winter. They can also be augmented with flowering plants for bright colour.

Composts and containers

Proprietary loam-based potting composts are best for tall plants. They make heavy ballast and a secure rooting medium for top-heavy plants which tend to be unstable in lightweight, soil-less and peat-based composts, even in heavy containers. Watering can also be more problematic. Repotting of mature plants is a major undertaking, but it is usually sufficient to replace the top 5-7.5cm (2-3in) layer with fresh compost.

Most shrubby indoor plants accept the removal of awkwardly-placed shoots and dying branches. The exception is the slow-growing Norfolk Island pine, which responds to pruning by dying back and shedding its foliage.

Plastic pots are too light for large plants, so where possible use heavier ceramic containers. Enamelled glassfibre tubs are more stable and blend particularly well with modern decor.

Tall plants in large containers filled with heavy compost are difficult to move once positioned. Place them far enough away from a wall to allow access for cleaning and general care. Choose plants which do not grow towards the light and therefore will not require regular turning – small-leaved species and plants with rigid fan-like leaves rather than broad-leaved or lax-stemmed varieties. Alternatively, set the containers on plant trays fitted with castors.

▼ **Lofty interior** A high-ceilinged studio apartment provides a light and spacious environment for a veritable jungle of tropical foliage plants. Tree-like scheffleras, a massive dracaena and a willowy weeping fig bring colour to this pale-coloured room.

▲ Yucca tree The exotic-looking yucca is a slow-growing house plant. Grown from trunk sections of varying lengths which sprout roots at one end and rosettes of dark green leaves at the other, several sections can create a mini-forest.

► Moisture-lover Indoor bamboos plants need plenty of headroom and a deep container filled with moist compost. Boston ferns hide their roots.

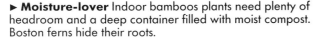

SCULPTURAL PLANTS

African hemp (*Sparmannia africana*)
Bamboo (*Arundinaria* species)
Banyan tree (*Ficus benghalensis*)
Canary date palm (*Phoenix canariensis*)
Dracaena fragrans
Dracaena marginata
False aralia (*Dizygotheca elegantissima*)
False castor-oil plant (*Fatsia japonica*)
Norfolk Island pine (*Araucaria heterophylla*)
Paradise palm (*Howeia forsteriana*)
Parasol plant (*Heptapleurum arboricola*)
Parlour palm (*Chamaedorea elegans*)
Silk oak (*Grevillea robusta*)
Spathiphyllum hybrids
Spineless yucca (*Yucca elephantipes*)
Umbrella tree (*Schefflera actinophylla*)
Weeping fig (*Ficus benjamina*)

◄ Weeping fig With age, the weeping fig (*Ficus benjamina*) develops into a miniature tree with a bare trunk and a head of small glossy leaves. It is tolerant of light shade, but enjoys good air moisture.

PLANTS FOR SCENT AND COLOUR

**Some house plants, especially forced bulbs,
are sweetly scented and many more have colourful
flowers and striking foliage.**

In nature, plant scent has two main functions: either to attract pollinating insects and other creatures, or to deter would-be pests. Many insects associate sweet scents with a supply of sugary nectar. Plants can thus attract pollinators from far and wide without the need for large or brightly coloured flowers, even in the darkest, shadiest rainforest where flowers are unlikely to be seen anyway.

Many highly scented flowers are white – fragrance provides the initial attraction, then insects can locate the white landing stage even at night. Generally, brilliantly coloured flowers emit less scent. Of the flowering house plants especially noticeable for their fragrance, angels trumpets, wax flower, wax plant, gardenia and white jasmine are among the most evocative. Their sweet, heady scents linger in warm air,

especially on summer evenings. Grow them near a doorway, where moving air currents will disperse the aroma around the room.

The white spider lily (*Hymenocallis caribaea*) is another summer-flowering pot plant with a pleasant scent, and most of the *Citrus* species are also deliciously fragrant from spring until summer. The calamondin orange (*C. mitis*) blooms at almost any time of year, even on quite young plants, and fills a room with a refreshing scent.

Aromatic foliage is fired by an accumulation of volatile oils which are close to the leaf surfaces. It usually acts as a warning that the leaves are either unpleasant or poisonous to eat. The aroma may be released continuously by evaporation – especially when the air is warm – as in the culinary thymes, or only when the leaves are bruised or touched.

The scented pelargoniums are a large group, varying in leaf size, flowers and fragrance. Generally, the flowers are smaller and less flamboyant than those on zonal and ivy-leaved pelargoniums, but their foliage is highly scented. Specialist nurseries offer varieties with leaves that smell of roses, apples, lemon or pine, or with the spicy aromas of balsam, nutmeg, camphor or peppermint.

Fragrance from aromatic leaves may be strongest when the plants are kept slightly dry. Grow these plants where the leaves will be brushed gently by passers-by – in a hallway or alongside a work-surface, for example. Unlike scented flowers, which may be rather transient, aromatic foliage provides year-round delight.

For a combination of beautifully coloured flowers and delicate

◄ **Grouped for scent** The wax flower (*Stephanotis floribunda*) is noted for the beauty and fragrance of its white flowers. It blooms in summer, at the same time as the little German violet (*Exacum affine*), which bears delicately scented, mauve flowers. The leaves of lemon-scented pelargonium add a sharp citrus aroma.

131

▲ **Double narcissi** Tazetta daffodils flower in the garden in mid-spring, but they can be forced into bloom in winter. 'Cheerfulness', with several creamy-white flowers to a stem, is sweetly scented and mixes well with early-flowering crocuses.

SCENTED PLANTS

Flowering plants
Angels trumpet (*Datura candida*)
Calamondin orange (*Citrus mitis*)
Coffee plant (*Coffea arabica*)
Dutch hyacinth (*Hyacinthus orientalis* varieties)
Florist's cyclamen (*Cyclamen persicum* varieties)
Gardenia (*Gardenia jasminoides*)
German/Arabian/Persian violet (*Exacum affine*)
Grape hyacinth (*Muscari armeniacum*)
Heliotrope (*Heliotropium hybridum*)
Jasmine (*Jasminum officinale* and *J. polyanthum*)
Lily-of-the-valley (*Convallaria majalis*)
Miniature roses (*Rosa* varieties)
Narcissi (*Narcissus* Poetaz, Tazetta and bunch-flowered varieties, such as 'Cragford', 'Geranium', 'Soleil d'Or', 'Paper White' and 'Cheerfulness')
Oleander (*Nerium odorum*)
Wax flower (*Stephanotis floribunda*)
Wax plant (*Hoya carnosa* and *H. bella*)

Aromatic foliage
Delta maidenhair fern (*Adiantum raddianum* 'Fragrantissimum')
Rosemary (*Rosmarinus officinalis*)
Scented-leaved pelargoniums/ geraniums, including: *P. crispum* (lemon-scented), 'Chocolate Peppermint', *P. fragrans* (nutmeg), 'Lady Plymouth' (rose-scented), 'Mabel Grey' (lemon-grapefruit, 'Prince of Orange' (orange), *P. tomentosum* (peppermint)

▲ **Indoor hyacinths**
Popular for forcing, Dutch hyacinths produce thick flower stems topped by 15cm (6in) long spikes of densely packed flowers. They are so richly scented that their fragrance can fill an entire room in winter and early spring. Bulb fibre is clean and easy to use and does not require drainage, so any attractive container can be used. The bulbs, however, are usually exhausted at the end of flowering and are best discarded.

▶ **Evening scent** The climbing wax flower (*Hoya carnosa*), with its thick, fleshy leaves, bears clusters of flesh-pink flowers from spring to autumn. Their sweet scent is especially strong in the evening, and as the flowers mature, they become sticky with nectar.

scent, choose red, pink or white dwarf cyclamen or oleander. Miniature roses have the widest colour range – everything except blue – but be careful to choose a fragrant variety (such as 'Golden Pin' or rose-pink 'Sweet Fairy'), since some are disappointing.

The strongest scent comes from bulbs forced for indoor flowering. Dutch hyacinths are especially useful – they produce flamboyant white, pink, red, blue or yellow flower spikes which emit a powerfully sweet scent during the fullest periods of mid to late winter. Keep them in a cool place, such as a window-sill, for the longest show.

Some of the single early tulips are also scented, especially pastel-coloured types, such as the golden 'Bellona' and the yellow-orange 'De Wet'. Bunch-flowered narcissi, too tender for outdoor flowering, often bloom in time for Christmas, wafting their sweet springtime scent in the midst of winter. The pure white 'Paper White Grandiflora' is the most outstanding.

Freesias, admired for their long-lasting scent, are pre-treated and can be brought into flower in summer or winter; they are unlikely to bloom indoors more than once, but the small corms are inexpensive and easy to replace.

German violets, grape hyacinths and heliotrope can also be grown in pots for their blue, mauve or purple scented flowers. Widely used for perfumery, the fleshy rooted lily-of-the-valley has the most exquisite fragrance, and specially prepared roots are available from nurseries. Potted up in bowls at three-week intervals, and forced in the dark, they can be in flower indoors for several months.

Colourful displays

Large house plants often look most spectacular when standing alone, but smaller ones – whether flowering or foliage types – are generally displayed to better effect in group arrangements.

Don't position house plants haphazardly on every empty shelf or table. Instead, choose a focal point in the room and select plants which complement the furnishings or fabrics.

Also make sure that the plant containers blend with their surroundings. You can either repot a plant from a container with un-suitable colours or shape into one with more pleasing characteristics, or simply stand it inside a second container. There is a vast range of plastic, ceramic and metal pots, troughs and bowls available from house plant stockists to suit every taste – some plain and brightly coloured, others in period designs.

The choice of flowering house plants, especially temporary varieties, is fairly large and covers every season of the year. You can opt for dazzling primary colours to enhance modern decor, or soft pastel shades to complement an attractive period setting. An otherwise drab room can be given an instant lift by placing a pretty and colourful bowl of flowering plants in a prominent spot.

▼ **Optical illusion** A painted blind depicting a country landscape and a vase of tulips forms a bright background for a row of flowering plants. In bloom for many months, gloxinia hybrids (*Sinningia speciosa*) bear clusters of velvety upturned bell flowers, more flamboyant than the dainty sapphire flower (*Browallia speciosa* 'Major') and salmon-pink Elatior begonia.

▲ Spring colour The small primulas come in a vast colour range and cheer up any room. Group them in single or mixed colours and dead-head regularly to extend the flowering season.

◄ Triangular display Contrasts give added interest to a group arrangement. Here, a red-flowered *Kalanchoë blossfeldiana* and the rat-tail spikes of *Peperomia griseo-argentea* climb up to meet a trailing *Campanula isophylla*.

▼ Study in white Long-flowering white *Streptocarpus* is an excellent partner for the billowing foliage and scented flowers of *Jasminum polyanthum*.

MULTI-COLOURED PLANTS

The following popular house plants are available in a number of different eye-catching colours. You should be able to find at least one to match or contrast with any interior colour scheme.

African violets (*Saintpaulia* hybrids)
Azaleas (*Rhododendron simsii* varieties)
Busy Lizzies (*Impatiens walleriana*)
Cape primroses (*Streptocarpus* hybrids)
Cinerarias (*Senecio × hybridus* varieties)
Elatior begonias (*Begonia × hiemalis* hybrids)
Florist's chrysanthemums (*C. × morifolium* hybrids)
Florist's cyclamen (*Cyclamen persicum*)
Geraniums (*Pelargonium* varieties)
Gloxinias (*Sinningia speciosa* hybrids)
Kalanchoë blossfeldiana hybrids
Plume flowers (*Celosia plumosa* varieties)
Primulas (*Primula malacoides, P. obconica, P. sinensis* and *P. vulgaris* varieties)
Rose of China (*Hibiscus rosa-sinensis* varieties)
Slipper flowers (*Calceolaria × herbeohybrida* varieties)

Equally, foliage can be spiky and imposing, or lacy and delicate. Some plants have vividly coloured leaves, so you can create a cheerful display all year round.

Ornaments, vases of cut flowers, and everyday household articles can enhance the effect of a living plant display. An extra sense of depth will be achieved by positioning plants near a large mirror or other reflective surface. And when natural light fades, the array can be subtly illuminated by a table lamp or spotlight.

Special lamps which can be placed above plants are available – they aren't as hot as conventional tungsten bulbs, and emit a colour spectrum more suited to plants. You *can* use ordinary bulbs, but make sure they're not too close to the plants as to cause scorching.

Coloured foliage

Flowers provide an attractive splash of colour in the home, but their season is often limited to a few weeks, or even days. For year-round colour there's a wonderful choice of plants which display vivid or subtle shades of red, orange, yellow, pink, purple, white or cream – sometimes all together – on their leaves.

Rich foliage colour is often enhanced by surface texture – the wrinkled or corrugated surfaces of *Begonia rex* hybrids are marbled so that the colours actually stand out prominently from the leaf surface. In other plants, attractive colour effects are heightened by intricate leaf patterns and shapes, many with incut margins.

The poinsettia (*Euphorbia pulcherrima*) can be considered here, too, since the brilliant red 'flowers' are really bracts – modified leaves surrounding the true but insignificant yellow flowers.

Some plants possess both attractive flowers and colourful foliage. For example, the zonal geraniums (strictly pelargoniums) include 'fancy-leaved' varieties, of which 'Mrs Henry Cox' is perhaps the most spectacular; it has salmon-coloured flowers above leaves ringed with yellow, copper, red and green.

Certain coloured-leaved plants, especially those with pale leaves, scorch much more easily than their green partners, so position them away from direct sunlight. Unlike true variegated leaves (those with white, cream, silver or gold patches) which lack life-sustaining green chlorophyll pigment in the pale areas, coloured foliage is green below the upper surface, and so usually tolerates low light levels without reverting to all-green colouring.

▼ **Colourful foliage** The exquisite colouring and delicate texture of angel's wings (*Caladium × hortulanum*) are maintained only with constant high humidity. The thin, arrowhead-shaped leaves, up to 38cm (15in) long, come in a range of colours and patterns.

COLOURED FOLIAGE
Multi-coloured
Angel's wings (*Caladium × hortulanum*)
Begonia rex
Croton (*Codiaeum variegatum pictum* varieties)
Dracaena marginata 'Tricolor'
Flame nettle (*Coleus blumei*)
Herringbone plant (*Maranta leuconeura erythroneura*)
Mother-of-thousands (*Saxifraga stolonifera* 'Tricolor')
Wandering Jew (*Zebrina pendula* 'Quadricolor')
Zonal geranium (*Pelargonium* 'Mrs Henry Cox')

Red/pink
Beefsteak plant (*Iresine herbstii*)
Calathea ornata
Christmas cheer (*Sedum rubrotinctum*)
Copperleaf (*Acalypha wilkesiana*)
Fittonia verschaffeltii
Polka dot plant (*Hypoestes phyllostachya*)

Purple
Purple heart (*Setcreasea purpurea*)
Velvet plant (*Gynura sarmentosa*)

Yellow/cream
Dumb cane (*Dieffenbachia maculata* varieties)
Golden hunter's robe (*Scindapsus aureus* 'Golden Queen')

▲ **Joseph's coat** Also known as croton, and correctly called *Codiaeum variegatum pictum*, these superb foliage plants come in an incredible variety of leaf shapes and colours. The foliage may be strap-shaped, oval or lobed, sometimes smooth-edged and sometimes twisted or wavy. The startling colours appear as speckles or large patches and frequently follow the leaf veins, often nearly obliterating the green background. In contrast, *Calathea ornata* displays its ivory-white stripes in a regular herringbone pattern.

▶ **Flame nettle** Almost as colourful as Joseph's coat, flame nettle (*Coleus blumei*) is considerably easier to grow. The coarsely toothed, multi-coloured leaves come in a variety of shapes; the small blue or white flowers detract from the beauty of the foliage and should be pinched out. Coleus are best grown as annuals but are easily raised from cuttings.

COLOUR ROUND THE YEAR

**There are a host of flowering plants and
indoor bulbs which can add bright colour to the
home in every season of the year.**

Although the majority of house plants are grown for their foliage, plenty of flowering pot plants are just as easy to grow, and many will be in bloom for most of the year given proper growing conditions. The African violets and many of the *Streptocarpus* hybrids have no particular flowering season.

More temporary flowering plants, often sold as florist's varieties, are short-term plants which were never intended by commercial growers to have more than one beautiful but short-lived display. Some are true annuals, such as gloxinias and cinerarias, and will die anyway after flowering. Others are perennials, such as florist's chrysanthemums, but are treated as annuals having been subjected to various dwarfing and delayed-flowering techniques which cannot be repeated by the amateur grower.

Some house plants combine handsome foliage with attractive flowers, for example the zebra plant (*Aphelandra squarrosa*). The striking Kaffir lilies (*Clivia*) have large fans of dark green, strap-shaped leaves and huge heads of attractive flame-coloured flowers which are produced at any time from early spring through to late summer.

There are flowering indoor shrubs, climbers and trailers, in addition to various specialist plant groups such as cacti, orchids and bromeliads.

Spring colour

Although cyclamen still bear their dainty flowers in spring, the main display is on the wane, and the freshest colours come from the little primulas and winter-flowering pansies. Indoor bulbs, however, are in their prime, either forced for early flowering (see page 33) or grown in pots in the open garden and brought indoors as soon as the colourful flower buds begin to appear.

Bulbs and corms look their best when planted *en masse*, whether outdoors or indoors. They do not have extensive root systems and can be grown successfully in quite shallow bowls or troughs, allowing you to create a miniature 'landscape' of blossom.

Most of the hardy bulbs popular in gardens can be cultivated indoors, though the shorter, more compact species and varieties are best – others become lanky and ungainly when grown in the rela-

▼ **Spring bulbs** The indoor garden comes into bloom while it is still winter outside. Potted here in bulb fibre and grown in functional white containers, sweetly scented hyacinths, trumpet daffodils, tiny blue squills and club-shaped grape hyacinths are the early harbingers of spring.

◄ **Early tulips** Forced tulips make a welcome change from the more usual hyacinths and cyclamens in early spring. The colour range is much wider and includes pastel yellow, pink and white, brilliant scarlet and orange, often on bicoloured blooms. The dwarf single tulips are the first to make a show, sometimes as early as Christmas, and are slightly ahead of the double varieties. Several Darwin Hybrid and Cottage Garden tulips are also suitable for pot culture and indoor flowering.

▼ **Miniature bulbs** Snowdrops and the little golden winter aconites do not respond well to forcing, but they can still be enjoyed indoors. Pot them up as soon as possible in autumn and leave them in the open until roots have developed and shoots are clearly visible. Bring them to the flowering stage indoors, in a well-lit position where the temperature does not exceed 10°C (50°F).

INDOOR BULBS

African corn lily (*Ixia* hybrids)
Amaryllis (*Hippeastrum* hybrids)
Belladonna lily (*Amaryllis belladonna*)
Blood lily (*Haemanthus*)
Brodiaea laxa
Chincherinchee (*Ornithogalum thyrsoides*)
Crocus (*Crocus* species and hybrids)
Dutch hyacinth (*Hyacinthus orientalis*)
Glory-of-the-snow (*Chionodoxa luciliae*)
Grape hyacinth (*Muscari armeniacum*)
Harlequin flower (*Sparaxis tricolor*)
Ipheion uniflorum
Iris (*Iris danfordiae* and *I. reticulata*)
Jacobean lily (*Sprekelia formosissima*)
Lily-of-the-valley (*Convallaria majalis*)
Narcissus (*Narcissus* species and hybrids)
Nerine species and varieties
Scarborough lily (*Vallota speciosa*)
Snowdrop (*Galanthus nivalis*)
Spider lily (*Hymenocallis × festalis*)
Squills (*Scilla* species and hybrids)
Tulip (*Tulipa* species and hybrids)
Winter aconite (*Eranthis hyemalis*)

tively poor light of most indoor environments.

You can plant bulbs in layers in ordinary pots. With narcissi, for instance, place three bulbs on a 5cm (2in) layer of compost in a 13cm (5in) pot, cover their necks with more compost, then set three more bulbs between them and repeat until the pot is full.

An attractive display can be created using a glass bowl or tank. Instead of compost, use washed pebbles – which are available in several colours – to support the bulbs. Though pebbles provide no nutrients, most bulbs will flower for one season using only their own food store – all they need is water.

Special clay pots – such as mini strawberry pots – can be bought for growing small bulbs in several layers. The pots have holes round the sides, and the bulbs are planted so that the flowers will grow out through the holes. Cro-cuses and snowdrops in particular, look very effective planted in this way.

Hardy bulbs such as narcissi, tulips, crocuses and hyacinths will not flourish indoors for a second year, especially if they were originally 'prepared' bulbs. Once the blooms have faded and the leaves begin to shrivel and die, lift the bulbs and replant them in the garden where they may take a year or so to recover, but will then eventually go on to flower successfully for many years. Buy fresh bulbs for flowering indoors the following year.

Summer colour
The outdoor summer garden traditionally brims with bright flowers, many of them annuals and bedding plants which are discarded after they have finished flowering. In the home, the requirements for summer are the same – lively colours and bold shapes. Many garden annuals, including marigolds, petunias, felicias and butterfly flowers (*Schizanthus*), can be grown in pots indoors, though they tend to become rather lanky unless kept in a very bright and airy place.

For the most successful and continuous display of colour indoors, however, grow perennial and shrubby plants, such as busy Lizzies, begonias, pelargoniums, Cape primroses, fuchsias and gloxinias. Many come in a vast colour range, so you can match them with almost any decorative scheme.

Flowering plants need a lot of natural sunlight – bud and flower drop are common symptoms of in-

▼ **Summer flowers** The popular and easy-to-grow gloxinias and Elatior hybrid begonias are available in a range of pastel and primary colours. The long-lasting flowers are set off by rich green foliage.

▲ **Busy Lizzie** Flowering for many months, the popular 'New Guinea Hybrids' come in vivid flower colours and have attractive green, red, bronze and yellow-variegated foliage.

▲ **Summer arrangement** This group of pot plants includes pink and mauve-flowered *Streptocarpus*, pink and white Madagascar periwinkle (*Catharanthus roseus*) and mauve achimenes. The pink-spotted polka dot plant provides a good foil.

▼ **Annuals for colour** Black-eyed Susan (*Thunbergia alata*) will bloom from late spring to autumn in a well-lit spot, bearing golden trumpet flowers on climbing or trailing stems. It associates well with the daisy flowers and silvery leaves of anthemis.

SUMMER-FLOWERING PLANTS

Achimenes hybrids — red-purple, mauve-blue or pink

Begonia species and hybrids — pink, red, orange or white

Black-eyed Susan (*Thunbergia alata*) — orange or orange-yellow

Bottle-brush (*Callistemon citrinus* 'Splendens') — red

Busy Lizzie (*Impatiens* hybrids) — pink, red, orange or white, often bicoloured

Cape leadwort (*Plumbago capensis*) — pale blue

Cape primrose (*Streptocarpus* hybrids) — violet, pink or white

Celosia species — red or yellow flower plumes

Flamingo flower (*Anthurium scherzerianum*) — red

Fuchsia species and hybrids, upright or trailing — purple, mauve, red, pink or white.

Geranium/pelargonium (*Pelargonium* hybrids) — red, pink, orange, mauve or white, sometimes bicoloured

Gloxinia (*Sinningia speciosa*) — red, violet, purple, pink or white, often bicoloured

Italian bellflower (*Campanula isophylla*) — blue or white

Jacobean lily (*Sprekelia formosissima*) — bronze-red

Madagascar periwinkle (*Catharanthus roseus*) — pink, lavender or white

Miniature rose (*Rosa* hybrids) — red, pink, yellow, orange or white, sometimes bicoloured

Pachystachys lutea — yellow

Paper flower (*Bougainvillea* × *buttiana* and *B. glabra*) — pink, red, mauve, orange or white

Yellow sage (*Lantana camara*) — yellow, orange, pink and red

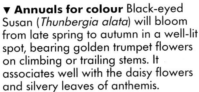

sufficient light and overwatering. Even with the correct amount of sunlight, however, you should keep a daily check on the soil moisture as the roots can dry out very rapidly. Plastic pots, though not the most attractive, help to prevent undue evaporation. Conceal them by standing them inside glazed ceramic, terracotta or wicker containers.

If you buy mature flowering plants rather than raising them yourself, select plants which have more buds than open blooms – fully open flowers often fall when a plant is moved to a new environment. Water and feed the plants regularly to ensure that they continue to grow steadily.

Autumn colour

Few indoor plants shed their leaves in autumn – with living room temperatures maintained at a fairly constant level all year, house plants are generally selected from the range of evergreen shrubs and perennials. Tender indoor fuchsias are the exception; they are herbaceous and drop their leaves in late autumn. The majority of house plants don't undergo a period of complete winter dormancy, though many have a rest period when they need less frequent watering as growth slows down, and when they tolerate, or even prefer, lower than normal room temperatures. However, this does not mean that autumn is a dull period for house plants. There are many species which give a superb show of flowers or fruits at this time.

Chrysanthemums are among the most popular autumn-flowering plants. With modern all-year-round production of so-called 'pot mums', these lavishly coloured daisy flowers can be bought from florists in any season, but they seem most appropriate during the autumn months. Colours range from pale cream and yellow through orange and red to deep purple. However, they are short-term plants and are often best discarded after flowering.

The florist's cyclamen is another example of a house plant with a long flowering season – it is available in shops during much of the year. But, like chrysanthemums, cyclamen plants are happiest when brought into flower in the autumn. Their butterfly-like blooms come in many shades of pink, salmon, red, mauve, purple or white, often with contrasting lacing or shading.

Several of the summer-flowering plants continue blooming into autumn, especially if they are kept in a bright spot where prolonged warmth and sunshine counteract the effects of shorter days – fuchsias, pelargoniums, flowering maples (*Abutilon*), leadwort (*Plumbago*) and the rose of China (*Hibiscus*) are effective and reliable examples.

Rosy fruits are traditionally associated with autumn. For an indoor display, the bead plant (*Nertera*) is a good choice. Masses of tiny orange-red bead-like fruits mature in late summer and remain on the plant for several months. Having a low-growing, carpeting habit, this plant makes a good underplanting for bushy

▼ **Hallowe'en still life** Russet autumn tints are captured here in an arrangement that includes Chinese lanterns (*Physalis alkekengi*) nodding above pots of winter-flowering indoor heathers (*Erica gracilis*). The fiery-coloured trumpets and deep purple foliage of *Fuchsia triphylla* complement an illuminated pumpkin.

▲ **Autumn calm** White cyclamen make a refreshing change from the usual shades of orange and red commonly associated with autumn. Their marbled leaves blend well with variegated ivies and pink polka dot plant.

▼ **Mellow fruitfulness** Although pot chrysanthemums can be bought throughout the year, their prominent scent and warm flower colours are reminiscent of the smell of wet soil and the rich tints of falling leaves in autumn.

▲ **Rose of China** Flowering well into the autumn, the rose of China (*Hibiscus rosa-sinensis*) begins life as a bushy shrub, but left unpruned will soon grow to tree-like proportions, with a stout main stem and a head of branching side-shoots. The large funnel-shaped flowers last for only a day or two, but new buds follow in rapid succession. Red, pink, yellow, orange and white varieties are available.

autumn plants grown in a bowl or trough. If you have 'green fingers', the dwarf pomegranate (*Punica granatum* 'Nana') may produce a few attractive, rose-hip-like fruits on a sunny window-sill in autumn.

For a really unusual autumn show, the red-hot cat's tail (*Acalypha hispida*) is well worth a try. It is a large shrubby plant, decked with bright green, slightly hairy leaves and drooping, brilliant red tassels, which are white in the variety 'Alba'.

Winter colour

Winter may be the dormant season in the garden, but there is a wide variety of brightly-coloured flowering plants which can cheer up the home during even the dullest months. Florist's cyclamen and indoor azaleas (*Rhododendron simsii*), in particular, are in abundance everywhere. Although they rarely survive for more than two years as house plants, azaleas are neat, compact shrubs with a wealth of flower clusters available in red, pink, white, orange and lilac, often bi-coloured and frequently with double, ruffled petals. Winter heaths (*Erica gracilis*), with their massed spikes of dark pink flowers, are also colourful additions to the home; like the azaleas, indoor heathers prefer cool conditions and bright light.

The poinsettias (*Euphorbia pulcherrima*) are probably the most flamboyant of all winter-flowering plants. The tall, vivid red types are more traditional, but newer varieties come in striking shades of salmon-pink, lime-green and creamy-white, often on more compact, dwarf plants.

Bulbs provide some of the brightest colours of all cultivated plants, both in the garden and indoors. Hyacinths, early single and double tulips, narcissi, Dutch crocuses, scillas, dwarf irises and chionodoxas are the most popular bulbs for planting in bowls from late summer to mid-autumn for winter colour.

Most of these bulbs give an extended flowering display if grown in a cool room in a light, airy position – warm central-heating does not encourage better flowers and can, in fact, cause rather disappointing results.

Apart from the colourful bulbs, there are several other attractive house plants – ranging from the succulent, exotic and colourful kalanchoës to the familiar and popular 'pot' chrysanthemums and cinerarias – which can be grown in a prominent spot in the living room for an instant feeling of summer. The many and varied all-year foliage plants can be grouped with them to create extra colour.

The Christmas cactus (*Schlumbergera/Zygocactus*), which does not look like a cactus at all, is in its full glory during the festive season. Its pendent branches are smothered with deep pink trumpet flowers from mid-winter onwards.

Cultivated strains of the wild primrose (*Primula vulgaris*) have become very popular, producing the widest range of flower colours of any one winter species – shades of red, pink, orange, yellow, cream, mauve, purple and white, usually with a yellow eye, are available. Modern strains withstand some forcing and are sold in florists' shops and garden centres from mid-winter. These plants are hardy and ideal for the coolest rooms in the house – the hallway, bedroom or cloakroom. After flowering, plant them out in the garden.

◄ **Winter colour** Poinsettias, brilliant red, pink and creamy-white, are synonymous with Christmas. Mid-winter flowering depends on a strict regime of day and night control, but it is possible to bring the plants into flower in subsequent years.

▼ **Indoor cyclamen** As popular at Christmas as poinsettias, the dainty cyclamens flower from autumn through winter, in shades of white, pink and red. Miniature varieties are also available, and all do best in a bright but cool spot.

▲ **Winter cherries** Species of *Solanum* include the 75cm (2½ft) Jerusalem cherry (*S. pseudocapsicum*) and the smaller winter cherry. Both bear cherry-like berries during winter, ripening from green through yellow to red. They will fruit again after a summer in the open.

▼ **Winter into spring** Double-flowered narcissi, such as orange-centred 'Flower Drift', can be forced into bloom weeks ahead of those grown outdoors. Like the mottled-leaved Greigii tulips, the bulbs can be planted out after flowering.

▲ **Temporary colour** Cinerarias (*Senecio* × *hybridus*) flower annually in late winter. The massive daisy flowers come in shades of blue, purple, red, pink and white or combinations of these, all with prominent eyes.

WINTER-FLOWERING PLANTS

Christmas cactus (*Schlumbergera* hybrids)
Chrysanthemum × *morifolium* varieties
Cineraria (*Senecio* × *hybridus* varieties)
Claw cactus (*Schlumbergera truncata*)
Dutch hyacinths (*Hyacinthus orientalis* varieties — forced bulbs)
Florist's cyclamen (*Cyclamen persicum* varieties)
Hippeastrum hybrids
Iris danfordiae
Iris reticulata
Jerusalem cherry (*Solanum pseudocapsicum*)
Kalanchoë blossfeldiana
Lily-of-the-valley (*Convallaria majalis* — forced 'pips')
Narcissi and daffodils (*Narcissus* varieties — forced bulbs)
Egyptian star cluster (*Pentas lancelolata*)
Fairy primrose (*Primula malacoides*)
Poinsettia (*Euphorbia pulcherrima* varieties)
Primula kewensis
Primula obconica
Primula vulgaris varieties
Snowdrop (*Galanthus nivalis*)
Tulips (*Tulipa* varieties — forced bulbs)
Winter cherry (*Solanum capsicastrum*)

Unusual house plants

Enthusiastic indoor gardeners will be tempted to try growing some of the rarer and more unusual plants. When given the right conditions, paying particular attention to temperature and humidity, a large number of the more flamboyant types can be grown successfully in the home. Many orchids are far less demanding than their exotic appearance would suggest, and their spectacular blooms last for many weeks. The striking bird of paradise flower can be brought into bloom in most indoor environments with good light, but it does demand ample room and a long winter rest for buds to form.

Bottle gardens and terrariums take up little space and are ideal for those miniature plants that need higher humidity than can be provided in a living room. Once planted up they need little attention.

Bonsais – miniaturized versions of ancient gnarled pines, trees and shrubs – cannot abide such rarefied atmospheres. Infinite patience is needed in the shaping and training of bonsai trees, and although they thrive only in outdoor conditions they may be brought indoors for a few weeks while they are in full flower.

The alluring air plants are much easier to grow in the home; they live literally on air alone and make few demands on their owners, unlike carnivorous plants. These are not the easiest plants to grow over a prolonged period but their almost grotesque shapes and voracious appetites can be fascinating.

Jungle effect A richly furnished bay window is a fitting setting for flamboyant amaryllis and exotic orchids.

EXOTIC TASTES

Though sometimes presenting a challenge to the amateur grower, exotic flowering and foliage plants make striking focal points in any home.

There is no clear-cut definition of an exotic plant, but any flower or foliage with an aura of mystery and intrigue – especially if it is reminiscent of the jungles and forests of the tropical world or of the colourful Far East – could be included.

Many curious plants originate from the humid African tropics, including species and varieties of *Clerodendrum* and *Dracaena*. From drier regions we get *Clivia* and *Strelitzia*, while South Africa is home to exotic bulbs such as *Haemanthus, Lachenalia* and *Sparaxis*. The warm Asian countries – notably India – supply us with many unusual house plants, including *Hoya* and *Colocasia*. And the South American continent gives us many unique bromeliads, such as *Billbergia* and *Vriesea*, as well as the arum-related genera *Anthurium* and *Philodendron*.

With other fascinating examples coming from China, Japan, Australasia, the Mediterranean and Central America, it is obvious that growing conditions vary widely within this large and diverse group of house plants. Before buying an exotic plant, make sure that its main requirements for light, temperature, humidity and water supply can be met in your home. If not, a sunroom or conservatory may provide a much better environment.

If you have difficulty in obtaining exotic plants from nurseries or garden centres, consider growing them from seed – many mail order and retail trade seedsmen offer very unusual species. Full cultural instructions are usually supplied on the packet. Most exotic seeds must be germinated in regulated conditions, so it is worth buying a small electrically heated propagating unit.

Humidity – required by many exotic plants – is often difficult to maintain in a home environment. In a conservatory or sunroom with a water-resistant floor, hose down the staging, pots and floor with water daily during warm weather. Indoors, this is not a practicable solution, so improve humidity by growing several plants in one large container or standing them in a tray filled with moist pebbles. In this way, you will create a humid microclimate around the plants.

► **Bird of paradise** The striking, long-stalked and crested orange- and blue-flowered bird of paradise flower (*Strelitzia reginae*) is rather large for the average living room. Complemented here by orange-flowered *Clivia* and footed by ivies, ferns and trailing red *Columnea*, the group needs a space of 1.2m (4ft).

▶ **Close relations** The little calamondin orange (*Citrus mitis*) flowers and fruits while still quite young, the tiny, bright orange fruit following clusters of white flowers. Its taller relation, the kumquat (*Fortunella japonica*), often achieves the stature of a miniature tree, growing up to 1.2m (4ft) tall. It bears single, sweetly-scented white flowers and oval or rounded edible fruits that ripen slowly to deep orange and persist for many weeks.

▼ **Palm house** In the controlled temperature and humidity of a conservatory, many foliage plants can begin to approach the size they attain in their natural environments. Palms' especially, develop typical, deeply furrowed trunks and huge arching leaf fans. Here, a hanging basket of trailing, ivy-leaved pelargoniums adds bright colour to a veritable jungle of dark green palm fronds.

▲ **Egyptian star cluster** Exotic in name and appearance, the Egyptian star cluster (*Pentas lanceolata*) is quite easy to grow, provided it is given bright light with some full sun. The lavender-pink, magenta or white flowers appear mainly from late autumn to mid-winter, though one or two may be produced at any time of year.

▲ ► **Glory lily** A spectacular climber from tropical Africa, the glory lily (*Gloriosa rothschildiana*) is best grown in a sunny conservatory where its 1.8m (6ft) tall stems can clamber through other plants. The exotic flowers, which resemble Turk's-cap lilies, are crimson, the petals crimped and wavy and edged with yellow. They are borne from early to late summer.

► **Colour harmony** Here, sprays of pink-flowered moth orchid (*Phalaenopsis*), curious crimson spathes of *Anthurium*, red-flowered begonia and cerise-pink azalea bring colour to a collection of foliage plants. This includes variegated ivies, weeping figs and calatheas.

EXOTIC FLOWERING PLANTS

Basket plant (*Aeschynanthus* species)
Bird of paradise flower (*Strelitzia reginae*)
Bleeding heart vine (*Clerodendrum thomsoniae*)
Blood flower (*Asclepias curassavica*)
Blood lilies (*Haemanthus* species)
Cape cowslip (*Lachenalia aloides*)
Cestrum (*Cestrum aurantiacum* and *C. elegans*)
Egyptian star cluster (*Pentas lanceolata*)
Flamingo flower (*Anthurium scherzerianum*)
Flaming sword (*Vriesea splendens*)
Ginger-worts (*Hedychium* species)
Glory lily (*Gloriosa rothschildiana*)
Golden trumpet (*Allamanda cathartica*)
Harlequin flower (*Sparaxis tricolor*)
Kaffir lily (*Clivia miniata*)
King's crown (*Jacobinia carnea*)
Marmalade bush (*Streptosolen jamesonii*)
Passion flower (*Passiflora caerulea*)
Queen's-tears (*Billbergia nutans*)
Rose grape (*Medinilla magnifica*)
Urn plant (*Aechmea* species)
Wax plant (*Hoya carnosa*)
Yellow sage (*Lantana camara*)

▲ **Bleeding heart vine** A vigorous twining shrub, the bleeding heart vine (*Clerodendrum thomsoniae*) makes a stunning feature with its glossy green foliage and huge sprays of striking red and white flowers from early summer into autumn.

It can grow up to 3m (10ft) high and is ideal for a large conservatory or sunroom where the high temperatures and humidity required for flower production can be maintained. In a living room, the plant's height can be controlled by regularly pinching out the shoot tips during the growing season.

▶ **Terrestrial bromeliads** Growing wild in tropical jungles, the spectacular bromeliads come in many unusual shades of green and grey. The curious flower head consists of a cluster of pointed, orange-red bracts, which droop as they open to reveal branched flower stems with upright yellow and red flowers.

Another characteristic is the water reservoir contained within the base of the leaf rosette. This must be kept topped up at all times, since the roots serve as anchors only and do not take up water from the soil.

CACTI AND SUCCULENTS

With their bizarre shapes, varied textures and often vivid flowers, cacti and other succulents are among the most fascinating of house plants.

Cacti form a large family of prickly succulents – plants which store water in swollen tissues. In common usage, the term 'cactus' extends to other succulents as well; although all cacti are succulents, not all succulents are cacti, i.e. they lack spines. Visually, they are very different from any other plants – they lack typical leaves, have a geometric shape and pattern of spines, and often bear exotic flowers.

A vast number of cacti are available – some are easy to grow, others are a challenge – making them very 'collectable' plants.

Many are rather modestly sized and tend to look out of proportion in individual pots. For a more appealing array, plant them in groups in a shallow trough, using gravel, stone-chippings or wood bark to 'landscape' the surface.

Most cacti come from deserts and enjoy bright sunlight, so a south- or west-facing window is ideal. However, a few come from tropical forests – epiphyllums, *Rhipsalidopsis* and *Schlumbergera* for instance – and prefer a shady east- or north-facing spot.

Desert cacti need a cold, dry winter rest in order to flower well.

In winter they should be kept in an unheated room, where the temperature remains between 5°C (41°F) and 10°C (50°F).

In the growing period, water desert cacti whenever the soil looks dry. When dormant they need no water, or just enough to stop the soil drying out completely. Forest cacti must never

▼ **Desert cacti** A group arrangement is the most effective way of displaying the different forms and textures of desert cacti. Most are slow-growing and shallow-rooted; they thrive in sharply drained soil and bright sun.

◄ **Cactus shapes** There is a huge diversity in the shape of cacti and other succulents. Some are sharply spiny plants, such as the rounded stem bodies of *Gymnocalycium* (left) and the cylindrical *Astophytum* (far left), with its clearly marked indentations. Others have shiny, fleshy leaf rosettes like *Aeonium* (centre) which are carried on top of thick stems.

Glazed ceramic pots complement the variety of extraordinary plant shapes. You can use containers without drainage holes, provided there is a generous layer of crocks in the bottom to improve drainage.

Special cactus composts are available, but any porous, free-draining type will do — John Innes potting compost No 1 plus ¼ by volume of coarse sand or grit is an ideal growing medium.

► **Cactus flowers** Some cacti never flower indoors while others readily bloom year after year. In general, most cactus flowers are short-lived, but they appear in succession to give a comparatively long display. Lobivia is one of the easiest cacti to bring into flower; its spiny body bears wide, funnel-shaped flowers of pink, bright red or yellow.

The stem-grafted *Gymnocalycium mihanovichii* is topped with curious pink or yellow flowers (foreground).

▼ **Desert garden** A shallow trough is transformed into an arid desert landscape occupied by cacti and succulents. They include the viciously spiny barrel cactus (*Echinocactus*) in the foreground and the smooth and shiny-leaved jade plant. Stone chippings covering the compost add to the desert-like effect.

dry out, even in winter, but don't overwater them – roots rot easily. When in flower and during active growth, give all cacti and succulents a liquid feed with tomato fertilizer every fortnight.

Succulents

Although the term cactus in popular usage covers all succulent plants, it should be correctly applied only to members of the *Cactaceae* family. This excludes the aloes, agaves, crassulas, euphorbias, kalanchoës and many other types. By loosely terming all succulents cacti, there is a danger in applying incorrect growing regimes to true succulents.

In those parts of the world where water is scarce or very seasonal, certain plants have evolved the ability to store water, as and when it *is* available, in swollen stems and leaves. Such plants are known as succulents. Their leaves and stems are often decorative and always distinctive. Although a few succulents are spiny – and a few cacti are spineless – they differ from cacti in being without areoles, the tiny swellings from which cactus spines and flower buds emerge.

As house plants, cacti and other succulents are especially valuable where regular watering cannot be guaranteed – many can survive for several weeks, or even months, without water. However, when they are watered, they prefer to have a good drenching before being left to dry out again. They rot at their base if kept constantly moist.

Some succulents flower reliably indoors – including *Kalanchoë blossfeldiana* and its hybrids, *Rochea coccinea* and many echeverias. Others, however, are grown for their colourful leaves or swollen stems and are unlikely to flower in the home.

Except for haworthias and gasterias, which tolerate some shade, all succulent house plants must be given as much direct sunlight as possible – remember that their native habitat is desert, except for a few forest types which prefer more subdued light. This means that the best spot for a succulent desert plant is in or near a south-facing window. Give plants a quarter turn every so often to prevent them from turning towards the light. A typical sign of insufficient light is elongated and floppy growth – especially noticeable with rosette-forming succulents, such as echeverias, which should remain low and compact.

The warmth and comparatively low humidity of centrally heated living rooms are perfectly suitable for most succulent plants throughout the year. Winter warmth does not normally affect flowering adversely in the way it does cacti. Some succulent species will not thrive, however, unless they are encouraged to have a cool winter rest period.

Like many house plants, succulents benefit from being placed outdoors in their pots during the bright, warm days of late spring and summer. When doing this, though, exercise some caution. In general, succulents with small, delicate leaves or with leaves that are coated with a decorative, white powdery bloom should not be left out in the rain. More resilient plants, such as agaves, can safely be left in a sunny outdoor position throughout the warmer months.

Always grow succulents in free-draining compost to prevent root rot – even if strict control is kept on watering. Special cacti/succulent compost can be bought, or mix a liberal amount of coarse sand or perlite with a conventional soil-based potting compost.

Natural clay pots and containers tend to look more in keeping with the desert-like character of succulent plants than plastic ones. Both types are perfectly suitable, however, and plants grown in plastic containers often need even less watering. Grow species which branch from their base or eventually form broad clumps in shallow troughs or half-pots for a more balanced shape.

► **Rocky landscape** Miniature gardens replicating the natural habitats of succulents can make arresting focal points. Here, string-of-beads (*Senecio rowleyanus*) tumbles trailing stems over a plant tray; the tiny grey-green leaves are perfectly bead-like. An attractive maroon-tipped houseleek looms over an ornamental rock at whose foot a bright, pink-flowered miniature succulent nestles.

INDOOR SUCCULENTS

Aeonium arboreum and varieties
Aloe species
Buttons-on-a-string (*Crassula rupestris*)
Century plants (*Agave* species)
Christmas cheer (*Sedum rubrotinctum*)
Crown-of-thorns (*Euphorbia milii*)
Devil's backbone (*Kalanchoë daigremontiana*)
Donkey's tail (*Sedum morganianum*)
Echeveria species and varieties
Flaming Katy (*Kalanchoë blossfeldiana* hybrids)
Houseleeks (*Sempervivum* species)
Jade tree (*Crassula argentea*)
Living stones (*Lithops* species)
Moonstones (*Pachyphytum oviferum*)
Mother-in-law's tongue (*Sansevieria trifasciata* 'Laurentii')
Pearl plant (*Haworthia margaritifera*)
Rat-tail (*Crassula lycopodioides*)
Rochea coccinea
Sedum sieboldii 'Medio-variegatum'
String-of-beads (*Senecio rowleyanus*)
Wart gasteria (*Gasteria verrucosa*)

◄ **Partridge-breasted aloe** A popular succulent, partridge-breasted aloe (*Aloe variegata*) rarely exceeds 30cm (1ft) in height. It produces offsets which form a spiky clump. They can also be potted up singly.

◄ ▼ **Century plant** Agaves are dramatic foliage succulents with rosettes of tough, sword-shaped leaves. The century plant (*A. victoriae-reginae*) forms a wide clump of dark green, white piped and spiny-tipped leaves.

▼ **Jade tree** The glossy-leaved jade plant (*Crassula portulacea*) eventually forms a small, branching tree. During early growth, it can share a container with tiny succulents such as *Lithops*.

BOTTLE GARDENS

**First developed in the Victorian era, the practice
of growing house plants in enclosed glass cases is both
attractive and beneficial to plant health.**

Many tropical plants and the majority of ferns require more humidity and constantly higher temperatures than can be provided in the home. Chiefly foliage plants, they flourish in filtered light and the steamy atmosphere of tropical jungles.

Such conditions can be difficult to re-create in the home. On a large scale, botanical gardens build huge hothouses with simulated jungle conditions; on a smaller scale, closed plant cases – bottle gardens, Wardian cases and terrariums – can provide similar microclimates. A closed plant case is in effect a mini-greenhouse – moisture from the compost condenses on the inside of the glass and runs back down, so the air and roots never dry out. Smoky and dusty air is also excluded from the plants so leaf pores never get clogged, and they are protected from draughts and sudden fluctuations in temperature.

Bottle gardens

Narrow-necked, clear glass bottles of various sizes make handsome containers – the only restriction being that the neck must be wide enough to let small plants through. Large carboys are especially good for bottle gardens, often having a neck wide enough to put your hand through. Plastic bottles and tanks can be used, but condensation tends to build up on the inside of plastic and obscure the plants – condensation runs off glass more readily.

When growing ferns and waxy-leaved plants a stopper can be inserted in the neck of the bottle to maximize humidity. However, for flowering plants or other soft or hairy-leaved plants, whose foliage is damaged by water drops, leave the neck open.

Choose small, slow-growing plants, such as miniature ferns, small-leaved ivies, fittonias, marantas and, for 'ground-cover', the mossy selaginellas, which need constantly moist conditions and rarely survive for long outside a bottle garden or terrarium.

If the bottle garden is to be viewed from all sides, set taller plants in the centre. Choose from slow-growing varieties of calatheas, dieffenbachias and dracaenas. The brilliantly coloured earth star (*Cryptanthus*) species are also ideal for bottle gardens and plant cases. These small bromeliads, only a few inches high, make marvellous centrepieces, although their vivid leaf patterns show up best through clear glass.

Plan the arrangement before placing plants in the bottle (see also pages 159-162). Ensure that small plants are not hidden behind taller ones, and are not too cramped – bank up the compost towards the back of the bottle to create a tiered effect.

Flowering plants are not generally suitable for a bottle garden since they have a short season of interest, then look rather dull; they are also difficult to deadhead. It is best to select plants with coloured leaves to provide highlights. Add pebbles or wood bark around the plants to improve the visual appeal.

Water the plants with a hand mist sprayer and, if necessary, clean the inside of the glass with a

◄ **Plant cases** Glass containers of many shapes and sizes are suitable for bottle gardens. Old-fashioned sweet jars, fish tanks, wide-necked bottles and carboys are useful, provided the glass is clear and not coloured. Moisture-loving foliage plants thrive in the enclosed, humid atmosphere and will need the minimum of attention.

155

◄ **Carboy bottle** Clear glass bottles are ideal, but lightly tinted green bottles are also suitable if placed in a well-lit position. Avoid direct sunlight, where delicate foliage can be easily scorched.

Moss ferns and true ferns are ideal for creating a lush green effect. Use variegated or coloured-leaved plants — polka-dot plant, ribbon plant or one of the variegated arrowhead vines, for instance — to add splashes of colour. Flowering plants can look lacklustre once their flowers have faded.

BOTTLE GARDEN PLANTS

Green foliage
Button fern (*Pellaea rotundifolia*)
Creeping fig (*Ficus pumila* 'Minima')
Ivy (*Hedera helix* dwarf varieties)
Maidenhair fern (*Adiantum capillus-veneris*)
Maidenhair spleenwort (*Asplenium trichomanes*)
Mind-your-own-business (*Soleirolia soleirolii*)
Moss ferns (*Selaginella* species)
Peperomia caperata
Watermelon peperomia (*Peperomia argyreia*)

Coloured foliage
Aluminium plant (*Pilea cadierei*)
Angel's wings (*Caladium* varieties)
Arrowhead vine (*Syngonium podophyllum* varieties)
Cretan brake fern (*Pteris cretica* 'Albolineata')
Croton (*Codiaeum variegatum pictum* narrow-leaved varieties)
Dumb cane (*Dieffenbachia maculata* varieties)
Earth stars (*Cryptanthus* species)
Goodluck plant (*Cordyline terminalis*)
Ivy (*Hedera helix*, small-leaved variegated types)
Mosaic plant (*Fittonia verschaffeltii argyroneura* 'Nana')
Mother-of-thousands (*Saxifraga stolonifera* 'Tricolor')
Polka-dot plant (*Hypoestes phyllostachya*)
Prayer plant (*Maranta leuconeura*)
Ribbon plant (*Dracaena sanderiana*)

◄ **Victorian terrarium** Adapted from the 'Wardian' plant case, a terrarium offers plants a similar environment to a bottle garden, but has the option of allowing more air to circulate if one or more panes are left unglazed. It is easier to plant up a terrarium, and to adjust the arrangement as plants become larger.

Here, an ivy tumbles from one side, breaking up the symmetry of the terrarium. Colour is provided by pink-tinted mother-of-thousands and a polka-dot plant. A green moss fern forms a delicate, contrasting backdrop.

piece of sponge attached to a wire or cane. Place the bottle in good light – the glass reduces the amount of light inside the bottle quite considerably – but not in direct sunlight. The display will be self-supporting for several months. When plants become too large, creating an overcrowded jungle effect, re-planting is often the best solution.

Terrariums

Terrariums have developed from the 'Wardian' case, invented by an English physician, Nathaniel B. Ward, a century and a half ago. He was experimenting with caterpillars and discovered by chance that a fern spore had germinated in one of the stoppered jars. After further experiments he found that certain plants would grow indefinitely in sealed glass containers, and thus the 'Wardian' case came into being. They were favoured by collectors, who for the first time could bring back sensitive tropical plants.

Ward's terrariums were popular in the Victorian era, and were often extremely ornate. Similar sealed containers can be made from an ordinary fish tank, with a cover made to fit closely over the top.

Although plants can live for years in sealed cases, condensation does cloud the glass, so some ventilation is preferable. Terrariums have the advantage over bottle gardens in being made from panes of glass, some of which can be removed or opened either permanently or for a few days when the glass becomes clouded.

Unlike bottle gardens, terrariums consist of a portable canopy of glass or plastic panes with metal or alloy glazing bars, which can be lifted off the plants growing inside with ease. This allows far more freedom when choosing suitable plants, since it is easier to replace overgrown specimens and to swap short-term flowering species – you don't have to work through a narrow neck.

The traditional brass-framed or leaded-light construction is very expensive, though, with care, such a container will last a life-time. Cheaper all-plastic or alloy-

▲ **Wall-mounted terrarium** A glass-sided double planter, open at the front and the top, makes an interesting feature on a wall. It needs watering more often than a closed plant case.

framed terrariums are becoming popular, but have less charm.

Neither glass nor plastic cladding transmits all the available light to the plants inside the terrarium, and some natural sunlight is also lost through the room windows – so all terrariums must be placed in a bright spot but out of direct sun, otherwise the glass will steam up too much.

Do not encourage the plants to grow quickly by over-feeding – the fertilizer in most potting composts will be sufficient to last for several seasons. Thereafter, use half-strength house plant fertilizer every six months only. Once a balanced environment has been established inside a terrarium, it should not need watering for several months or even years.

All of the plants recommended for bottle gardens are suitable for growing in terrariums. Small trailers and climbers can also be included if the terrarium has open sides. Flowering plants can be used, but are more liable to rot in an enclosed, humid environment than foliage plants, though orchids thrive in a terrarium. Avoid cacti and succulents, which prefer dry conditions.

◄ **Traditional terrarium** Mossy selaginellas and small-leaved mind-your-own-business (*Soleirolia*) thrive in the moist environment of a partially enclosed terrarium. The more vigorous ivies and tradescantias tumble through the open glass panes.

► **Wardian case** The traditional Victorian terrarium consists of an ornate brass or iron framework – this may be painted – which resembles a miniature conservatory, and is glazed with clear glass. It is ideal for growing and displaying humidity-loving plants such as ferns and mosses. Once planted, it will need little routine maintenance.

► ▼ **Modern terrarium** More suited to late 20th-century interior decor, contemporary terrariums are taller, brighter and more airy than the Victorian types. A slanting, hinged roof provides a little ventilation at all times.

▼ **Bell jar** A smaller version of the Wardian case, the solid glass dome of a bell jar provides a similarly enclosed environment, rather like a miniature greenhouse. Delicate ferns are ideal under the protection of bell jars, which can simply be up-ended over a plant pot on a waterproof tray or incorporated into an ornate wooden or stone plant stand.

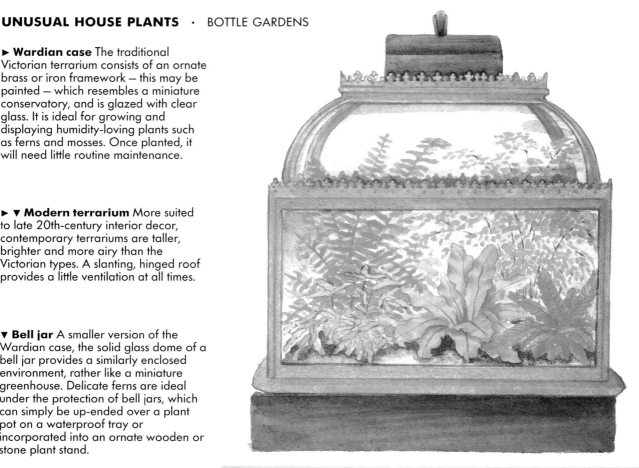

PLANTING A BOTTLE GARDEN

The creation of a bottle garden demands dexterity and ingenuity, but the result is a long-lasting, low-maintenance house plant display.

As keen model-makers relish the challenge of building a galleon inside a wine bottle, indoor gardeners derive much pleasure from planting and growing a miniature jungle in a carboy or other similar large bottle.

In fact, house plants can be grown very successfully in almost any large, transparent container, including glass flagons, wine-making demijohns, old-fashioned sweet jars and other storage jars, bell jars, powder bowls – even a goldfish bowl is suitable. Aquariums can also be used – they give much more scope for 'landscaping' the miniature garden and don't demand the same skills in planting them up.

Ideally, the glass should be non-coloured and crystal clear so that as much light as possible will pass through it. Pale green, very pale brown or slightly smoked glass can also be used, but the choice of plants is then restricted to shade-loving species. Dark green or dark brown glass bottles are not suitable for planting in.

Clear plastic containers *can* be used for bottle gardens, but tend to lack the charm of glass types. Plastic also has the unfortunate characteristic of allowing condensation to build up on it, obscuring the view of the plants inside. Glass, on the other hand, is smoother and cooler, and condensation runs off more freely. However, the big advantage of plastic is that it is light to handle and won't shatter into sharp pieces if it is dropped – an important consideration where children or pets are present.

The smaller the neck of the container, the more difficult it is to plant up, but there is no real limitation on the proportions. Beginners to this art should choose a wide-necked container, but with experience very young plants of many kinds can be inserted through a neck as small as that of a wine bottle. All that is needed is a few home-made improvised tools, some patience and imagination, and a steady hand.

Apart from looking highly decorative, a bottle garden also provides the extra humidity and protection which most jungle plants miss in modern centrally heated rooms. Such plants usually respond to this improved environment by growing healthier, often with more richly coloured foliage.

Provided the plants are free from pests when they are first planted in the bottle, infestation is almost completely prevented when the neck is narrow, especially if it is corked. Fungal diseases and rots – whose spores are carried in the air or may multiply in the compost – can be a problem, but only if the bottle garden is neglected or overcrowded.

Miniature plants
Many garden centres and nurseries offer very young house plants in tiny pots for quite modest prices. However, make sure that they are well rooted specimens and not merely new and as yet unrooted cuttings. To check this, inspect the drainage holes in the bottom of the pot for signs of roots.

▶ **Miniature bottle garden** Moisture- and humidity-loving plants flourish in a closed environment. Their contrasting leaf colours, shapes and textures are more vividly displayed than in the dry air of a living room.

1 Thoroughly wash and disinfect the bottle before planting it up — moulds and other organisms growing on the inside will infect the plants and dirt will reduce light transmission.

2 When the bottle is dry, add a drainage layer of pebbles mixed with a little charcoal to keep it sweet. Lay a piece of muslin or fine mesh over it, then add the compost mix.

3 Using a long-handled spoon, spread the compost and firm it gently. Bank the compost up towards the back of the bottle to facilitate a tiered display. Then make the first planting hole.

4 Lower the first plant into its planting hole. Either use two canes or pieces of dowel-like chopsticks, or grip the root ball between two long-handled spoons. Then infill the hole.

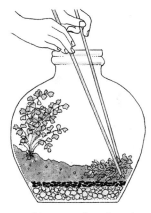

5 Repeat this procedure for plants at the sides and front of the bottle. You will find it easier to insert the lowest growing species first, building up the planting in tiers.

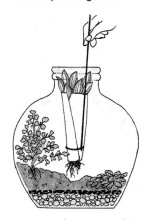

6 As you get to the centre of the planting, the foliage cover may make insertion of the last plant difficult. Wrap a paper tube round it, and slip it off later.

Alternatively very gently pull the plant's main stem upwards from the soil – if it is well-rooted there should be little or no movement.

A still cheaper way of obtaining the plants for a bottle garden is to propagate your own. Young seedlings or rooted cuttings can be used straight from the seed tray or propagating frame. Bare-rooted plants lifted from a sand bed, or those rooted in water or a proprietary rooting gel, are easier to manoeuvre into a bottle without soiling the surrounding plants already set in position.

Suitable cuttings can be taken from your own stock of house plants or from that of a friend; make sure the plants are completely free of pests and diseases. Seed can be either collected or bought from a shop – many seed merchants offer house plant selections.

Preparing the bottle

It is very important to clean the inside of the bottle thoroughly before attempting to plant it up. Deposits of dirt will impair the transmission of sunlight through the glass, look unsightly and possibly harbour troublesome fungal and viral diseases.

Rinse the inside of the bottle with detergent, then flush it out with cold water. If the inside has signs of mildew or mould growth on it, rinse with a liquid fungicide before the detergent. Bad stains on the glass can be removed by rinsing with cleaning crystals sold for wine-making purposes. When clean, allow the bottle to air dry in a warm place for a day or so.

Once thoroughly dry, prepare the bottle for planting by covering the base with a 2.5-5cm (1-2in) deep layer of drainage material. Make this by mixing a handful of charcoal chips with clay aggregate pebbles – the type sold for use on greenhouse benches is ideal – or washed stone pebbles with a diameter not exceeding 6mm (¼in). The charcoal helps to keep the compost sweet.

Cover the drainage layer with a sheet of muslin or fine gauze to prevent compost from being washed down into it and clogging the pores.

Using a rolled paper funnel or chute, add a 5-10cm (2-4in) layer of sterilized potting compost. This should not be of a type that contains a lot of fertilizer and so encourages growth – the plants must remain very slow-growing and compact, yet healthy. A mixture of two parts by volume of a proprietary loam-based potting compost, two parts of coarse sand and one part of sphagnum moss peat suits most recommended plants.

7 When all the plants are in place, firm down the compost using a cotton-reel wedged on to the end of a bamboo cane. Make sure that none of the leaves are buried.

8 Any remaining bare patches can be filled with fresh moss, pieces of wood bark or cork, or pebbles. Use a wire hook to insert moss, or a paper or plastic tube to scatter pebbles.

9 Moisten the compost and foliage with tepid water using a hand sprayer with a fine nozzle. If the compost is very dry, use a plastic tube and funnel to apply water directly to its surface.

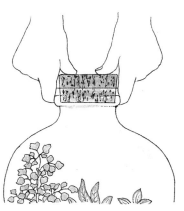

10 Leave the bottle unstoppered for a few weeks until the amount of moisture condensing on the inside of the glass is minimal. When the moisture balance has equalized, insert a cork stopper.

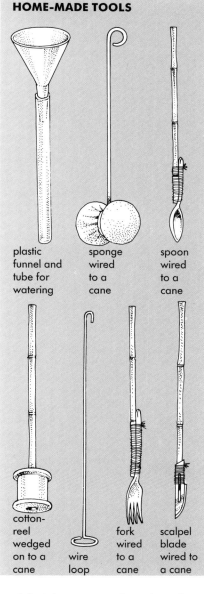

HOME-MADE TOOLS

plastic funnel and tube for watering

sponge wired to a cane

spoon wired to a cane

cotton-reel wedged on to a cane

wire loop

fork wired to a cane

scalpel blade wired to a cane

Unless you plan to view the bottle garden from all sides, bank the compost up towards the back so that a tiered effect can be created more readily.

Planting up

Select attractive plants in a range of sizes – taller but slow-growing ones for the back or centre; shorter, compact ones for the front or edges and for ground-cover in-fills. Also select plants which have differing colours, textures and shapes, and which complement each other.

As a general rule, avoid including flowering species in the plant grouping, since they usually only have a limited season and may be difficult to replace or dead-head. This does not mean that bright colours are excluded – there are many coloured-leaved plants to choose from and these give an attractive all-year-round display.

For the actual planting process you will need a number of special tools. These can generally be made from ordinary household spoons and forks, cotton-reels and stiff wire – such as copper mains earthing wire – each attached to a small bamboo cane or a length of dowel. Unless the neck of the bottle is really wide, never try to squeeze your hand inside to plant or tend the garden – it may get stuck. Also warn children of this danger.

It is best to begin by inserting plants close to the edge of the bottle and then work towards the middle. For a tiered planting effect, begin at the back, then fill the sides and front before completing the centre.

Low-growing plants should always go in before the taller ones to minimize the danger of bruising their leaves. With rounded jars and bottles, remember that there is more available headroom for taller plants in the centre than at the sides – plants which have their leaves squashed against the glass look unsightly and the leaves may rot if they remain permanently wet with condensation.

Use a long-handled spoon to smooth the surface of the compost and then make a hole for the first plant. Remove the plant from its pot and shake or tease away any excess potting mixture from its roots. Holding the plant's root ball gently but firmly between two long-handled spoons – or simply between two sticks (like chopsticks) – lower it into the scooped-out hole. Use two spoons or canes to firm the compost over the roots and keep the plant upright.

Repeat this procedure until the planting is complete. When inserting a tall, floppy-leaved plant, you may find it easier to wrap it in a collar of paper before manoeuvring it into position. This will protect the leaves from damage – both to themselves and to surrounding plants – and the collar can be removed quite easily once the plant is in place. If you make the collar or tube of paper sufficiently deep, you may be able to hold on to the top of it and guide the plant down to the compost without using the spoons or sticks. Alternatively, guide the collar with a long-handled wire hook. Develop your own preferred techniques.

When all the plants are positioned, tamp down the surface of the compost using the cotton-reel tool. If desired, you can then decorate any bare patches of compost by dropping in pebbles or small pieces of sterilized wood bark, cork or driftwood. Alternatively, press small pieces of moss into the gaps. These will soon spread in the humid atmosphere and provide an attractive ground-cover.

Spray the bottled plants with a fine mist of tepid water. Aim to get the compost evenly moist but not wet. If a lot of water is required to moisten the compost, add it by means of a plastic funnel and tube.

Finally, if necessary, clean off any compost or plant debris from the sides of the bottle using a piece of sponge attached to a cane or length of stiff but flexible wire. Place the bottle garden in a bright place near to a window, but not in direct sun.

Aftercare
During the course of the first few weeks after planting, water vapour will escape slowly through the neck of the bottle. Excess moisture will also condense on the inside of the bottle. The correct humidity level is reached when there is just the slightest trace of condensation on the inside of the glass. A lot of condensation indicates that the compost is too wet; none at all suggests that it is too dry and more water should be added. Wipe off excess condensation using a piece of sponge attached to a cane.

When this fine moisture balance is achieved, insert a cork stopper in broad-necked bottles. Those with very narrow necks may be left open. Remove the stopper for a few days from time to time to allow some fresh air in. A sealed bottle

ROUTINE MAINTENANCE

1 Wipe away excess condensation and any plant debris or compost sticking to the inside of the bottle with a small piece of sponge fastened to the end of a cane or piece of stout wire.

2 Apply small amounts of water, and any liquid fertilizer that may be required from time to time, using a plastic funnel and tube of the type commonly sold for wine-making.

3 Sever dead or diseased shoots, leaves and flowers as soon as they are seen. Use a scalpel blade or razor blade fixed to the end of a cane. Remove the prunings with a wire hook.

4 Remove dead plants or any that have become overgrown or unsightly by twisting a wire hook into the root ball and lifting the crown upwards. Replace with a new plant as before.

should only need watering very infrequently, but an open one must be given a sprinkling occasionally to prevent drying out of the compost.

Once a balanced internal environment has developed the bottle garden needs very little further maintenance. Dead leaves, flowers, whole shoots or entire plants must be removed immediately to avoid rotting. This is best done by using an improvised long-handled cutting tool consisting of a razor blade or scalpel blade attached to a thin bamboo cane with wire or adhesive tape. Severed plant material can be extracted from the bottle with a wire hook.

Unless the plants seem stunted, discoloured or are otherwise unhealthy, feeding bottle garden plants is not recommended, since it would encourage excess growth, swamping the display. If it is con-

sidered essential, apply half-strength liquid house plant fertilizer directly to the compost via a funnel and tube.

Terrariums
Terrariums or glass cases provide similar growing conditions to bottle gardens, but, since the environment inside is not usually so tightly sealed, the rooting medium dries out more quickly and humidity is lower – terrariums require more frequent routine maintenance.

The planting procedure is the same as for a bottle garden, but you won't need such specialized tools – most terrariums have removable panels or unglazed sections through which you can work unhindered. The choice of plants for a terrarium need not be as limited as for a bottle garden because replacement is easy.

EYE-CATCHING BONSAI

The ancient Oriental skill of growing woody plants in tiny containers can produce an exciting range of miniature trees and shrubs.

The term 'bonsai' derives from two words which are the same in both the Chinese and Japanese languages – *bon-sai* meaning potted tree. The art of bonsai aims to duplicate all the characteristics of a mature and shapely tree or shrub in a miniature plant, which can be moved indoors for a short but stunning display.

The technique involves confining the plant to a very small container – a shallow dish or bowl – by pinching out the top growth and pruning the roots throughout its life. Bonsais must be trained carefully in order to create the individual charm of a gnarled and twisted mature forest tree.

Most trees can be grown as bonsais, but those with imposing shapes and small leaves give the best results. Conifers, such as cedars, firs, hemlocks, junipers, pines and spruces, and broadleaved trees including ashes, beeches, birches, hornbeams, maples and oaks, are all popular favourites. These have beautiful foliage – some with brilliant autumn tints – and flowering and fruiting species such as hawthorns, crab apples, quinces, and cherries are also suitable.

Bonsais require constant care and attention. Plants must be watered according to weather conditions, container size, season and leaf type – the frequency is high for much of the year since the restricted roots soon dry out. The site must be sheltered from strong winds which desiccate all but the toughest species. Bonsais are not strictly house plants – the best place for them is outdoors on a patio, terrace or balcony. They can be brought indoors when they are in full display, but must be moved outdoors again within a week or so. Indoors, they must have as much light and fresh air as possible – stuffy and poorly lit rooms are not suitable.

Growth styles

Three major bonsai types are recognized – single trunk plants, multiple trunk plants and multiple plant groupings. Single trunk plants can be trained into many different forms:

☐ Formal upright – branches grow uniformly in all directions from a straight trunk.

☐ Informal upright – usually an S-shaped trunk with branches radiating from the outer curves.

☐ Slanting – branches grow in all directions from a leaning trunk.

☐ Windswept – branches grow from one side only of an arching trunk.

☐ Literati – branches restricted to the top third of a subtly twisted and slanting trunk, with relatively little foliage.

☐ Broom – upright trunk with branches spreading out like an up-ended besom broom.

☐ Umbrella – upright trunk with a broad crown.

☐ Weeping – upright or slanting trunk with pendent branches.

☐ Cascade – pendent trunk hanging over the edge of the container,

◄ **Windswept bonsai** Almost a century old, yet no more than 60cm (2ft) tall, this miniature Chinese juniper has been carefully trained to mimic the windswept contours normally associated with buffeted hillside trees.

▲ Informal upright This style needs little forced training of branches and trunk. To ensure a good crop of fruit on a crab apple (*Malus baccata mandschurica*), the flowers must be hand-pollinated if the tree is moved indoors away from bees and insects.

◄ Formal upright Japanese maples are among the most beautiful of trees suitable for bonsai culture, acquiring stunning autumn tints from bronze and yellow through orange to intense scarlet. The branches of the formal upright style are elegantly tiered, setting the foliage off to its best advantage.

► Bonsai shrub Normally bushy shrubs, such as red-fruited cotoneasters, can be trained into small tree-like bonsais with a gnarled elegance.

▼ Weeping miniature An antique Chinese pot enhances the oriental theme of a weeping willow. As bonsais, willows produce masses of foliage and need constant trimming.

similar in style to trees growing out from a vertical rock face.

□ Semi-cascade – near-horizontal trunk, characteristic of trees growing by a lakeside.

□ Exposed root – roots form the lower part of the above-ground tree.

□ Root-over-rock – tree standing on a rock with roots spreading across its face.

□ Rock-grown – tree rooted in a crevice in a craggy rock.

□ Driftwood – sections of trunk and branches carved and stripped of bark to look like driftwood.

BONSAI STYLES

The basic style must be planned from the propagation stage, but individual characteristics can be brought out and enhanced as the plant matures.

Buying bonsais
Bonsai trees and shrubs are often sold by garden centres and nurseries. Having been trained and grown for many years, their price is relatively high. Ensure that the plant is healthy and has not been displayed under spot-lights or in a hot shop for too long.

Much satisfaction can be gained from growing your own bonsais from seeds or cuttings – although a tree will take 10-50 years to develop its full character.

Basic cultivation
Bonsais need fresh air, nutrients, light and water. In summer, the compost in their small and shallow containers dries out extremely quickly, so they need watering daily, or even twice a day during hot spells. Broad-leaved species can die within days if they are left unattended.

Saturate the soil at each watering, applying it from above until water runs out of the drainage holes. At other times of the year, keep the compost just moist. Don't

water in winter unless there is a prolonged period of dryness.

Grow bonsais in full sunlight at all times – shady conditions encourage weak, spindly growth. However, light shading does prevent leaf scorching from hot sun.

A good general compost consists of equal parts by volume of peat substitute, sand and loam. Add extra sand for pines and use an acid mix for azaleas.

The dwarf habit of bonsais is not achieved by starvation – they actually need more regular feeding than other container plants, since the compost is kept to a minimum. However, dilute liquid fertilizers to half their normal recommended strength to avoid burning exposed roots, but apply at twice the normal frequency.

In spring and early summer, use a high-nitrogen fertilizer; in mid to late summer, use a high-potash fertilizer to induce fruiting and flower bud initiation and to harden the wood. Water before applying fertilizer – whether liquid, granule or powder types. Special bonsai fertilizers are available, but ordinary house plant feeds are equally suitable. Do not feed plants for a few weeks after repotting or after root pruning.

Maintain humidity, especially when bonsais are growing indoors – stand the pots in a tray filled with moist pebbles.

Propagating bonsais
Bonsai plants can be grown from seeds, cuttings or layers.
Seeds The digging up of seedlings from the wild is discouraged by conservationists and may be ille-

Plants can be allowed to develop their natural, albeit dwarf, growth form, but many artificially induced shapes are produced to mimic the stunting and ageing processes of extremes of nature.

1 Cascade
2 Multi-tree
3 Windswept
4 Slanting/ exposed roots
5 Root-over-rock
6 Informal upright

GROWING BONSAIS FROM SEED

1 Tree or shrub seedlings with two or more true leaves are ready for potting up individually. To encourage fibrous roots, pinch out the tap root.

2 If a free-branching or multi-trunk bonsai is required, pinch out the seedling's growing tip. Don't pinch out those intended for other styles.

3 Further pinching out of side-shoots will induce a bushy habit if desired. Time the pinching out according to the trunk and branch length required.

gal. However, tree seedlings often appear in your own garden and these may be lifted and potted up. Alternatively collect and sow seeds yourself.

The best time to sow tree seeds is in spring. Use a proprietary seedling compost, covering the seeds to a depth equivalent to two or three times their diameter. Germinate them in a cold frame outdoors. Some seeds may take a year to germinate, but dormancy can be broken by placing the seeds in a moist plastic bag in a refrigerator for a few weeks prior to sowing. When large enough to handle, pot up the seedlings individually.

Cuttings form a slightly quicker means of getting actively growing plants. For deciduous trees, softwood heel cuttings taken in early to mid-summer are the most successful. Evergreens are best grown from hardwood cuttings taken during the growing season.

Air-layering produces small rooted trees very quickly.

Choosing containers

A wide selection of special bonsai pots are available. They are mostly stoneware and usually glazed. Porcelain containers are much more expensive.

Improve drainage by placing a shallow layer of gravel or clay pebbles in the bottom of the pot before filling with compost.

Shaping and pruning

You can use conventional small secateurs, pruning knives and household scissors for pruning bonsais, but enthusiasts may prefer to buy special bonsai tools.

Gouging tools, chisels and other small carpentry tools are required for crafting certain bonsai styles, such as driftwood.

Branch pruning is necessary to develop and maintain the desired shape. Aim to produce a tree with well-spaced branches.

Use secateurs or concave branch cutters which give a clean cut flush with the trunk, to remove entire branches. Regularly trim others to the desired length, cutting close to and away from a bud. Use your finger and thumb to rub out any unwanted buds.

The best time to prune is during dormancy. Begin by pruning out poorly shaped branches and those which are inappropriately positioned for the desired form. Then shape the plant by selecting and snipping off any surplus branches. Aim to produce branches which taper evenly from trunk to tip.

Wiring Curving and contorted shapes rarely occur naturally – young shoots must be forced into the desired shape or position by wiring them until they are woody enough to remain rigid – this may take several years. Wiring is best done in early summer when growth is most flexible.

Use wire which is thick enough to overcome the plant's natural springiness, but not so thick as to be obtrusive or stifle the plant. Never use ferric metal wires, which will rust. Insead, use copper or aluminium wire. Toughen copper wire before use by heating it to a high temperature in a fire. Aluminium wire remains more pliable than copper wire and does not oxidize so readily.

GROWING FROM AIR-LAYERS

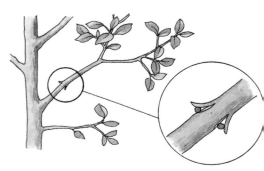

1 An advanced bonsai can be obtained by inducing the branch of a full-sized tree to grow roots. Nick the bark and wedge it open with matchsticks.

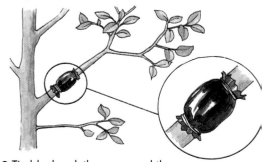

2 Tie black polythene around the branch and pack moist coir around the wound. Secure the rooting medium by tying the top of the polythene.

3 When well rooted – after six to twelve months – remove the polythene. Sever the branch, cutting just below the roots, and pot it up.

REPOTTING AND ROOT PRUNING

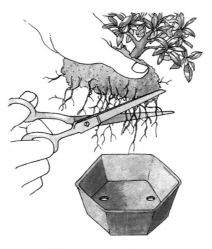

1 Every one or two years, or when pot-bound, remove the bonsai from its pot. Using a small fork, tease away the old soil and loosen the congested or spiralling roots.

2 Trim off the longest, oldest roots, reducing the root ball to such a size that it will fit back into the original container with enough space all round to take a little new compost.

3 If the tree is top-heavy, support it temporarily by looping string round the trunk and threading it through the pot's drainage holes. Add drainage material before repotting the plant.

Other methods of shaping branches include tying them with to the pot with string, in the style of guy-ropes, and weighing them down. However, these techniques tend to be more hazardous, often resulting in branch breakage.

Root pruning and repotting must be carried out every one to two years to ensure that the bonsai does not choke itself to death in its tiny pot. Old trees can be left for up to ten years without repotting. Unlike most containerized plants, bonsais should not be moved into progressively larger pots. Instead, make space for fresh compost and the growth of new, fibrous roots by pruning the old roots.

Remove the plant from its pot, rub away some of the old compost and tease out the roots. Cut off the excessively long roots, then repot and water. Unstable trees can be tied in to the pot's drainage holes to keep them upright.

Leaf pruning aims to reduce the leaf size of broad-leaved species, to encourage twiggy growth and to improve autumn colours. In early or mid-summer, use fine scissors to cut off the leaves where the stalk joins the leaf – take care not to damage the growing bud at the base of the leaf stalk. A second flush of smaller leaves will subsequently appear.

Never leaf-prune weak trees, and don't do it for more than two consecutive summers. Build up the plant's strength before leaf pruning by applying fertilizer. Flowering plants should never be leaf-pruned.

Pinching out of the growth tips is another form of pruning, used mainly for scaly-leaved conifers, including many of the junipers. Using your fingers, gently pull away new growth buds, taking care not to damage the tip – never slice off the buds with a knife.

Needle-leaved evergreens, such as *Juniperus rigida*, can be pruned in a similar way. As new growth begins to elongate in spring and late summer, pinch out the centre of each tuft.

Special techniques

Each of the different growth types requires individual treatment over a period of many years – no two bonsai plants are the same, and your own personal taste will influence your approach.

Informal upright style is one of the easiest to achieve, since it is

WIRING TRUNKS AND BRANCHES

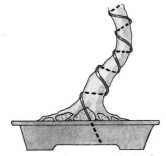

1 Train the trunk into the desired curves by binding it with wire. Anchor one end, then twist the wire firmly but not too tightly in a spiral up the trunk. Leave it in place for one year.

2 Bend branches in the same way, but anchor the wire to the trunk or to an adjacent branch. Never wrap it across leaf nodes. Remove the wire in autumn to avoid scarring the swelling bark.

ROOT-OVER-ROCK

When planting, sit the base of the trunk in the crotch of a suitably shaped rock. Drape the roots over the rock, anchoring their tips in the compost. Wire in until stable.

the natural form of many trees. Begin pruning a young newly potted tree for shape and balance immediately after the first season's growth. Remove one-third to a half from the ends of each strong branch. This will encourage side branches and also minimize unwanted growth.

It is essential to cut back the top growth after each growing season to divert energy into developing side branches. Re-align any branches which point in the wrong direction by wiring them, and cut out branches which grow from the inside curves of the trunk – branches should be spaced more or less evenly up the trunk. The overall shape of the plant should be conical, with the lowest branch coming from one-third of the way up the trunk.

Formal upright style demands a straight trunk. This is achieved by wiring, unless the tree is naturally upright. Cut out more branches from the viewing side than from the back of the tree to create a feeling of depth. Also remove any branch which overshadows the one below.

Slanting style requires the trunk to lean at about 45° from the vertical. Again, wire the trunk in place until it is firm and woody. Check the wires each year, rewiring if necessary to avoid strangling the bark. Encourage slightly exposed roots on the side away from the angle of lean, in order to create a visual sense of stability.

Windswept style is achieved in the same way as the slanting type, but cut out all branches forming on the 'windward' side. Naturally windswept trees frequently have ripped and broken branches, some of which may have been severed completely, leaving only a jagged stump. This characteristic can be imitated on a bonsai by a process known as jinning.

This involves selecting an unwanted but otherwise healthy branch and making a slanting cut about half-way through the wood, slanting away from the trunk. Then, pulling towards the trunk, snap off the branch with a twisting and tearing action, leaving a rough end. Don't clean up the bark or wood around the wound, but treat it with lime sulphur to prevent disease – after a year or so of natural healing, the jin will look like genuine wind damage.

Root-over-rock style has gnarled

▲ **Bonsai collection** A group of mature and young bonsai trees creates an unusual focal point on a sheltered patio. They need outdoor conditions and plenty of light.

roots clinging firmly to the rock. This takes many years to achieve and demands extra care and attention, but the final effect is very rewarding. Maples, beeches and junipers respond particularly well to this style.

Begin by encouraging a seedling tree – or one grown from a cutting – to develop long roots by planting it in a deep container. In three to six years when these roots have formed, lift the small tree and tease out the roots.

Select a piece of rock which has fissures or a rugged surface which the roots can grip. Drape the long roots over the rock and bind them to it with wire or plastic raffia. Then plant the tree and the rock together in a bonsai dish, burying the ends of the roots in the compost around the sides. Leave the root-over-rock planting undisturbed for at least five more years before repotting.

Multiple trunk bonsais fork into two, three or more separate trunks at or near ground level. Grow and train the tree in the same way as

an informal upright, but prune it carefully to avoid cross-over of branches between each trunk. One of the trunks should be allowed to dominate the others in height and scale. Ready-grown multiple trunk bonsais can often be obtained by air-layering a forked branch.

Group plantings can be made to look just like miniature dense forests, or, with the inclusion of a bare space, can also resemble an open landscape. This style can make use of immature trees which lack suitable characteristics to form specimen plants.

Grow a group planting in the same way as a formal upright. Their roots become entwined and the group can be lifted from the pot as one. Don't try to separate them when re-potting, unless one dies or becomes unsightly.

EASY-TO-GROW AIR PLANTS

**Air plants, as their name suggests, really do
live on air alone and will thrive in almost every
home with minimal care and attention.**

The term 'air plant' applies to a small and very specialized group of bromeliads belonging to the genus *Tillandsia*. These unusual plants have two features in common – they have little or no root system and absorb most or all of the water and food they need through their leaves. Air plants range in size from tiny, lichen-like plants to immense leaf rosettes, though the smaller ones are the most suitable as house plants. Their native habitats range from humid tropical rainforests to arid deserts.

The key to the air plants' survival lies in a mass of minute scale-like growths on the leaf surfaces, which extract moisture from humid air and nutrients from floating particles of dust. These scales give all tillandsias a greyish or silvery hue. Unlike most other plants, they do not need soil for anchorage or food and water supply, and so can be fastened on to almost any surface.

Many nurseries and florists supply air plants attached to pieces of bark or gnarled wood, coral or decorative sea-shells. This practice probably stems from the fact that most air plants resemble, to some extent, sea-living organisms – especially sea-anemones. Pieces of lichen are frequently used to conceal the adhesive material. The effect is particularly eye-catching, and air plants so mounted form an interesting link between living plant displays and purely ornamental objects.

The best-known air plant is *Tillandsia usneoides*, the Spanish moss. It consists of thread-like stems covered with silvery scales that are, in reality, minute leaves. In the wild this virtually rootless plant hangs from trees and rocks in long, tangled festoons. Spanish moss, therefore, is not used as a conventional pot plant. Instead, gardeners attach a few sections of the tangled mass to a small piece of cork or bark, tying the fine stems on loosely with plastic-coated or copper wire and hanging the bark on a hook.

As with most bromeliads, the air plant rosette generally flowers only once and then gradually dies, but this process takes several years. Offsets are produced from leaf bases, and these may be detached and used for propagation or can be left in place after the withered old rosette has finally been removed.

Air plants do best in bright but filtered light. They grow all year round if the temperature is kept reasonably warm, but will not tolerate cold conditions. Though water is needed in negligible amounts, it is advisable to mist-spray plants regularly as central heating dries the air unduly. For this reason, avoid placing air plants over a radiator or other heat-source, and don't mount them near fabrics or furnishings which might be damaged by mist-spraying. Apart from these minor limitations, air plants can be displayed almost anywhere – they can even be stuck to mirrors and glazed tiles.

◄ **Air plant** Although the true flowers of air plants are short-lived, the bracts which enclose them remain attractive for much longer. The yellow bracts of *Tillandsia fasciculata* 'Tricolor' contrast well with the grey, mauve-tinted leaves.

◄ Medusa's hair The twisted and curling, silver-scaled leaves of *Tillandsia caput-medusae* arise from a swollen base, which can be mounted on a piece of wood bark or cork. Flower bracts develop rich red tones, and tiny blue flowers peep out along the length of the spike on mature plants.

▼ Mounted tillandsias Air plants make ideal companions for cacti and succulents, all of them needing relatively little routine care. Sections of bark are easy to hang on a vertical surface by means of wires and hooks, allowing the spidery leaf rosettes to fan out into the room, where they absorb moisture and nutrients from the air.

▲ Artistic tillandsia The display of tillandsias demands some creativity. Try to match the form of the plant with the shape of the mount.

▼ Driftwood plants The curious leaf arrangements of *Tillandsia filifolia* and diminutive *T. ionantha* are complemented by driftwood. Lichen adds to the charm of the arrangement.

INSECT-EATERS

**Needing animal matter to supplement
their diet, carnivorous plants are fascinating
to grow in the conservatory or home.**

Carnivorous plants are different from all other plants in their feeding habits – they have adapted to environments in which certain nutrients, especially nitrogen, are deficient in the soil. More in character with animals than plants, these curious species trap small insects and other creatures, and digest them to acquire the missing nutrients. Enzymes are secreted on to the ensnared creatures which dissolve their bodies – the resulting 'soup' is absorbed directly into the tissues of the plant trap.

There are two types of trap. Some are passive traps – insects drop into some form of pitfall while in search of nectar. These include the jungle pitcher plants (*Nepenthes* and *Sarracenia* species), which produce large jug-shaped receptacles filled with water. Some pitchers have hinged lids or hoods to complete the trap; all eventually drown their prey.

Active traps have touch-sensitive triggers which cause a special leaf organ to clamp shut around visiting insects. The Venus fly-trap is a well-known example which has hinged, two-lobed traps edged with long spines capable of rapid closure. Sundews operate by a similar mechanism, but instead of capturing their prey in a small prison until they die and can be digested, these small bog plants glue unsuspecting insects to their folding leaves with a sticky secretion – sundews are sometimes known as living flypapers!

Traps are often brightly coloured, and many carnivorous plants also produce unusual, showy flowers which attract insects. The dainty European butterwort, for instance, bears streptocarpus-like blue-purple flowers in summer. And sarracenias produce striking red or greenish-yellow nodding flowers, whose drooping petals form another type of trap – this time for capturing pollinating insects, though they often successfully escape uninjured to pollinate the next flower.

Most insect-eating plants have special cultural needs. Use free-draining yet moisture-retentive compost – a 50:50 mix of peat substitute and fine sand is suitable, or choose a lime-free compost containing vermiculite. Plastic pots are best since they retain more water. Stand each pot in a saucer part-filled with water. Don't use tap-water – carnivorous plants hate the lime and chlorine in hard, purified water. Instead, water plentifully with rain-water, or distilled or spring water.

No fertilizer is required, but, assuming your home is not plagued by flies, drop tiny pieces of meat or cheese (or dead flies) into the traps occasionally. Grow in normal room temperatures in a bright spot, but out of hot sun.

▲ **Sundew plants** Insects are attracted to the foliage of sundews (*Drosera*) which is covered with reddish, stalked, sticky glands. A leaf slowly wraps itself around the creature, which is unable to escape from the glue, and is then slowly digested. Plants are rarely more than 15cm (6in) tall.

▼ **Insect trap** Pitcher plants, such as *Nepenthes coccinea*, have leaves shaped like a pitcher, often with a hinged lid. These fill up with water into which a digestive enzyme is secreted. Small insects, attracted by the bright spotted colouring of the trap, crawl inside and drown.

CARNIVOROUS PLANTS

Butterworts (*Pinguicula caudata,
  P. grandiflora* and *P. vulgaris*)
Cobra plant (*Darlingtonia
  californica*)
Huntsman's cup (*Sarracenia
  purpurea*)
Huntsman's horn (*Sarracenia
  flava*)
Pitcher plants (*Nepenthes
  coccinea, N. hookeriana,
  Sarracenia×catesbaei, S.
  leucophylla* and *S. psittacina*)
Sundews (*Drosera aliciae, D.
  binata, D. capensis* and
  D. rotundifolia)
Venus fly-trap (*Dionaea muscipula*)

◄ **Cobra plant** The unusual pitcher-like
traps which resemble the heads of
cobra snakes — when mature, they even
have a darker-coloured forked tongue!
— are fatal to insects. Each trap grows
up to 60cm (2ft) tall. Nodding, green
and deep crimson flowers appear on
wiry stalks in mid to late spring. Keep
the roots cool by watering several times
a day in hot weather.

◄ ▼ **Huntsman's cup** Low-growing
but deadly, *Sarracenia flava* produces
short, fattish traps which are veined and
heavily tinted wine-red. Pinkish red
flowers may also appear on mature
plants. A cool conservatory provides
the best growing conditions for this
insect-eater, which needs good
ventilation yet moist air.

▼ **Venus fly-trap** Native to American
boglands, Venus fly-traps are the most
fascinating of all carnivorous plants.
Their spiny-armed 'jaws' spring closed
when an insect touches a tiny trigger
hair on the inner surface of the hinged
trap — the action is rapid and can be
fired by touching the hairs with the
point of a pencil.

INDEX

Plants are listed under both the common name and the botanical name (which appears in italics). However, where both names are almost identical, page numbers follow the botanical name only.

ACKNOWLEDGEMENTS

Photographer's credits

Anaglypta ltd 114; Arcaid (R Einzigt) 109; Biofotos 171(t), 172(bl,br); Guy Bouchet 10(r); Linda Burgess 10(l), 44(b), 44-45(t), 55; Camera Press 35(t); Brian Carter 131; Eric Crichton 43, 44(tl), 45(tr), 46(tl), 59, 67, 75, 87, 106(b); 115, 133, 134(tl), 139, 149(tl), 168; Arnaud Descat 135, 136(b), 146, 149(b); Eaglemoss/John Suett front cover; Garden Picture Library (Lynn Brotchie) back cover, 36(b), (Linda Burgess) 4-5, (Brian Carter) 154(br), (Mayer/LeScanff) 36(t), (Perdereau/Thomas) 159, (J S Sira) 148(b); Robert Harding Picture Library 6, (IPC magazines) 83; Annet Held 128(b); Jan den Hengst 127; Jacqui Hurst

164(bl); Insight (Linda Burgess) 141, (Michele Garrett) 50(t); Patrick Johns 71, 79; Lamontagne 9, 11, 13, 50(br), 51, 52, 91, 124(tl,b), 125(t), 136(t), 137, 140(tl,b), 142(t), 151, 172(t); Andrew Lawson 99(b), 149(tr), 169, 170(t); Maison de Marie Claire 29, 95, 107, 110(tl), 121, 153; Philippe Perdereau 126(br); Photos Horticultural 2-3, 14, 17, 33, 35(b), 37(l), 54, 99, 104, 125(b), 126(tl,tr) 132(tl,b), 140(tr), 143(l), 144, 150, 154(tl,b), 163, 164(tl,tr,br), 171(b); Annette Schreiner 118(b), 124(tr), 142(br), 152, 158, 170(br); Harry Smith Collection 20, 31, 37(r), 63, 116(tl), 155, 156(b), 157, 170(cl,bl); Jean-Paul Soulier 50(bl); Elizabeth Whiting and Associates 46(b), 116(tr), 123, (Karl-Dietrich Buhler) 106(tl), 122, 130(tl), 132(tr), 138, 142(bl), (Michael Crockett) 46(tr), (Michael

Dunne) 45(b), 106(tr), 111, 112(tl,b), 117, 118(t), 119, 129, 130(tr,b), 134(b), (Andreas von Einseidel) 128(t), (Geoffrey Frosh) 105, 120(br), (Clive Helm) 34(tr), (Frank Herholdt) 110(tr), (Neil Lorimer) 108(c), (Michael Nicholson) 108(t), (Orbis Library) 21, (Spike Powell) 113, (Jerry Tubby) 108(b), 112(tr); Worldwide Syndication/Strauss 148(t); 100 IdÇes 47, 48(br), 49.

Illustrators

Elisabeth Dowle 18-20, 64-66, 72-74, 147, 165-167, Christine Hart-Davies 1, 12, 14, 16, 22-28, 30-32, 34, 38-42, 56-58, 60-62, 68-70, 80-82, 84-86, 88-90, 92-94, 96-98, 100-102, 160-162; Claire Wright 158.

Index compiled by Hilary Bird

Typesetting SX COMPOSING, ESSEX; Printing & Binding PRINTER INDUSTRIA, GRÁFICA S.A. BARCELONA
Separations COLOURSCAN OVERSEAS CO PTE LTD, SINGAPORE; Paper PERIGORD-CONDAT, FRANCE

53-010-1